European History

DeMYSTiFieD®

DeMYSTiFieD® Series

Accounting Demystified

Advanced Statistics Demystified

Algebra Demystified

Alternative Energy Demystified

ASP.NET 2.0 Demystified

Biology Demystified

Biotechnology Demystified

Business Calculus Demystified

Business Math Demystified

Business Statistics Demystified

C++ Demystified

Calculus Demystified

Chemistry Demystified

Commodities Demystified

Corporate Finance Demystified, 2e

Data Structures Demystified

Databases Demystified, 2e

Differential Equations Demystified

Digital Electronics Demystified

Electricity Demystified

Electronics Demystified

Environmental Science Demystified

Everyday Math Demystified

Financial Accounting Demystified

Financial Planning Demystified

Financial Statements Demystified

Forensics Demystified

Genetics Demystified

Grant Writing Demystified

Hedge Funds Demystified

Human Resource Management Demystified

Intermediate Accounting Demystified

Investing Demystified, 2e

Java Demystified

JavaScript Demystified

Lean Six Sigma Demystified

Linear Algebra Demystified

Macroeconomics Demystified

Management Accounting Demystified

Marketing Demystified

Math Proofs Demystified

Math Word Problems Demystified

Mathematica Demystified

Matlab Demystified

Microbiology Demystified

Microeconomics Demystified

Nanotechnology Demystified

OOP Demystified

Operating Systems Demystified

Options Demystified

Organic Chemistry Demystified

Pharmacology Demystified

Physics Demystified

Physiology Demystified

Pre-Algebra Demystified

Precalculus Demystified

Probability Demystified

Project Management Demystified

Public Speaking and Presentations Demystified

Quality Management Demystified

Real Estate Math Demystified

Robotics Demystified

Sales Management Demystified

Six Sigma Demystified, 2e

SQL Demystified

Statistical Process Control Demystified

Statistics Demystified

Technical Analysis Demystified

Technical Math Demystified

Trigonometry Demystified

UML Demystified

Visual Basic 2005 Demystified

Visual C# 2005 Demystified

XML Demystified

The Demystified Series publishes over 125 titles in all areas of academic study. For a complete list of titles, please visit www.mhprofessional.com.

European History
DeMYSTiFieD®

Stephanie Muntone

McGraw Graw Hill

New York   Chicago   San Francisco   Lisbon   London   Madrid   Mexico City
Milan   New Delhi   San Juan   Seoul   Singapore   Sydney   Toronto

ISBN   978-0-07-175421-7
MHID   0-07-175421-0

e-ISBN 978-0-07-175422-4
e-MHID   0-07-175422-9

Library of Congress Control Number   2011922821

McGraw-Hill books are available at special quantity discounts to use as premiums and sales promotions, or for use in corporate training programs. To contact a representative, please e-mail us at bulksales@mcgraw-hill.com.

Contents

How to Use This Book

The important questions a historian asks are "What happened?" and "Why did it happen?" This book should help you to answer those questions on the topic of modern European history—that is, from the Italian Renaissance to the end of the Cold War and the formation of the European Union.

History students are often confused by a wealth of information being thrown at them at once—names, dates, monarchs, and battles following one another in a bewildering array. The easiest way to sort out the confusion is to think about how events connect with one another. History is a long story of causes and effects. For example, the Italian Renaissance led indirectly to the Protestant Reformation, and both the Renaissance and the Reformation were necessary first steps toward the Enlightenment. Provisions of the peace treaty signed at the end of World War I created conditions that led to World War II. And so on. It's much easier to remember events when you understand how they relate to one another.

This book tells you the political history of Europe in a narrative format, emphasizing the key ideas so you will understand why they are important— why a revolution broke out when and where it did, what caused a major intellectual movement to occur in a certain time and place, or why one nation industrialized its economy long before the others. Each chapter deals with an important era or event in history, such as the Age of Monarchy or the Industrial Revolution. Chapter topics can overlap in time, but the order of topics is basically chronological. The book is divided into three major sections:

- Part I describes early modern Europe from the Renaissance to the seventeenth century.

- Part II picks up the story with the seventeenth-century Scientific Revolution and ends just after 1900.
- Part III narrates the course of European history in the twentieth century.

Each chapter ends with a ten-question quiz. Each section ends with a 50-question section exam, and there is a 100-question final exam at the end of the book. The questions are all multiple choice, similar to the sorts of questions used on standardized tests. Many of the questions ask you about causes and effects: Why did this event happen? What happened as a result of that decision?

You might try taking the chapter quiz first, before reading the chapter. This will tell you which sections of each chapter you already know well and which sections you need to study further. Read and study the chapter, then take the quiz again. Keep working on each chapter until you can answer at least nine of the ten questions correctly.

Take the section exam after you finish reading the section, and take the final exam once you have mastered the entire book. Check your work against the answer key; if you answer at least 92 of the 100 questions correctly, you can consider that you have mastered the subject satisfactorily. Go back and study any areas of the book that cover the questions you did not answer correctly.

If you are using this book as a course companion, follow along at the same pace your professor is taking. Use the book for extra tutorial and practice in addition to what is covered in class. If you are using the book as a substitute for taking the course, or to prepare yourself for an exam, then allow yourself time to get the most out of it. Allow three months, one month for each section of the book, to complete your study. Read the narrative, take the quizzes, and make a list of questions on aspects of European history that aren't clear to you. Use the sources recommended in the Bibliography, or similar titles in the library or bookstore, to find the answers. When you're done with the course, you can use this book, with its comprehensive index, as a permanent reference.

Introduction

Understanding the Themes of European History

History, like a great work of literature, has themes—major motifs and concerns that arise again and again over the course of time. Understanding these themes helps the student make sense of history. Themes show connections—causes and effects that can help you understand not only what happened but also why it happened. Themes show you the important factors that shape the course of history of a nation, a region, and a continent.

Geography

The history of any nation is inseparable from its geography: its position in relation to other nations, its climate, its topography, its natural resources, whether or not it has a seacoast, the location of its major rivers, and similar factors. Here are some examples of how geography affects history:

- Russia is so vast in its physical size that no Western nation ever succeeded in conquering it. Additionally, its bitter winter temperatures, much more severe than winters in Western Europe, have served it well as a defensive weapon. Both an 1812 French invasion and a 1941 German invasion resulted in humiliation and disaster for the invaders.

- Britain is geographically detached from the continent. The English Channel served as both a defense against invasion and an assurance against British aggression for those on the European continent. Britain was never invaded during the early modern period; only with the twentieth-century development of fighter planes did it become vulnerable to attack.

- France was the largest nation-state in central Europe until German unification in 1871. This made it the dominant European power until the downfall of Napoleon in 1815. A contiguous landmass like France is much easier to defend than an empire made of small states scattered over the map.

- Germany's central geographical position on the continent was the direct cause of the aggressive foreign policy begun under the Prussian kings in the seventeenth century. Being in the center, Germany was vulnerable to attack on all sides; equally, it was in a strategic position to attack others.

War and the Force of Arms

The nations of Europe all have one thing in common in their history: the desire for territorial expansion. All nations wanted to acquire more natural resources, to expand their power bases, to control major trade routes, and to secure their borders from attack.

Another powerful motivation for war is domination or suppression of what the attacker perceives as a hostile or unfriendly culture. Many of the European wars before 1700 were caused by deep differences over the question of religious faith.

There is one basic historical axiom about the force of arms: the nation with bigger, stronger, or more guns always wins the fight. Although a small army has very occasionally defeated a larger one, it has always been because of greatly superior strategy.

The same force of arms is responsible for all of history's successful dictatorships. Only the loyalty of the army has allowed military dictators to rise to power and keep it—for the simple reason that guns are a powerful deterrent to any attack on the dictator. Armies have always been loyal to dictators, because under dictators they occupy a privileged position in society and government. The people fear and obey them—not out of patriotism or personal loyalty to the dictator, but because the army has the guns.

Balance of Power

This is crucial to the peace of Europe as a whole. When any one nation became too dominant, other nations would unite to put down the aggressor.

- In the seventeenth century, when the royal Hapsburg family acquired power over too many European states, France and Sweden worked with other nations to break the ties between the Hapsburg's Spanish and German possessions.

- In the nineteenth century, France's attempt to conquer all of Europe under Napoleon failed because Germany, Russia, Austria, and Britain all worked together to crush France.

- In the twentieth century, Germany's attempt to establish a vast "Aryan" empire under Adolf Hitler failed because most of the nations of Europe united to crush Germany.

Religion

In today's world, as in the past, religion is a powerful emotional force. It can work to unite or divide people who, in many cases, seem deaf to any reasonable discussion of their faith.

For a thousand years, almost all Western Europeans were Catholic. Europe had a small Jewish population, and North African Muslims had occupied Spain for eight hundred years, but for the most part, all nations shared the same religious faith. Administratively, the pope controlled the Catholic Church from Rome; in all nations, the archbishops, bishops, and cardinals answered to his central authority. This shared religion was a strong unifying force, especially among scholars, all of whom could read and speak Latin. It promoted a sense among Europeans that all was fair, because the same rules applied to people of all nations. In addition, the pope was a secular head of state over a sizable Italian principality that included Rome. In Eastern Europe, primarily in Russia and Greece, the Orthodox Catholic Church held sway.

This all began to change in the 1500s with the Reformation, which can accurately be called the Protestant Revolution. Three major new Christian denominations—Lutheranism, Anglicanism, and Calvinism—came into existence, converting at least half the population of Western Europe. Tension between Catholics and Protestants erupted into major wars on a number of occasions.

Rank or Class

Through most of European history, social class was a deciding factor in a person's life. A person was born into a certain social position, and had very few choices as to his or her own future. Artisans married other artisans; shopkeepers passed down their businesses to their children; aristocrats arranged marriages with other aristocrats; and princes and princesses married other royal persons in arrangements based on international diplomacy.

Change came about gradually. The rise of literacy meant that a person could get an education, and an educated person could find ways to rise in class. In most nations, the hereditary nobility was so cash-poor that families sometimes arranged their children's marriages to the children of wealthy commoners. The noble family gained cash, and the bourgeois family gained prestige. Over time, it became possible to rise in society according to talent, luck, and ambition.

Part I

Early Modern Europe: The Renaissance to the Seventeenth Century

The Renaissance, 1350–1517

The European Renaissance began in Italy in the early 1300s and continued, spreading northward, through the late 1500s. It was by no means a complete break from the Middle Ages that preceded it. The European population was still devoutly religious, not secular, in its ways of thought and behavior. Ideas of universal equality were still a long way in the future. All human achievements were still dedicated to the glory of God (at least on the surface).

However, two important factors did make the Renaissance different from the centuries that came before. One was the rediscovery of the Classical era, the great age of Rome and to a lesser extent Greece. It was this interest in ancient literature, philosophy, science, and art that gave the Renaissance its name; the era marked a "rebirth" of Classical values and ideas.

The second factor was the questioning of Church teachings. For a thousand years, the Church had held sway over every aspect of European life and society. During the Renaissance, this began to change due to a variety of factors. The Church's inability to stamp out the Black Plague made people begin to question its claims of unlimited power. Great scholars began to study subjects other than theology. The development of movable type made printed books widely available, and thus literacy rates rose. Cultural exchanges led to the study of ancient texts unaffected by Church tradition. This trend of questioning the Church's accuracy and authority would eventually lead to the sixteenth-century Reformation and the eighteenth-century Enlightenment.

CHAPTER 1 OBJECTIVES

- Define the term *Renaissance* and explain its importance in European history.
- Explain how the Church began to lose its authority during the Renaissance.
- Identify the major figures of the era and match each person to his or her accomplishments in government, politics, the arts, and/or science.

Chapter 1 Time Line

- **1348–1350**   Black Death (bubonic and pneumonic plagues) decimates European population
- **1397**   Medici Bank established in Florence
- **1438**   Council of Florence
- **1455**   Johannes Gutenberg publishes the Vulgate Bible, the first book in Europe printed with movable type
- **1495–1498**   Leonardo da Vinci paints the mural of *The Last Supper* in Milan
- **1508–1512**   Michelangelo completes the frescoes on the ceiling of the Sistine Chapel in the Vatican
- **1511**   Erasmus publishes *Praise of Folly*
- **1513**   Machiavelli publishes *The Prince*
- **1517**   Luther publishes Ninety-Five Theses at Wittenberg

The Renaissance

The word *renaissance* means "rebirth." The 250-year period of European history beginning about 1350 is called the Renaissance because it marked the rebirth of a certain way of thinking—a return to the values of the Classical era. A variety of conditions gave rise to the Renaissance. First, the Black Death decimated Europe, striking down almost half of the population. Second, survivors of the plague began migrating to the cities, causing them to grow and prosper. This prosperity in turn meant that wealthy citizens had disposable income to spend on culture and the arts. Third, the perfection of the printing process brought about the possibility of near-universal literacy and education.

The Renaissance in Italy

The earliest stirrings of the ideas that would make historians label this era "the Renaissance" occurred in the Italian city-states. Several factors were responsible for this. First, Italy was the location of the Roman Empire, whose great artistic and intellectual achievements became so important to the era. It was natural that the Italians would be the first to celebrate the cultural past, which could be seen, touched, and studied literally on their very doorsteps. Second, Italy was enjoying a period of great economic prosperity. This meant that there were enormously wealthy families who had money to spend on major artistic and architectural projects. Third, the Catholic Church, which was headquartered in Rome, had begun to depend financially on wealthy Italians like Cosimo de' Medici. This financial dependency gave these wealthy businessmen and politicians a certain amount of power over Church policies. Fourth, Italy's location in the center of the Mediterranean, between the Middle East and the West, had always made it a place of cultural and intellectual exchange.

The Black Death

The Black Death is the name given to a severe epidemic of bubonic and pneumonic plague that spread across Europe from about 1348 to about 1350. The plague originated in the Crimea and was brought westward on trading ships. It was highly infectious and was spread by flea and rat bites and by close contact with the infected. Symptoms included raging fever, delirium, aching joints, vomiting, and ugly, painful swellings in the armpits and groin. Very little could be done to make a sick person comfortable, let alone cure him or her. Most of the plague's victims died within a week of catching the disease.

Historians estimate that the Black Death killed 30 to 60 percent of Europe's population. The loss was highest in cities, where people were crowded together in unsanitary conditions: the populations of Florence, Paris, and London were cut in half. The death rate was comparatively lower in isolated rural areas, where there was less chance of infection.

Naturally, this was a time of terror throughout Europe. Medical science was at a primitive stage, and no one understood where the disease had come from or what caused it. Many people believed it was a sign that the world was coming to an end. People turned to the Church for help, as it was the universal authority of the time. However, the Church could do nothing to combat the epidemic. Priests who cared for the sick caught the plague and died like anyone else.

The Black Death helped to bring about the Renaissance in a number of ways. First, survivors began moving to cities looking for work as the disease receded. Cities grew larger as a result. Second, so many workers and artisans had died that those who were left found that their services were in greater demand. Third, people began to doubt that the Church was as omnipotent as it had always claimed to be. If it was so helpless in the face of real disaster, what power did the Church really have?

The Church in the Renaissance

For a thousand years before the Renaissance, the Roman Catholic Church had held universal, undisputed sway over all aspects of life in Western Europe. This began to change during the Renaissance for a number of reasons.

First, the Church proved powerless in the face of the Black Death. This shook the faith of the ordinary people. Second, secular authorities such as the powerful merchant families of Italy arose; they proved powerful rivals to the Church's authority. Third, the Church itself encouraged and eased the cultural exchange that led to such developments as the study of Greek and Middle Eastern texts and ideas. Fourth, the Church embraced the Classical revival that played a part in undermining its own authority. Fifth, the availability of printed books in Europe after 1450 meant that more people were reading and learning to think for themselves.

Beginning in 1414, the Church sponsored a series of councils—international gatherings of scholars and church officials. The goal of the councils was to repair a schism in the Church that had led to rival papacies throughout much of the fourteenth century, one in Avignon and one in Rome. Once the Church was reunited under one pope, the next goal was to reunite the Roman and Eastern Orthodox churches, which had been split since the year 1054. This was the purpose of the Council of Florence, convened in 1438. It was sponsored in part by money from the Medici family.

Scholars and officials from Greece, Ethiopia, Russia, Cairo, and Trebizond came to Florence for the council. It thus became an unprecedented exchange of ideas from the various cultures. Eastern and Western scholars were able to trade books and manuscripts and hold long debates and discussions on questions of science and philosophy. While the Eastern guests admired new Italian works of art and architecture, Western scholars pored over texts by Euclid, Plato, and Aristotle—works to which they had never before had access.

The council not only failed to reunite the Roman and Orthodox Churches, but, ironically, by making the spread and exchange of knowledge possible, it weakened the authority of the Church. As knowledge continued to spread and literacy continued to rise, people questioned the Church more and more. Only another eighty years would go by before Martin Luther began the Protestant Reformation that would change everything.

Politics and the Economy

In the days of the Black Death, Italy was not a unified nation. It was a collection of politically independent city-states whose people shared a common ethnic, cultural, religious, and linguistic heritage. These city-states were ruled by wealthy middle-class families who seized and clung to political power because this was the best way to further their business interests.

Florence was especially important in the Renaissance because its economy recovered quickly from the Black Death and the city enjoyed a period of great prosperity. The Medici family ruled the city of Florence for most of the 1400s. This stupendously wealthy family of bankers and importers used and invested its money in two areas. The first was patronage of the arts; the Medicis sponsored many of the most significant artistic achievements of the period. The second was financial loans to the Church. By being the Church's banker, the Medici family gained a significant amount of influence over Church policies. Strong family ties to the papacy gave the Medicis virtual control of Rome as well as Florence. In the 1480s, a Medici married the son of Pope Innocent VIII. In 1513, Giovanni de' Medici became Pope Leo X.

This table shows the most prominent members of the Medici family and their major achievements.

THE MEDICI FAMILY

Name	Political Achievements	Contributions to the Arts and Letters
Cosimo de' Medici (1389–1464)	Sponsorship of the Council of Florence in 1438	Built up family library into one of the largest and most important in Europe
Lorenzo de' Medici (Lorenzo the Magnificent) (1449–1492)	• Organized army against Turkish invasion in 1480 • Arranged marriage between his daughter and son of Pope Innocent VIII	• Founded academy for artists in Florence • Patron of Michelangelo • Accomplished poet • Continued to add to family library
Giovanni de' Medici (Pope Leo X) (1475–1521)	• By 1512, had returned Medici family to power lost in 1494 • Became Pope Leo X in 1513 • United central Italian states politically	Ordered and oversaw reconstruction and restoration of the Vatican and St. Peter's Basilica in Rome, including major contributions by Michelangelo, Bramante, and Raphael

The political insights of Niccolò Machiavelli, born in Florence in 1469, remain highly influential even today. Machiavelli's most famous work is a short discourse titled *The Prince*, published in 1513. In an obvious bid for employment, Machiavelli dedicated *The Prince* to Giuliano de' Medici. It is a treatise explaining how to gain and hold absolute political power. What made the book so revolutionary was its frank assertion that a prince should not hesitate to act treacherously or dishonestly in order to keep his power. He should not be swayed by considerations of ethics or religion. Machiavelli's realistic approach to politics is as relevant today as it was in his own time.

Michelangelo

Born in Florence in 1475, Michelangelo Buonarroti is one of the towering figures of art. He achieved great fame in his own lifetime and forever after as a sculptor, architect, painter, and poet. During his career, Michelangelo received many important commissions from members of the Medici family.

The frescoes that Pope Leo X commissioned for the ceiling of the Vatican's Sistine Chapel constitute Michelangelo's greatest claim to fame. Michelangelo eschewed the usual practice of the time, in which the master artist would design the overall plan but have assistants help him on the actual painting. Instead, Michelangelo himself painted the entire ceiling (a surface of more than ten thousand square feet) over a four-year period from 1508 to 1512. He planned an ambitious, daring scheme of Old Testament scenes framed and surrounded by painted architectural elements and Classical figures.

From the historian's point of view, the Sistine Chapel ceiling is most notable for its mix of biblical and Classical elements. Michelangelo set aside twelve large, prominent spaces for portraits of ancient prophets of the birth of Jesus. Seven male prophets from the Old Testament alternate with the figures of five female pagan sibyls—prophets from the Classical world. Michelangelo treated these figures equally in terms of placement, size, and scale, with no suggestion that either the artist or the patron saw any incongruity. Given that the Sistine Chapel was at the very heart of the headquarters of the Catholic Church, and that the Church itself sponsored the project, this alone makes it clear that Renaissance Europeans had no sense that these elements were contradictory.

The ceiling frescoes show a clear break with medieval artistic traditions in their style as well. The figures are heroic in size and scale, bursting out of frames that cannot contain them. They are shown in a great variety of poses, from every angle and point of view—a complete break from the medieval style. These figures also show that Michelangelo had a thorough knowledge of human anatomy; the depiction of the bones and muscles beneath the skin is perfectly accurate. The faces reveal recognizable emotions that make the frescoes a celebration of the human being. All these elements mark the Sistine ceiling as a product of the Renaissance. Sixteenth-century art historian Giorgio Vasari later wrote that the Sistine ceiling "restored light to a world that for centuries had been plunged into darkness."

The Perfection of Printing

Woodblock printing was invented in China before A.D. 220 and remained the main method of printing on cloth and paper for centuries. However, this method was not practical for printing multiple copies of long texts. Movable type, in which each block was an individual letter or character, made the process much more efficient. Printers first tried movable wooden type, but soon turned to metal because it was much more durable.

The Koreans were the first to print entire books with movable metal type, perhaps as early as the 1200s. The world's oldest surviving book printed with movable metal type is a Korean guide to Buddhism published in the late 1300s.

Like all other Asian inventions, the technology of printing eventually traveled westward. Europeans were producing printed textiles and fabrics by the twelfth century. When paper became widely available around 1400, they began trying to develop an efficient method of printing texts on it. Born around 1398 in the city of Mainz, the artisan Johannes Gutenberg achieved the first and best success at movable-type printing in Europe. He invented the modern printing press and also arrived at a combination of metals that made his type the clearest and most durable. In fact, his recipe continued to be used until digital printing became near-universal at the beginning of the twenty-first century.

The first European printed book was the Vulgate Bible, the Latin translation commonly used throughout Europe at that time. It is often called "the Gutenberg Bible" in honor of the printer.

The importance of the development of movable type and the printing press cannot be underestimated. Printing may be the single most important invention of the millennium. The widespread availability of books led directly and swiftly to a rise in literacy. For the first time, literacy and knowledge were not exclusive to priests and wealthy people, but came within the reach of everyone. For the first time, texts (including the Bible) became available in the languages people actually spoke, not just in Latin.

Humanism

The word *humanism* refers to a Classical course of study at European universities, many of which were founded between about A.D. 1000 and 1200. Humanism meant the study of the seven liberal arts, "liberal" because in ancient Rome this was regarded as the proper course of study for a free man (in Latin, *liberus* means "free"). The liberal arts consisted of grammar, logic, rhetoric, arithmetic, music, geometry, and astronomy.

The humanist course of study focused on Classical texts, from both the Greek and Roman eras. Roman texts predominated for two reasons. First, they were written in Latin, which was much easier for Europeans to understand than Greek. All the Romance languages of Western Europe, especially Italian, were closely based on Latin, and Latin had been kept alive by constant use in the Church. Second, Italy was the seat of the Roman Empire; the Roman manuscripts and scrolls were physically handy, relatively easy to obtain and copy for study purposes. Only time, travel, and cultural exchange would eventually bring the Greek manuscripts west for study.

Humanist scholars of the Renaissance focused their interest on the human being as a unique individual, with his or her own way of thinking about the great questions of philosophy and the meaning of life. All of this, however, was firmly in the context of the human being as God's creation, with all human achievement being dedicated to God's glory. In this era, the word *humanism* did not have the secular connotation it has in our own time.

Desiderus Erasmus, born in Rotterdam in 1466, is probably the best known of the Humanists. Erasmus' work shows that he embraced both biblical and Classical studies. He published a Latin translation of the Greek New Testament in 1516, but also completed translations and scholarly commentaries on Classical texts, including the works of Plutarch and Seneca. He corresponded with most of the great European scholars of his day and was widely regarded as the hub of the intellectual world.

QUIZ

1. **The word *Renaissance* refers to**
   A. the reawakening of interest in Classical values and ideas.
   B. the gradual loss of authority of the Catholic Church.
   C. the loss of half of Europe's population during the Black Death.
   D. the role wealthy merchants played in the development of art.

2. _____ **is an important historical figure because he perfected the process of printing books with movable type.**
   A. Michelangelo Buonarroti
   B. Cosimo de' Medici
   C. Martin Luther
   D. Johannes Gutenberg

3. **One important reason Italy was the birthplace of the European Renaissance was**
   A. its geographical status as the center of the Roman Empire.
   B. the greatness of its writers, scholars, and artists.
   C. its strong political unity as a nation.
   D. the economic depression that followed the Black Death.

4. **Western scholars of the fourteenth and early fifteenth centuries primarily studied Roman texts instead of Greek ones because**
   A. Greek texts were not as well written as Roman.
   B. Greek texts were scarcer and harder to understand than Roman.
   C. Greek texts were older than Roman.
   D. Greek texts showed a different way of thinking than Roman.

5. **The Black Death was one powerful factor that caused ordinary Europeans to question the omnipotence of**
   A. humanism.
   B. medical science.
   C. the Church.
   D. the economy.

6. _____ **excelled as a sculptor, painter, architect, and poet.**
   A. Michelangelo Buonarroti
   B. Lorenzo de' Medici
   C. Desiderus Erasmus
   D. Martin Luther

7. **Pope Leo X commissioned** _____
   A. the restoration of the Vatican and St. Peter's Basilica.
   B. the printing of the Vulgate edition of the Bible.
   C. the Council of Florence.
   D. the founding of the Medici Bank.

8. **The Medici family ruled** _____ **for most of the fifteenth century.**
   A. Rome
   B. Florence
   C. Italy
   D. France

9. _____ wrote a political treatise stating that princes should not hesitate to commit unethical acts in order to hold on to their power.
   A. Michelangelo Buonarroti
   B. Johannes Gutenberg
   C. Desiderus Erasmus
   D. Niccolò Machiavelli

10. **The most important effect of the Council of Florence was**
   A. the official reunion of the Roman and Orthodox Catholic Churches.
   B. a major exchange of books and ideas among Eastern and Western scholars.
   C. Pope Leo X's decision to restore the Vatican and St. Peter's Basilica.
   D. the publication of the first Bible printed with movable type.

chapter 2

The Reformation, 1455–1600

The Reformation is the name given to the era in which discontent with the practices and policies of the Catholic Church boiled over, causing widespread attempts at reform (hence the name "Reformation"). Because the Church resisted change, thousands of Christians abandoned the Catholic Church and joined new Christian denominations. These new churches came to be known as Protestant denominations, so-called because they were born in protest against the original Church.

The word *catholic* means "universal." Before 1517, the Catholic Church was the universal Christian church in Western Europe and had controlled many aspects of people's lives for close to a thousand years. In 1517, however, the birth of the Lutheran Church put an end to the unquestioned spiritual authority of the Catholic Church. By 1600, thousands of Europeans were worshiping in Protestant churches: Lutheran, Calvinist, and Anglican.

In response, the Catholic Church made serious efforts to reform itself from within, in what is generally called the Counter-Reformation. Positive efforts included founding seminaries all over Europe where young men could be educated and trained for the priesthood. Negative efforts included forcible attempts to stamp out Protestantism (or heresy, as the Church called it) through the Inquisitions in Spain, Portugal, and Italy. The Church's reforms succeeded to a large extent; however, the Protestant churches continued to thrive. The era in which one Christian church ruled all of Western Europe had definitely come to an end.

CHAPTER 2 OBJECTIVES

- Define the term *Reformation* and explain its importance in European history.
- Explain what caused the widespread protests against the Catholic Church.
- Identify the major Protestant denominations and explain how and why each one came into being.
- Identify the major figures of the era.
- Describe the Catholic response to the Reformation.

Chapter 2 Time Line

- **1455**   Johannes Gutenberg publishes the Vulgate Bible, the first book in Europe printed with movable type
- **1517**   Luther publishes Ninety-Five Theses
- **1521**   Diet of Worms
- **1534**   Act of Supremacy declares Henry VIII Supreme Head of the Church of England
- **1540**   Society of Jesuits is founded
- **1541**   Calvin establishes theocracy in Geneva
- **1545–1563**   Council of Trent; Catholic Reformation (Counter-Reformation)
- **1555**   Peace of Augsburg
- **1598**   Henry of Navarre becomes King of France; issues Edict of Nantes

Causes of the Reformation

The rise of Protestantism had multiple causes. They included a growing realization that the Church was not as powerful as it had claimed, a rise in secular political power, and the perfection of the printing process stimulating a rise in literacy (see Chapter 1). The spark that finally pushed people into widespread, open rebellion against the Church was the trade of indulgences for financial contributions to the Church.

The Catholic Church functioned on a system of the forgiveness of sins. A person sinned, repented, confessed to a priest, and received absolution in exchange for some form of penance. This might involve repeating a certain number of prayers or doing good work in the community. A sinner who was granted an indulgence did not have to go through such a penance; an indulgence was an official promise that the Church forgave earthly punishment for sins already committed. The first indulgences were granted to soldiers who had fought in the Crusades, as forgiveness for sins committed in the course of war. Of course, God might still choose to punish sins after death; the Church could only forgive earthly punishment.

The practice of granting indulgences quickly became corrupt. Both the Church and its agents, most notably Johann Tetzel in Germany, grew greedy for money and began offering indulgences in exchange for financial donations. People were assured that if they donated money, their sins would be forgiven, not only on earth but also after death. They were also told that they could purchase heavenly forgiveness for family members who were already dead. The idea that one could buy forgiveness for sins with money, or that the Church could preempt God's power to forgive sin after death, deeply offended many devout Catholics. The most notable of these was Martin Luther.

Martin Luther

Martin Luther was born in 1483 in the German state of Saxony. He became a theological scholar and a professor of scripture at Wittenberg University. A devout Catholic, Luther was outraged by the notion that salvation could be bought and sold. His Ninety-Five Theses, which appeared in 1517, were propositions for debate that questioned and criticized many aspects of the Catholic Church, including a prominent and harsh reference to the sale of indulgences. The Ninety-Five Theses were printed and widely circulated, and many people were convinced by Luther's arguments. The pope ordered Luther to recant his criticisms of the Church on pain of excommunication; Luther refused.

At this time in history, the German city-states of north-central Europe were bound in a loose alliance known as the Holy Roman Empire. Each state had its own prince, with one emperor ruling over all. The rulers of the provinces were called electors because the emperor was chosen by election. Over time, the election had become purely ceremonial; since 1440, the title had been passed down in the ruling Hapsburg (spelled "Habsburg" in some sources) family in the same manner as any hereditary monarchy in Europe. In 1519, Charles I of Spain was crowned Holy Roman emperor, succeeding his grandfather Maximilian I. He would rule as Emperor Charles V.

In 1521, Charles called all his princes together for a diet—an official assembly—at the town of Worms. Summoned to appear before the diet, Luther refused to recant his statements. Ordered to leave the empire, he instead accepted an offer of protection from the elector of Saxony. Luther continued to write and publish and, to his own astonishment, soon realized that instead of bringing about reform in the Catholic Church, he had founded a new denomination.

The most important idea behind Lutheranism is the notion that salvation depends on faith. Each believer must read, study, and understand scripture for himself or herself—in effect, each soul would serve as his or her own priest, instead of relying exclusively on an ordained priest to interpret the word of God. Part of what made this possible was, of course, the technology of printing, which before long brought a Bible into every household. Luther's German translation of the Bible appeared in 1534. For the first time, Germans could read the Bible in their own language rather than having to learn Hebrew, Latin, or Greek.

Luther advocated a simple worship service, arguing that the communion between the individual and God took place in the individual's heart and mind. The elaborate ceremony of the Catholic mass, to Luther, was merely an outward show that had no spiritual significance. Luther also argued that worship services should be conducted in the language of the people, so that they could understand exactly what was being said and think about it for themselves. These ideas and reforms appealed to thousands of Germans.

Several of the German princes became enthusiastic Lutherans as well. When Lutheranism became the state religion, the Church's vast wealth and property passed from the pope's control into the hands of the prince. This was a powerful practical reason for adopting Lutheranism, above and beyond questions of spirituality. However, many princes remained devoutly Catholic.

At first, Charles V tolerated Lutheranism, but as it spread, various groups began using it as a basis for social and political revolt. In 1529, the emperor decreed a ban on Lutheranism. It was during this period that the term *Protestant* first came into use, describing the Lutheran princes and people who *protested* against the emperor's decree. War eventually broke out between the German states over this issue. In 1555, the Peace of Augsburg settled the matter by declaring that each German prince could determine the religion of his own state.

Lutheranism took firm hold in Germany and also spread north to the Scandinavian countries. Meanwhile, a rather different form of Protestant Christianity developed in Switzerland.

John Calvin

John Calvin was born in France in 1509. He studied philosophy, law, and humanism and learned both Latin and Greek. Like Luther, Calvin came to believe that the Catholic Church needed reform. When he spoke out on this issue, he found himself so unpopular in France that he fled to Switzerland. Here he eventually acquired so much power and influence that many historians describe the city of Geneva as a theocracy—a state ruled by religious laws.

The central idea of Calvinism is predestination—the belief that God predetermines everything that will happen on earth. According to this belief, human beings are already marked for salvation or damnation at birth, and no amount of faith or good deeds can earn salvation. Calvin argued that those who were saved would naturally perform good works and lead exemplary lives; therefore, all believers must live this way, because it was one sure sign that they were among the saved. Calvinism strictly regulated every aspect of a person's life: it made church attendance mandatory, encouraged simplicity in dress, and forbade many forms of enjoyment such as dancing, singing, and playing cards.

Despite its harsh rules and its intolerance of other forms of worship, Calvinism gained many converts. Calvin's followers spread his ideas and practices throughout Switzerland, the Netherlands, and France. John Knox transported many of Calvin's ideas home to Scotland, where the religion was called Presbyterianism after the *presbyters*, or elders, who ruled the church. In 1560–1561, Parliament made Presbyterianism the state religion of Scotland.

In France, Calvin's followers were called French Protestants or Huguenots. Despite tens of thousands of individual converts to Protestantism, France as a whole was not sympathetic to the Reformation. The French monarchs sided with the Catholics throughout a series of civil wars fought from 1562 to 1598, helping to ensure that Protestantism could not establish itself securely. Thousands of Huguenots were massacred, and many more fled France to settle in Holland, Belgium, and England.

The 1580s saw a struggle for the French throne known as the War of the Three Henries. These were King Henry III and two of his kinsmen, Henry of Guise and Henry of Navarre. With the support of Philip II of Spain, Henry of Guise made a bold move to take the throne, but he was taken by surprise by supporters of Henry III and assassinated. When a fanatic assassinated the king the following year, Henry of Navarre inherited the throne. He would rule as King Henry IV of France.

Henry IV was a Calvinist, but his religious convictions were not nearly as strong as his political ambition. His main goal was to strengthen the monarchy, and he believed that siding with the religious majority was a crucial step to achieving security on his throne. Therefore, Henry converted to Catholicism. In 1598, he issued the Edict of Nantes, which established Catholicism as the state religion of France and its territories, but allowed Protestants to worship as they saw fit, without molestation. This ended the French civil wars of religion. Henry was enlightened enough to understand that tolerance in the matter of private worship would lead to domestic accord in the population and would therefore benefit the kingdom.

Henry VIII and the Church of England

The Anglican Church, also called the Church of England, is unique in history for two reasons. First, it was created solely for political reasons, not religious ones. Second, it was the most sweeping assertion of secular authority in the history of Europe.

By the 1520s, King Henry VIII of England and the Spanish princess Catherine of Aragon had been married for several years. Although Catherine had given birth to several children, only one, a daughter, had survived past infancy.

Lacking a male heir, Henry dreaded possible rival claims to the throne and a return to the civil wars that had battered England throughout the 1400s. He was also personally tired of Catherine. Therefore, Henry petitioned Pope Clement VII for an annulment of his marriage. The king had fallen in love with lady-in-waiting Anne Boleyn, who was several years younger than Catherine and seemed likely to provide him with healthy children. (Ironically, only one daughter of their marriage would survive; Henry would have to marry yet again in order to produce a son.)

Henry VIII never tolerated opposition at any time in his life. When the pope refused to grant him his annulment, the king determined to find another way to get what he wanted. In 1533, he named Thomas Cranmer, a loyal official of the court, the new archbishop of Canterbury. Archbishop Cranmer granted Henry his annulment and then married him to Anne Boleyn. The new pope, Paul III, excommunicated both the king and the archbishop for violating the sacrament of marriage.

In 1534, the British Parliament retaliated against the pope by passing the Act of Supremacy. This act acknowledged the king as the Supreme Head of the Church in England, thus creating a new Christian denomination and eliminating any papal involvement in British affairs. In effect, the British monarch now had the same authority over England that the pope had over the rest of Europe. No secular government had ever asserted such power in a thousand years of Church authority.

It is important to note the role of Parliament in the creation of the Church of England. The king did not create the Anglican Church with a wave of a royal scepter; instead, the duly elected representative government passed the Act of Supremacy according to the laws of the land. Thus, Henry VIII could claim with some reason that the English people and the government fully supported his desire to break away from the Catholic Church.

In a clear sign that Henry's action had been politically and not spiritually motivated, the Anglican Church continued to hear confessions and celebrate mass in just the same manner as the Catholic Church. Under Henry's son and successor, Edward VI, the clergy introduced various reforms, such as permission for priests to marry. In 1549, Archbishop Cranmer published *The Book of Common Prayer*, which contained the prayers and proper forms of all Anglican services—in English, not Latin. During the next century, the status of the Church of England fluctuated according to the personal faith of the monarch. (See Chapter 4.)

The Counter-Reformation

Meanwhile, the Catholic Church was well aware of the need to reform itself from within. However, reform depended largely on the personality of the pope in power at any given time. This made for inconsistency; reform proceeded slowly, by fits and starts. Some popes felt a genuine need to reform corrupt practices, others hoped to reclaim Protestants who had left the Church, and still others stubbornly refused to support any changes.

Pope Paul III called for a council of high Church officials to meet in the city of Trent to devise a plan for reform. Due to strong opposition from within the Church, the Council of Trent did not meet until 1545 and took more than fifteen years to reach any conclusions. In the end, it supported all doctrines that Protestants had criticized, banned the sale of indulgences, and required the founding of hundreds of new seminaries for the education and training of priests.

Paul III appointed many pro-reform cardinals in the hope that they would continue to elect popes who would fight corruption in the Church and try to restore it to its former glory. This attempt was largely successful; the popes who followed Paul III continued to support reform.

In 1542, Paul III created the Congregation of the Holy Office of the Inquisition. Its purpose was to supervise the Roman Inquisition, whose job was to try people accused of heresy. The Roman Inquisition generally assessed penalties such as fines or public whippings. The most serious sentence it could hand down was one of life imprisonment. However, if the Inquisition handed a prisoner over to secular authorities, it almost certainly meant the person would be executed. It began as a sincere attempt on the part of reformers to root out heresy within the Church. Under some of Paul III's successors, it became a byword for torture and terror. Portugal and Spain had their own Inquisitions; these, however, reported directly to the monarchs rather than being supervised by the Church. (See Chapter 4.)

Paul IV, who served as pope from 1555 to 1559, was a particularly strict reformer, focusing his energy on a variety of targets. He came down especially hard on the practice of simony, or the sale of Church offices; although this was a dependable source of income for the Church, it was clearly corrupt. Paul IV also made the Church bureaucracy more efficient by eliminating many unnecessary positions. In 1559, the Church published the *Index of Forbidden Books*; this document listed all books that, according to the Holy Office, contained heretical ideas and thus were off limits to Catholics because of their corrupting influence. Not content with banning the books, the Church also burned thousands of copies. Owning a copy of a forbidden book made the possessor liable to punishment under the Inquisition.

The founding of the Society of Jesus, also known as the order of the Jesuits, was a more positive Catholic reform. Its founder, Ignatius Loyola, was born in the Basque region of Spain in 1491. An active military career led to severe injuries and wounds; while he lay still recovering, Loyola passed the time with books, studying the life and teachings of Jesus. Greatly impressed by Jesus' simplicity and humility, Loyola vowed to emulate him. He took vows of poverty, wore the simplest of clothing, and spent his days serving and helping the poor. He published a work called *Spiritual Exercises,* which advocated a period of intense contemplation and study for any man wanting to devote his life to serving the Church.

In 1540, the pope approved Loyola's petition to found the order of the Jesuits. The society grew quickly as many men joined, attracted by Loyola's high ideals. Like their leader, the Jesuits lived simply and chastely, indifferent to physical comforts or luxuries. Jesuit schools offered the best education then available to children in Europe; pupils from all income levels and all ranks of society were welcomed and treated equally. The Jesuits were characterized by reforming zeal, preferring to persuade non-Catholics to convert, rather than resorting to the bullying techniques of the Inquisition. Their missionary ambitions eventually led them to the most remote areas of the world, far beyond Europe's borders.

The Jesuits were not the only order founded during the Counter-Reformation. The Ursuline order of nuns and the Capucine order of priests, among others, provided both men and women with the opportunity to teach, preach, and serve. Because these orders, like the Jesuits, turned their backs on the pomp, ceremony, and display that Luther and Calvin had found so objectionable, the common people were impressed. Seeing that these Catholic orders practiced the simplicity and purity that they preached, thousands of people were inspired to follow them. The activities of these orders, especially the Jesuits, helped to counteract the effects of the Protestant Reformation and to strengthen and improve the Catholic Church as an institution.

QUIZ

1. **The Edict of Nantes decreed**
   A. that Catholics were forbidden from reading anything listed in the *Index of Forbidden Books.*
   B. that the people of France had the right to worship in the church of their choice.
   C. that each elector in the Holy Roman Empire could choose the religion for his own electorate.
   D. that the monarch was the supreme head of the Church of England.

2. _____ **presided over a virtual theocracy in Geneva during the Reformation.**
   A. John Calvin
   B. John Knox
   C. Henry IV
   D. Paul III

3. **The term *Protestant Reformation* refers to**
   A. the campaign of reform carried out in the Catholic Church in an attempt to recover lost ground.
   B. the attempt to reform Protestant churches that grew gradually corrupt during the sixteenth and seventeenth centuries.
   C. the creation of several Christian denominations in a protest against the practices of Catholicism.
   D. the pilgrimages made by both Catholic and Protestant missionaries to distant lands to win converts.

4. **What was the most important effect of Henry IV's declaration of religious toleration in France?**
   A. It ended the religiously based civil wars.
   B. It earned him the lasting hostility of England and Spain.
   C. It led directly to the Peace of Augsburg.
   D. It forced thousands of Huguenots to flee the country.

5. **The publication of** _____ **was the spark that created the Reformation.**
    A. the Edict of Nantes
    B. _The Book of Common Prayer_
    C. the Bible in German
    D. the Ninety-Five Theses

6. _____ **is an important historical figure because he founded the Society of Jesus in 1540.**
    A. Thomas Cranmer
    B. Henry of Guise
    C. Ignatius Loyola
    D. John Calvin

7. **The main purpose of the Council of Trent was**
    A. to establish Church supervision of the Roman Inquisition.
    B. to reunite the Catholic and Protestant denominations.
    C. to devise a plan for the reformation of the Catholic Church.
    D. to persuade Martin Luther to recant the Ninety-Five Theses.

8. **Which Protestant denomination preached the doctrine of predestination?**
    A. Anglicanism
    B. Calvinism
    C. the Church of England
    D. Lutheranism

9. **The overall main point of the Ninety-Five Theses was that**
    A. believers would win salvation by a combination of faith and good works.
    B. God predetermined everything that happened on earth.
    C. people should abandon the Catholic Church and found a new denomination.
    D. the Catholic Church had become corrupt and needed reform.

10. **Anglicanism differed from other Protestant denominations in that**
    A. it was the result of discontent among the people.
    B. it was embraced and made official by the head of state.
    C. it was founded for political, not spiritual, reasons.
    D. it was not a Christian religion.

Early Czarist Russia, 1380–1613

In 1380, the nation we know today as Russia was a small collection of principalities—Muscovy, Novgorod, and others—paying tribute to the Tatars. By 1600, it had become an empire under Russian rule and had expanded its borders far beyond its original size. It was to grow much larger over the next century, eventually encompassing one-sixth of all the land on earth.

The major goals of the early Russian princes and czars were fourfold. First, they wanted to break away from the stranglehold of Tatar authority. Second, they wanted to consolidate power into the hands of one absolute monarch, with a capital city as a central power base. Third, they wanted the central government to consolidate and control all the elements of society, from the boyars (hereditary nobles) through the peasants. Last, they wanted to expand the empire to both the west and the east for strategic and trade purposes.

Although present-day Russia has one foot in Asia, this was not the case in its early history. Historically and culturally, it is an Eastern European nation with its roots in the western portion of the country, in the area bordering Poland and Scandinavia. Russians are a Slavic people, like most Eastern Europeans.

Russian is written in the Cyrillic alphabet, not the Roman one used throughout the West. Therefore, the student may find variations, in both primary and secondary sources, in the English transliterations of Russian proper names and other Russian words. For example, both *czar* and *tsar* are acceptable Western spellings of the Russian emperor's title. In addition, Russian names are sometimes anglicized; for example, Pyotr becomes Peter and Yekaterina becomes Catherine.

CHAPTER 3 OBJECTIVES

- Identify the early Russian principalities on a map.
- Trace the progress of Russian expansion under the early princes and czars.
- Compare and contrast government in Russia with government at the same period in Western Europe.
- Describe the major turning points in Russian history between 1380 and 1613.

Chapter 3 Time Line

- **1380** Moscow defeats Tatars in Battle of Kulikovo; Muscovite expansion begins
- **1453** Fall of Constantinople to Ottoman Turks
- **1469** Ivan III marries Zoe, niece of emperor of Byzantium
- **1480** End of Tatar authority in Russia
- **1547** Ivan IV is crowned Czar of All the Russias
- **1598–1613** Time of Troubles
- **1613** Mikhail Romanov becomes new czar; dynasty will continue to 1917

The Grand Principality of Muscovy

The principality of Muscovy, with the city of Moscow at its center, became the core of the Russian empire through a combination of geographical and political factors.

Geography

Muscovy had no natural borders to define it, nor any geographical features such as mountain ranges to protect it from invasion. This explains its conquering mentality: Moscow could maintain its position of power only by remaining constantly on the attack. Successful attacks gave the rulers of Muscovy control over major rivers, which were essential for transportation and trade. Conquering more territory also enriched the royal treasury because it meant a larger population paying tax to the crown. In addition, Moscow was unifying Russia by consolidating power into the hands of one prince.

Politics

Moscow's ruling family, the Danilovitch, was abler and more shrewd than ruling families of the other principalities. As part of their policy of achieving a greater position of power in Russia, they arranged several important dynastic marriages to create alliances between Muscovy and the other principalities. Family connections, like territorial annexation, helped to unify the various states into one empire.

The Orthodox Catholic faith also served as a unifying force in the creation of the Russian empire. As Muscovy expanded far beyond its borders into sparsely inhabited territory, a shared form of worship helped to establish a sense of community and belonging. The Orthodox Church supported political unity among the principalities of Russia, because a strong central rule meant greater control over the people. Orthodox leaders saw political control as a useful supplement to religious control. By the 1400s, the metropolitan (head of the Orthodox Church in Russia, analogous to the archbishop of Canterbury in England) had accepted Moscow as the center of the empire.

Russian Society and Government

The Tatars, from the Asian lands we now refer to as Mongolia, invaded and conquered most of Russia under Genghis Khan in the 1200s. Under Tatar rule, the Russian princes had to pay annual tributes to the khan, but were more or less left to the details of governing on their own. Once the Tatars were overthrown and Moscow became the center of Russia, the Russian emperor was an absolute monarch—far more of an autocrat than any Western European ruler at this period of history. The emperor had advisers, usually drawn from the boyars (hereditary nobles) and the upper clergy, but these men had no power or privileges other than what the emperor chose to grant them. Nor did the Russian government have any form of popular representation. The emperor truly was the state.

The Russian climate and the geography were major obstacles to the formation of a prosperous mercantile middle class such as existed in Italy and other European nations in the early modern period. The countryside was bleak and barren and the weather was often bitterly cold; these factors combined to make travel difficult. Travel meant trade, and without frequent travel, trade did not become an important part of the local economy. Nor did Russia enter into trade or cultural exchange with the rest of Europe until somewhat later in its history.

With travel so difficult, and with the population as widely scattered as it was, a typical Russian estate provided for all its own needs. This contrasted with the economic system in Western Europe, where people either bartered or sold their surplus crops or livestock to obtain necessities and luxuries they could not produce themselves.

The End of Tatar Rule

Prince Dmitri, known to history as Dmitri of the Don, led the Russian army against the Tatars in the Battle of Kulikovo (1380). The Russian victory was a major blow against Mongol authority in Russia. The khan retained much of his power, but he agreed to recognize Moscow as the central Russian authority and to allow the princes of Moscow to appoint their own successors.

During the mid-1400s, the Khanate lost strength as the Russians gained it; by about 1430, the Great Khanate had broken into four smaller ones. On the Russian side, there was infighting among rival claimants to the throne of Moscow. By 1450 Vasili II emerged as the victor, declaring that only his own direct heirs would rule after him. This was a major step in the process toward unified central rule of Russia.

Vasili II and his successors carried out a policy of expanding the army by offering land to anyone willing to serve the state in the military. These land grants were made for life, and most of them could be passed on to the landowner's heirs. With such a powerful incentive, many men joined the ranks of the army; they included hereditary princes, boyars, and wealthy non-noble families. (In Russia, the title "prince" does not necessarily refer to the ruler of a province or a member of the royal family; it is a title of the higher nobility similar to the English titles "duke" and "earl.") Peasants and other commoners were required to serve their community in proportion to the local population.

Ivan III

Ivan III, Grand Prince or Grand Duke of Moscow, married Zoe (sometimes called Sophia) Palaeologos, niece of the Byzantine emperor, in 1469. Zoe's cultural and family background was to have a major influence on the style of the Russian court; with her arrival, it gained a great deal of ceremony and pomp. Ivan and Zoe made the Byzantine double-headed eagle the official emblem of the Russian state. By adopting this symbol, Ivan declared himself the last defender of the Orthodox faith, in the wake of the fall of Constantinople to the Turks and the failure to unite Orthodox and Roman Catholicism at the Council of Trent (see Chapter 2).

The real beginning of the history of Russia as a nation-state dates to 1480, when Ivan withheld the annual monetary tribute to the Tatars. This led to a confrontation of the Mongol and Russian forces on opposite sides of the Oka River. A stalemate resulted, as neither side seemed willing to begin the attack. In the end, the Tatars withdrew, ending the long period of Mongol authority in Russia.

With the Tatars gone, Ivan could assert his own authority as the supreme ruler of Russia, starting the tradition of autocracy that would continue until the Revolution of 1917. In 1493, for instance, Ivan forced the kingdom of Lithuania to grant him the title "Lord of All Rus." He also began using the title czar, a Russian form of *Caesar*. This had originally been a family name with no secondary meaning, but because the Caesar family ruled Rome for so long, it eventually became synonymous with *emperor*. Symbolically, the use of the imperial title reinforced Ivan's claim that he was descended from the Caesars and that after the fall of Constantinople, the New Rome, Moscow was "the Third Rome," the center of the world. Officially, however, he remained Grand Prince of Moscow.

Partly due to Zoe's cosmopolitan influence, Russia experienced a certain degree of cultural exchange with the West during Ivan's reign. Ivan established diplomatic relations with Western nations, and an exchange of embassies took place. Russians were curious about Westerners but also contemptuous of them because they were not Orthodox Christians. Europeans no doubt felt similar emotions toward the Russians, whose society seemed to them both more exotic and more primitive than their own. Ivan hired several Italian architects and artists, notably Petrus Antonius Solarius, to rebuild the Kremlin—the heart of Moscow—with four strikingly beautiful cathedrals and the czar's mansion ranged around a large open plaza, all surrounded by strong, fortified walls.

Under Ivan, Russia expanded into an empire more than three times the size of the original Grand Principality of Muscovy. Ivan III took control of Novgorod and its territories, which included vast tracts of land to the northeast and northwest of Muscovy. Vasili III, who became emperor on Ivan III's death in 1505, added the Baltic province of Pskov and the province of Riazan on the Oka River. Access to these bodies of water was important for trade, since it was much easier to transport quantities of goods by water than over land.

Ruling a larger empire brought with it both advantages and disadvantages. A substantial rise in population meant a larger army and greater revenue from tributes and taxes, but a larger population was more difficult to control and monitor. A larger bureaucracy became necessary in order to take care of the routine of governing at the local level. Because most of the empire was geographically far from Moscow, a great deal of everyday authority remained in the hands of local officials, which of course invited corruption on a large scale since there was no oversight. Ancient Rome had also faced the challenge of ruling a large and far-flung empire; this attempt was successful because the Roman bureaucracy was highly efficient, with clear lines of authority and a chain of command. Such was not the case in Russia. The harsh climate made travel slow and difficult, the postal service was unreliable, and local officials were generally free to carry out their responsibilities (or not) as they saw fit, without any fear of inspection or reprimand by superiors.

Ivan IV

Born in 1530, Ivan IV succeeded to the imperial throne at age three. He became known in Russia as Ivan Grozny, which has traditionally been translated into English as "Ivan the Terrible." However, this is a misleading translation; *grozny* means "terrifying" rather than "terrible." The czar is more accurately called "Ivan the Formidable" or "Ivan the Awe-Inspiring."

Because the new emperor was only a toddler, the boyars seized control of the administration. However, they could not agree on any chain of command or choose a leader among themselves; for a decade, Russia somehow functioned with total chaos in the capital city. Ivan proved his formidable qualities as soon as he turned thirteen; he asserted his authority in a manner that impressed everyone and convinced his subjects of his strength and determination. Four years later, he became the first Russian ruler to have himself crowned Czar of All the Russias. (Ivan III had used the title "czar" only in his private correspondence.)

Ivan's early experience of the boyars taught him that they were unreliable; he believed, with justification, that they were likely to quarrel among themselves, conspire against him, and overthrow him if they could. This distrust of the boyars convinced Ivan that he must rule as an absolute autocrat. Rather than allowing the boyars to play any role in government policy, Ivan chose advisers he felt were personally loyal to him as the head of the state. Partly to counteract the boyars' resentment and partly to protect his own place on the throne, Ivan also passed the first laws restricting mobility of the peasant class. Similar actions taken by his successors would eventually lead to their becoming serfs—the literal property of their noble landlords, with few rights of their own.

The policy of territorial expansion begun under Ivan III continued under Ivan the Terrible. Over a nearly forty-year reign, the czar conquered the last remaining Tatars and extended Russia's eastern border far beyond the Volga River, taking over a swath of territory stretching from the Caspian Sea in the south to the Arctic Ocean in the north. With the Tatars finally crushed, the way was open for expansion to the Pacific Ocean.

Under Ivan, the large Russian army began improving in quality. His predecessors had enlarged the army but had not trained it. Under Ivan's rule, military commanders created specialized divisions such as musketeers and artillery.

The Fall of Ivan IV

After a promising beginning, Russia's strong czar collapsed during the second half of his reign. His behavior grew more and more eccentric and his decisions more strange. In 1581, he struck and killed his son and heir Ivan in a fit of rage in front of several witnesses. Historians believe that Ivan IV suffered from paranoia, severe mental illness, and possibly also a spinal disability that meant constant physical pain.

Everyone close to the throne could see that Ivan the Formidable was no longer capable of ruling, but there was no peaceful means of deposing him. Russia was an absolute monarchy with no legislative or representative assembly, no constitution, no balance of powers, and no apparatus in the government for replacing an unstable or incompetent czar.

In 1564, Ivan mapped out an area covering about half the czardom and decreed that he would rule this area as his personal absolute kingdom. He created a bureaucracy for his new realm, confiscated land and property at will, and dismissed and executed any authority figures he saw as a threat. Ivan also formed the Oprichnina, an organization of secret police whose members were called *oprichniki*. The *oprichniki* were officially civil servants; in fact, they were murderous thugs, responsible to no one but Ivan, with total authority to crush anything they saw as opposition to the czar's authority. The *oprichniki* would operate until 1572. Creating a climate of fear and secrecy, they proved ruinous to the stability of Russian society, and Ivan was finally persuaded to disband them.

Time of Troubles

When Ivan IV died in 1584, he was succeeded by his son Feodor I. Feodor was mentally simple and childlike, incapable of governing; he was glad to hand his responsibilities over to his able brother-in-law Boris Godunov, who ruled in fact although not in name.

Feodor died in 1598. Hereditary rule had been the law in Russia since 1450, but since Feodor was the last of his family, a successor would have to be chosen by other authority figures. A council of six hundred boyars, clergy, and military officers elected Boris Godunov. His election began an era known in Russian history as the Time of Troubles. Although Boris was an intelligent and capable ruler, he had many enemies and was not popular among his subjects. For one thing, he had been an *oprichnik* and his wife was the daughter of the leader of this feared and hated gang; for another, many people suspected him of having murdered Feodor's younger brother Dmitri, who had been discovered stabbed to death in 1591 in a mystery that historians have yet to solve. In addition, the boyars opposed Boris's plans to reorganize the administration and make it more efficient. They preferred to cling to the privileges and personal advantages they enjoyed in an inefficient system.

The Time of Troubles was a period of chaos on many levels. First, there was social unrest within the Russian population. Second, there was a struggle for power among a variety of candidates for the throne. Third, fighting broke out among the armies of Sweden, Poland, and Russia as part of the struggle over who would rule the empire.

Social Unrest

In 1597, Boris issued a ukase, or royal edict, restricting the liberty peasants to move freely throughout the empire. In 1601, however, crop failure resulted in famine that caused thousands of peasants to defy the ukase, since remaining on barren land was tantamount to a death sentence. Many peasants roamed the countryside looking for food; others moved into towns and cities looking for work that would pay wages. By 1603, there was widespread social unrest; the czar had to muster the army to put down rebellion among the peasants and other members of the poorer classes.

The Struggle for Power

After the death of Feodor, Russia reverted to the days before Vasili II, when power was taken by violence and conquest rather than inheritance. Boris Godunov was a duly elected regent, but despite his intelligence and undoubted administrative ability, he was unable to unify and control the diverse elements within his realm. The situation was ripe for the appearance of a strong leader, but although several men tried to grab power, none could hold on to it.

In 1601, the first claimant appeared, declaring that he was Dmitri, Feodor I's younger brother. According to his story, the body identified in 1591 as Dmitri's had been someone else's; he, the real Dmitri, had been smuggled out of Russia and grown up in safety. The claim was false; historians believe the False Dmitri to have been a Russian nobleman. Whoever he really was, the False Dmitri won the support of the Polish army by promising to turn over some territory to King Zygmunt III on his accession to the Russian throne. Despite a triumphal march into Moscow two months after Godunov's death in 1605, with thousands of Poles and Cossacks in his train, the False Dmitri could not maintain power, and the boyars, who had never believed his claim of royal birth, murdered him in 1606. The boyar Vasili Shiuskii then assumed power, with the support of his fellow nobles, but although he did succeed in putting down a major peasant uprising, he was eventually forced out.

The Invasions from the West

In 1607, a second False Dmitri appeared, again from Poland. Poland invaded Russia with the new claimant and soon established a rival Russian government in the Upper Volga region. The early success of this group forced Shiuskii to summon Swedish mercenaries to help him put it down. However, Shiuskii soon found himself trying to fight both the Poles and the Swedes, both of whom saw strategic advantages to be gained by opposing rather than supporting him. Poland and Russia began discussing the possibility of a Polish czar in exchange for an end to the fighting, but there were loud outcries of anger in the Orthodox Church against this plan, since the Poles were not Orthodox. In the end, a national uprising led to the election of a new Russian czar, the sixteen-year-old boyar Mikhail Romanov, in 1613. His direct heirs would rule Russia until the Revolution of 1917.

QUIZ

1. _____ was a key factor in preventing the rise of a prosperous mercantile class in Russia.
   A. Orthodoxy
   B. Geography
   C. Politics
   D. Absolutism

2. Boris Godunov contrasted with his predecessor czars because
   A. he was chosen by election.
   B. he was a capable and strong leader.
   C. he drove the Tatars out of Russia.
   D. he tried to establish control over the boyars.

3. Many Russian nobles joined the military in the 1400s because
   A. they believed it was their duty.
   B. they were eager to show their loyalty to the throne.
   C. they were required by law to serve.
   D. they were given hereditary titles to land.

4. Which of the following describes one result of contact with Western Europe under the early czars?
   A. The Russian military was greatly expanded.
   B. The Moscow Kremlin was rebuilt with striking works of architecture.
   C. Russian citizens began to have a greater voice in their government.
   D. The Orthodox and Roman Catholic churches were reunited under one pope.

5. **Which best describes the Russian government under the early czars?**
   A. a constitutional monarchy
   B. an oligarchy of aristocrats and clergy
   C. an absolute monarchy
   D. a parliamentary democracy

6. **Despite his mental instability, Ivan IV continued to rule because**
   A. he remained stronger than any of the rival claimants to the throne.
   B. the Orthodox Church remained loyal to him.
   C. he murdered his son and heir.
   D. the system of government contained no procedure to remove a monarch from office.

7. **One major cause of Boris Godunov's unpopularity was**
   A. his having served in the *oprichniki*.
   B. his status as Czar Feodor's brother-in-law.
   C. his weakness and indecisiveness in matters of policy.
   D. his refusal to consult the boyars in affairs of state.

8. **During the Time of Troubles, Poland hoped to**
   A. take over the Russian empire.
   B. gain territory from Russia.
   C. establish formal diplomatic and trade relations with Russia.
   D. convert the Russians to Roman Catholicism.

9. **Which czar's decision marked the real beginning of Russia's status as a nation-state?**
   A. Vasili II's decree that only his direct heirs could inherit the throne
   B. Ivan III's refusal to pay the annual tribute to the Tatars
   C. Ivan IV's creation of the Oprichnina
   D. Feodor I's decision to turn over most of his powers to Boris Godunov

10. **What caused Boris Godunov to revoke the decree that prohibited peasants from moving?**
   A. He did not want them to continue dying of starvation during the famine.
   B. He needed to recruit them for military service against Poland.
   C. He wanted to appease the boyars.
   D. He wanted to gain popularity among the clergy.

chapter **4**

Europe to 1618

The sixteenth century was a chaotic time in Europe. At the beginning of the century, monarchies were largely hereditary estates with monarchs who had to be constantly on the alert for assassination or invasion—either from within, by local rivals, or from without, by hostile neighboring countries. By the end of the era, most nations had taken important steps toward achieving modern centralized governments. Some nations succeeded much better than others.

The landowner of a hereditary estate could run his property as he pleased, with no interference from others. In the same way, the early monarchs believed that they had the absolute right to rule over their much larger properties— their kingdoms. However, monarchs had to maintain the loyalty of their subjects if they wanted to remain on their thrones. The nobility wanted privileges and power, the advisers and court officials wanted influence over policy, the courts wanted control over the justice system, the military wanted to fight, and the people wanted the monarch's protection and a healthy economy in which they could support their families. Balancing all these elements called for skills in diplomacy and realism; if the monarch did not possess such skills, the kingdom could not be a dominant power.

CHAPTER 4 OBJECTIVES

- Explain the goals of Ferdinand and Isabel of Spain and how they achieved them.
- Describe the reigns of Queens Mary and Elizabeth of England.
- Describe the results of Charles V's division of Hapsburg lands between his heirs.

Chapter 4 Time Line

- **1469** Crowns of Aragon and Castile are politically united
- **1478** Establishment of Spanish Inquisition
- **1492** Expulsion of Jews from Spain
- **1499** Expulsion of Muslims from Spain
- **1497** Juana marries Philip the Handsome of Ghent
- **1500** Birth of Charles of Ghent; will become Charles I of Spain in 1516 and Holy Roman Emperor Charles V in 1519
- **1509** Catherine of Aragon marries Henry VIII of England
- **1553** Mary Tudor becomes Queen of England
- **1558** Elizabeth Tudor becomes Queen of England
- **1588** Defeat of the Spanish Armada
- **1603** Death of Elizabeth I

Spain

North African Muslims invaded the Iberian Peninsula in the early 700s and controlled much of the territory for more than seven hundred years. It was only toward the end of the Middle Ages that Christian armies began to drive them from power. During the 1400s, the expansion of the Spanish military led to success in this venture. This retaking of the lands that would eventually become the nations of Portugal and Spain is known as the *Reconquista*.

At this time, Spain was not a unified nation but a collection of principalities. The two strongest were Aragon in western Spain and Castile in eastern Spain. Each of these provinces had annexed others until they achieved the status of kingdoms. In 1469, Ferdinand of Aragon married Isabel of Castile, uniting the crowns and consolidating Spanish power. Both were monarchs in their own right, but there was no European tradition of female monarchs; therefore, Isabel considered it politically expedient to share some of her authority with Ferdinand. Isabel was queen of Castile, where Ferdinand had limited authority but could not act without her counsel and consent. Ferdinand was king of Aragon, where Isabel had no power or authority except as his consort.

The major goal of the Spanish monarchs can be summed up in one word: control. Control over the nobility would make their position on the throne secure. Control over the population would prevent any threats of uprising or civil war. Control over the other Spanish provinces would unite the kingdom and give the monarchs greater power and authority in Europe.

Control of the Nobility

Relations between the Spanish monarchy and the aristocracy were based on an exchange of favors for loyalty. The monarch needed to control the hereditary nobles, quelling any desire they might have to depose, assassinate, or rise up against royal authority; on their side, the nobles depended on the monarch for privileges. Isabel and Ferdinand offered the nobles major privileges: salaried offices and the titles that accompanied them, substantial rewards for military service, and grants of land that they could pass on to their heirs. In exchange, the Spanish nobles were remarkably loyal to the throne; as was usual in an absolute monarchy, the nobles were conservative, with no incentive to alter a system that brought them rich rewards in return for relatively little effort.

Control of the People

In 1478, Isabel and Ferdinand established the Spanish Inquisition, which reported directly to the monarch rather than operating under the authority of the Church. Although the Muslims had been driven from power, many Muslims still lived in Spain; the peninsula also had a substantial Jewish population. The monarchs believed that for the good of the state, the people should all have the same faith. This would prevent civil unrest, conflicts, and possible uprisings. A homogeneous nation, according to the monarchs' way of thinking, would be more peaceful.

Jews and Muslims were faced with three choices: convert to Christianity by choice, convert by force, or leave the country. In 1492, all Jews were ordered to convert or leave Spain; in 1499, the same order was issued against Muslims.

Naturally, many Jews and Muslims chose to convert, not wishing to give up home, friends, livelihood, and family. They remained objects of suspicion in the eyes of the Inquisition, which questioned the sincerity of their conversions; by Spanish law, it was a crime to practice any non-Christian religion, even in the privacy of one's home. If someone observed that the Jewish converts next door never ate pork, for example, the neighbor could denounce the family to the Inquisition on suspicion of practicing Judaism. The Inquisition would arrest such people, then use a variety of interrogation techniques to find the facts. In cases of high crimes, the Inquisitors used torture, which had been standard under the Roman laws on which the Inquisition was based. The Inquisition was an enormously effective royal tool for maintaining control by means of fear.

Control of the Lands

In 1492, the Spanish army completed the *Reconquista* by capturing Granada, the last Muslim stronghold. With the war over, Isabel could turn her attention to her longstanding interest in establishing a viable sea route to Asia. Her sponsorship of the first voyage of Christopher Columbus marked the beginning of the cultural exchange between Europe and the Americas (see Chapter 7). After Isabel's death, Ferdinand continued to acquire more land; he annexed provinces in Italy and France and even expanded as far as Oran in North Africa.

Isabel and Ferdinand cemented or established important foreign alliances by arranging dynastic marriages for their children. Princess Catherine of Aragon married Arthur of England; when he died, she married his younger brother Henry, who would rule as Henry VIII. Princess Juana married Philip of Ghent (sometimes called "Philip the Handsome"), son of Holy Roman Emperor Maximilian I. By birth, Philip would inherit all the considerable Hapsburg lands in central Europe; he was also the likely successor to his father as Holy Roman Emperor.

Spain in the 1500s

Queen Isabel died in 1504; although Juana inherited the throne of Castile, she was not mentally or emotionally stable enough to perform her duties. Knowing of her daughter's condition, Isabel had arranged for Ferdinand to serve as regent until Juana's son Charles of Ghent, born in 1500, was old enough to rule.

Ferdinand died in 1516; on his grandfather's death, Charles of Ghent inherited both Castile and Aragon and was crowned King Charles I of Spain. He also inherited all Hapsburg lands in central Europe, which put him in possession of more territory than any one individual had ever ruled in Europe. At first, Charles was much more interested in the Holy Roman Empire than in Spain; his Spanish subjects interpreted his long absences as disrespect, and rebelled. Once his loyal supporters had put down the rebellion, Charles agreed to reform his habits. He returned to Spain and remained there for the balance of his life, overseeing his responsibilities as his subjects had expected.

Charles had several sisters, all of whom married heirs to various thrones in Denmark, Hungary, Portugal, and France. These marriages solidified alliances between Spain and these European states. In 1519, he was elected Holy Roman Emperor, making him Charles I of Spain and Charles V of Germany.

A devout Catholic like all the Spanish monarchs, Charles engaged in a series of wars to try to wipe out Protestantism and reunite Europe under the Catholic faith. These efforts were costly, time-consuming, and ultimately unsuccessful. With the Peace of Augsburg of 1555, which established that each elector in the empire could choose the religion of his own state, Charles abdicated. He turned the Holy Roman Empire over to his brother Ferdinand and abdicated the throne of Spain in favor of his son Philip, who would rule as Philip II.

Philip II and the Fall of Spain

Philip II inherited perhaps the most prosperous and powerful kingdom in Europe. By the 1550s, Spain boasted a thriving wool industry, a powerful navy, a stable aristocracy, religious unity (albeit enforced), and great wealth coming in from the American colonies. In addition, Philip's close family ties to several rulers in Austria and central Europe created strong national alliances for Spain.

By the time Philip inherited the throne, Spain had reaped tremendous profits from trade with its American colonies. Spain had always been a shipping economy, since it had long stretches of coastline and its ships were accustomed to navigating the Mediterranean as well as the Atlantic. This high degree of maritime skill was one reason Spain had been the first nation to sponsor transatlantic voyages.

Philip established Spain's first national capital in the city of Madrid. Until his accession to the throne, the royal court had traveled throughout the provinces, settling first in one city, then another. Philip, whose natural bent was for administration rather than war, preferred a stable working environment and thus a stationary court. He chose Madrid because it had two advantages. First, it was centrally located in the realm. Second, it was an insignificant town at the time; by choosing Madrid, Philip did not create regional rivalry among the more established centers of learning, industry, and culture. Had he chosen a city such as Seville, it might have created resentment among the wealthy residents of the cities he rejected.

Like all the Spanish monarchs, Philip was a devout Catholic. Unlike Henry IV of France, who had converted for reasons of political expediency, Philip had no religious tolerance in his nature. He refused to allow the practice of any religion except Catholicism anywhere in his realms, including the distant American colonies.

The Holy Roman Empire

As you read earlier, Holy Roman Emperor Charles V was also King Charles I of Spain. Charles divided his Spanish and central European lands between two family members. His brother Ferdinand would rule the empire as Ferdinand I. Although the formal transfer of power did not take place until 1556, Ferdinand had already been ruling the Austrian Hapsburg lands for thirty years.

Ferdinand's major foreign-policy goal was to withstand the constant threat of Turkish invasion. In 1529, the Turks under Suleiman the Magnificent laid siege to Vienna. The next seventeen years saw repeated Turkish invasions that the Austrians managed to repel; however, the Turks could always be counted on to come back and try again. In 1547, a peace treaty divided Hungary into three zones: Royal Hungary under Ferdinand's rule, Transylvania under its own rule, and the rest—the largest share—under Turkish control.

As Holy Roman Emperor and also king of both Bohemia and Hungary, Ferdinand ruled over a diverse population that included ethnic Germans, Czechs, Poles, and Hungarians. His subjects were also religiously mixed, including both Lutherans and Catholics. Ferdinand believed that the only way to manage such a varied population was to maintain a centrally controlled, efficient civil service. He established three councils of government: one executive, one administrative, and one judicial. He retained the loyalty and cooperation of the great landlords by allowing them most of the responsibility for day-to-day government at the local level. He also allowed his subjects freedom of worship; as a Catholic, Ferdinand would have preferred to rule a Catholic realm, and as

Holy Roman Emperor he was obliged to favor the Catholic cause. However, his attempts to do so involved persuasion rather than force, and he certainly preferred Lutheranism to the Islam practiced by the Turks. Like other successful monarchs of the sixteenth and seventeenth centuries, Ferdinand realized that no government would ultimately succeed in dictating the personal faith of its subjects.

Ferdinand I had laid the foundations of a united Austrian state. Although he divided his lands among his sons on his death in 1564, Austria would emerge from the Thirty Years' War as a relatively strong, unified empire. (See Chapter 5.)

England and the Triumph of Protestantism

In 1553, Mary Tudor inherited the throne of England, succeeding her half-brother Edward VI. Like her Spanish mother, Catherine of Aragon, Mary was a Catholic; on assuming the throne, she restored Catholicism as the state religion. In 1554 she married Philip, her cousin and fellow Catholic and then-heir to the throne of Spain. The marriage was highly unpopular in England, because Philip was Catholic, foreign, and father to a son from a previous marriage; the English did not welcome the idea of a foreign and Catholic heir (at age thirty-seven, Mary seemed unlikely to bear healthy children of her own). The marriage was purely an affair of state on Philip's side; occupied with military strategy and administrative tasks in Spain, he spent almost no time in England.

Mary was given the nickname "Bloody Mary" for the number of Protestants who were executed during her reign. By her order, between 250 and 300 Protestants were executed or burned at the stake; however, due process of English law was observed in all these cases. The accused were tried in court and executed.

Mary reigned for only a short time; she was well past her youth when she became queen, and she was not physically robust. She died childless in 1558 and was succeeded by her half-sister Elizabeth, daughter of Anne Boleyn.

Queen Elizabeth

Elizabeth I had a thoroughly pragmatic attitude toward religion and, in fact, toward almost every affair of state. Elizabeth was hardly likely to profess or practice Catholicism, since the Church had excommunicated her father for marrying her mother (see Chapter 2). However, she was tolerant for a monarch of her era. She restored Anglicanism as the state religion, but believed that faith was a personal matter and should not be dictated by the crown. Elizabeth felt far more interest in managing affairs of state than in waging religious warfare.

One important aspect of Elizabeth's realistic attitude toward ruling was her belief in the importance of personal popularity. It is clear from her actions and her writings that Elizabeth believed firmly in the divine right of kings (and queens); she considered herself an absolute monarch. However, she also knew that absolute monarchs could be overthrown or assassinated, and she knew that England's only other experience with a female monarch, under Mary, had not inspired confidence in a woman's ability to govern. Elizabeth's goal as monarch was to rule a peaceful and prosperous realm. She understood that she would be able to achieve much more with a loyal population of subjects, and therefore cultivated popular goodwill as a matter of policy. She was highly successful: two of her people's nicknames for her were "Gloriana" and "Good Queen Bess."

Another aspect of Elizabeth's pragmatism was her refusal to marry. Since she was a woman, she would have had to share her power with whatever prince she married, just as Isabel of Castile had recognized the wisdom of sharing her authority with Ferdinand. Elizabeth was only twenty-five when she became queen; therefore, it seemed quite likely that she would marry. In fact, she received several proposals, including one from Mary's widower, Philip II of Spain, and another from Henry III of France. Any nation considering a matrimonial alliance with Elizabeth had to maintain good relations with England; therefore her single status, especially during her childbearing years, was very useful to her as a diplomatic tool. In fact, she never married. When she died in 1603, the Tudor dynasty ended and the crown passed to her cousin James Stuart, king of Scotland.

The period from about 1550 to 1650 is often known as the Elizabethan era. It is also called "the English Renaissance" due to a great flowering of music, visual art, poetry, and drama. Playwright and poet William Shakespeare (c. 1564–1616), who can safely be called the most important English-language writer in history, was active in London theater during Elizabeth's reign. His colleagues included Christopher Marlowe, Ben Jonson, John Webster, and John Ford. Poets John Donne and John Milton, organist and composer Henry Purcell, and painter Hans Holbein (who had been active under Henry VIII and painted a number of the most famous images of the Tudors) were other notable creative artists of the era.

The Defeat of the Armada

During the 1500s, England realized that Spain was beginning to reap enormous profits from the New World. The Spanish galleons carried home considerable prizes in money, jewels, and other treasures. This led to the beginnings of piracy on the high seas. An English ship would attack a homebound Spanish vessel, murder or capture its crew, and commandeer the treasure for the queen. The pirates were rewarded for their exploits with a fixed share of the proceeds. Elizabeth even knighted the fearless pirate Captain Francis Drake as a reward for his many successful ventures.

Hostility had existed between England and Spain for some time. After Queen Mary's death, Philip had attempted to arrange a marriage with her younger sister, but Elizabeth rejected his offer. As a Catholic, Philip was a natural enemy of any Protestant nation; additionally, he resented Elizabeth's support of Protestant uprisings in France and the Netherlands. On Elizabeth's side, she was displeased over Philip's support of Mary Queen of Scots, who had attempted to wrest the throne of England from her royal cousin. The queen's encouragement of piracy against Spanish ships was what finally persuaded Philip to attack England and wipe out its navy.

In 1588, the Spanish armed fleet, called the Armada, sailed toward the English Channel. The Armada consisted of 130 ships and thousands of soldiers. The fleet looked very impressive and intimidating, but the English navy was more technologically advanced, with ships that were smaller, lighter, better armed, and easier to maneuver.

The English had set aside a number of ships that were no longer seaworthy, loaded them with explosives, and manned them with skeleton crews. In the darkness, the few sailors on board steered each of these ships directly toward the Armada, setting them on fire along the way, and only jumping overboard once the course was set and the ship was well alight. When the Spaniards saw these burning ships bearing down on them, apparently by magic, they panicked. The formation of the Armada descended into chaos and disorder as each captain ordered his crew to turn the ship and run away. When a fierce storm then came up, the English knew they had won. This battle marked the end of Spanish supremacy in European history.

QUIZ

1. _____ marked the end of a period in which Spain was a dominant European power.
   A. The conquest of Granada
   B. The death of Queen Mary
   C. The defeat of the Armada
   D. The marriage of Ferdinand and Isabel

2. Juana was unable to rule as queen of Castile because
   A. she was a woman.
   B. she was too old.
   C. she was unmarried.
   D. she was mentally unstable.

3. The officials of the Spanish Inquisition reported directly to
   A. the Church in Rome.
   B. the military.
   C. the monarch.
   D. the civil courts.

4. What was one practical reason for the Spanish government to insist that all the people must practice the same religious faith?
   A. to avoid the need for popular elections
   B. to avoid the possibility of domestic conflict
   C. to keep the monarchs more securely on their thrones
   D. to maintain the union of Aragon and Castile

5. The term *Reconquista* refers to the Spanish takeover of
   A. the Holy Roman Empire.
   B. colonies in the Americas.
   C. provinces in France and Italy.
   D. the Iberian peninsula.

6. _____ is still considered the greatest English writer who ever lived.
   A. John Donne
   B. Hans Holbein
   C. John Milton
   D. William Shakespeare

7. **What explains Elizabeth I's belief in the importance of her subjects' personal affection?**
   A. The people were more likely to vote for a popular monarch.
   B. The people were less likely to rise up against a popular monarch.
   C. The people would not pressure a popular monarch to marry.
   D. The people would not support the policies of a popular monarch.

8. **Charles of Ghent ruled over Spain and all the central European Hapsburg lands by right of _____.**
   A. inheritance
   B. military conquest
   C. popular election
   D. royal appointment

9. **Charles V abdicated as Holy Roman Emperor in the wake of**
   A. the conquest of Granada.
   B. the Peace of Augsburg.
   C. the marriage of his son Philip.
   D. the defeat of the Armada.

10. **Why did Ferdinand I consider it important to establish a centrally controlled bureaucracy?**
    A. to enable his armies to defeat the Turks
    B. to run a diverse empire effectively and efficiently
    C. to maintain the loyalty of the major landowners
    D. to suppress the practice of Lutheranism

The Thirty Years' War, 1618–1648

The Thirty Years' War marked the end of one era and the beginning of another. It began an era in which nation-states struggled for territorial and political power. It ended the dominance of the powerful Hapsburg family and began the era in which France was the strongest nation in Europe. It ended an era of Spanish military domination. It also ushered in an era in which states completed the long process of centralizing their governments, becoming what we recognize today as modern nations.

The Thirty Years' War was fought over religious, dynastic, and political/territorial issues. It was a religious war fought between Catholics and Protestants, with much bitterness on both sides. It was a war of two powerful families, the Catholic Hapsburgs and the Protestant Wittelsbachs. It was a political war in which nations fought for territorial expansion and to gain stronger positions in the balance of European power.

Many historians have described the Thirty Years' War as the last religious war in Europe. This is an exaggeration; religion is a powerful motivating factor in some present-day European conflicts, such as those within the United Kingdom and in the Balkans. However, it is true that from 1648 on, European leaders have openly claimed political, territorial, and economic reasons for warfare, but not religious ones.

CHAPTER 5 OBJECTIVES

- Identify the causes of the Thirty Years' War.
- Describe the major provisions of the Peace of Westphalia.
- Identify the major figures of the era and match each person to his or her role in the Thirty Years' War.

Chapter 5 Time Line

●	1617	Ferdinand Hapsburg becomes king of Bohemia; revokes Letter of Majesty
●	1618	Defenestration of Prague; Thirty Years' War begins
●	1619	Ferdinand II elected Holy Roman Emperor; Bohemians crown Frederich Wittelsbach king, deposing Ferdinand
●	1620	Battle of White Mountain
●	1629	Edict of Restitution bans Protestantism throughout Holy Roman Empire
●	1635	France declares war on Spain
●	1648	Peace of Westphalia; Thirty Years' War ends

Thirty Years' War

The Thirty Years' War is the name given to a series of religious and political wars fought in the Holy Roman Empire from 1618 to 1648. In religious terms, Catholics and Protestants struggled for ascendancy. In political terms, two prominent ruling families each tried to dominate the other, and several nation-states fought to improve their position.

As you read in Chapter 2, the Holy Roman Empire was not a nation; it had no form of central government. It was a loose collection of seven electorates, covering present-day Austria and Germany and parts of the Czech Republic. The emperor was chosen by the seven ruling electors. The people of the empire spoke German, French, and Czech. In Chapter 4, you read that the Peace of Augsburg (1555) stated that each elector could choose the state religion of his own principality. In 1600, three of the electorates were Protestant and the other four were Catholic. Of course, Catholics and Protestants hated one another, but there was also quite a bit of conflict within the Protestant portions of the empire. For instance, Calvinists loathed Lutherans, believing that they were far too lax in their approach to religion.

In the early modern era, European rule was a family affair rather than an official form of government as we understand government today. National borders changed with bewildering rapidity as monarchs died and passed their authority and their lands on to their children. Kings, princes, and electors of Europe ran their territories in much the same way that a lord ran his estate. The territory was considered to be similar to private property; the king owed his subjects his protection in return for their obedience.

The two most important and influential ruling families in the Holy Roman Empire were the Wittelsbachs and the Hapsburgs. As of 1600, there was religious dissension within each family, although the Hapsburgs were mainly Catholic and the Wittelsbachs were mainly Protestant. One major figure emerged in each family in the early 1600s: Ferdinand Hapsburg, elected king of Bohemia in 1617 and Holy Roman Emperor two years later, and his rival Frederich Wittelsbach.

The Thirty Years' War falls into three major phases, although fighting continued in various parts of the empire throughout the entire span of time.

Bohemian War, 1618–1620

In the years leading up to the outbreak of war, the situation between Catholics and Protestants in Bohemia had become tense. A 1609 document called the Letter of Majesty had extended the rights of Protestants within the state. The result of this tolerance was a mostly Lutheran landed gentry whose members resented being controlled by Catholic officials in the civil service. The two sides could not get along.

The Catholic side gained an important victory when Ferdinand Hapsburg was elected king of Bohemia in 1617. A zealous Catholic, Ferdinand revoked the Letter of Majesty, thus creating many enemies among the wealthy and powerful Bohemians. Hostility between the two sides came to a head one day in Prague Castle, when a group of discontented Lutherans threw several of the hated civil servants through the upstairs windows onto a compost heap in the courtyard below. This event, called the Defenestration of Prague, marked the start of a major Protestant uprising in Bohemia. It ended with the Protestants declaring that Ferdinand could not be their king; they deposed him and replaced him with Frederich Wittelsbach in 1619.

Ferdinand, of course, fought back against the Protestant defiance. By this time the Holy Roman Emperor had died, and Ferdinand had been chosen in his place. This gave him a much greater position of power from which to fight for control of Bohemia.

The electorates and free cities within the empire lined up on opposite sides along religious lines, with the Catholics supporting the emperor. The Protestant armies under King Frederich fared badly against the Catholic armies under Maximilian of Bavaria. In 1620, the Catholic side won a decisive victory at the Battle of White Mountain. Frederich hastily decamped to The Hague in Amsterdam, abandoning Bohemia to a brutally enforced program of conversion back to Catholicism.

Swedish War, 1630–1634

As Holy Roman Emperor, Ferdinand now had much more authority to pass laws against Protestantism. In 1628, he decreed that all Protestant landowners in Inner Austria must leave the country, turning over their property to the state. Many of them converted in order to avoid banishment. In 1629, Ferdinand signed the Edict of Restitution, which banned Protestantism throughout the Holy Roman Empire. It also stated that any originally Catholic lands and property must be restored to the Church.

Ferdinand did not realize that the time for such high-handed conduct had passed into history. Instead of meekly obeying his edicts, his Lutheran and Calvinist subjects abandoned their own quarrel and united against him as their common enemy. Not even Ferdinand's fellow monarchs and ministers of state sympathized with him. The Lutheran nation of Sweden immediately made preparations to march into Germany and fight for the Protestant side. Even France, always a reliably Catholic nation, considered the ban and the Edict of Restitution reactionary and dangerous. For the moment, however, the French bided their time.

Gustav II Adolf succeeded to the throne of Sweden in 1611, at age seventeen. Like all successful absolute monarchs, he turned his energies toward streamlining the civil service to make it more efficient and expanding the military to aid in foreign conquest. Spiritually, Gustav was a devout Lutheran; on practical grounds, he believed that a culturally and religiously homogeneous Sweden would be more stable and easier for the monarch to control. With this goal in mind, he banned the practice of Roman and Orthodox Catholicism from his realm; of course, this meant that all Church land and riches became the property of the crown. Sweden became a Lutheran state that tolerated other forms of Protestantism. This tolerance proved practical on Gustav's part once Sweden entered the fighting in the empire.

Sweden entered the Thirty Years' War to assist an ally, but also with an eye to expanding the Swedish empire by picking up new territory on the Baltic. If Sweden could take over all the land around the Baltic Sea, it would be able to control the trade routes, an enormous advantage over other nations in the region.

In 1631, Gustav led his troops to a major victory over veteran General Count Johann Tilly's imperial forces at Breitenfeld, near the town of Leipzig. Gustav then formed alliances with most of the Calvinist leaders in areas such as Brandenburg. Over the course of the next year, Gustav and his forces marched south, progressing in triumph all the way to Munich. Gustav fell at the battle of Lützen in 1632. Despite this disaster, Sweden's great generals maintained the advantage on the battlefield.

Franco-Swedish War, 1635–1648

As a Catholic nation, France should have been the natural ally of Ferdinand II in his attempts to impose Catholicism on his subjects. The chief French minister of state, in fact, was a cardinal of the Catholic Church. However, France fought on the Protestant side and played a decisive role in the Hapsburg's defeat.

Born into the minor French nobility in 1585, Armand Jean du Plessis de Richelieu became a cardinal in 1622. Richelieu was also the king's chief minister; as such, his goal was to make France the most powerful nation in Europe. Logically, this meant France's foreign policy would be to weaken other nations as much as possible.

Up to this time, the Holy Roman Empire and the Hapsburg family had always been a thorn in France's side. Geographically, the empire occupied a very strong central position on the continent. In addition, the Austrian Hapsburgs were related to the Spanish royal family and had been acquiring more and more authority in the empire. All this created potential for a strong, united

German state under Hapsburg rule, with Spain as a powerful ally. Richelieu wanted to avoid this at all costs; France's geographical position between two strong allied nations would be very vulnerable.

This situation indicates that religion was by no means the central issue in the Thirty Years' War, at least not in the minds of all the combatants. Richelieu's position as a minister of the Church took second place to his position as minister of France. When Jules Mazarin—also a Catholic cardinal—succeeded Richelieu on the latter's death in 1642, he continued Richelieu's policies. Both were hardheaded men with great common sense who excelled at the politics of realism as described by Machiavelli in *The Prince* (see Chapter 1).

The French watched the progress of Gustav II Adolf and the Swedish army. Their decisive military success inspired Richelieu to offer substantial monetary support to the Swedes. French troops finally joined the fighting in 1635. The combined French and Swedish troops continued to win victories for the next ten years.

By 1644, Gustav's daughter Kristina had reached the age of eighteen and was old enough to rule Sweden in her own right, assisted by the canny advice of her chief minister Axel Oxenstierna. Sweden was also fortunate to have some brilliant generals, who achieved an impressive series of military victories. The Swedish army had reached Bavaria by 1646 and Prague by 1647; by the terms of the Peace of Westphalia in 1648, Sweden annexed several important territories.

Results of the Thirty Years' War

The Peace of Westphalia cemented the work begun under Ferdinand—the creation of a unified Austrian nation-state, which would before long become the Austro-Hungarian Empire. The Hapsburgs would continue to rule Austria into the twentieth century.

Provisions of the Peace of Westphalia

- Restored borders within the Holy Roman Empire to their 1624 locations
- Revoked the Edict of Restitution
- Gave Alsace to France
- Recognized Switzerland and the Netherlands as independent nation-states

- Made Bavaria, Prussia, Saxony, and Wurttemberg self-governing, independent states within the Holy Roman Empire
- Created a unified Austrian empire including Bohemia, Moravia, Silesia, and parts of Hungary

Since the war had been fought entirely within the Holy Roman Empire, the Germans suffered most from the violence. Of a total ethnic German population of about 17 million, historians agree that between 3.5 million and 7 million died; additionally, millions of acres of farmland were laid waste, and foreign troops released from combat duties were roaming the countryside, looting and murdering. German unification, which had seemed possible in the early 1600s, was set back for some time to come.

With north central Europe devastated by the war, France emerged as the dominant nation-state. Spain had lost its navy during the defeat of the Armada, Italy was still a collection of city-states that were constantly being invaded by Austria or France, and England, as always, maintained a measure of isolation on the far side of the English Channel. By contrast, France was a large, continuous landmass with a strong central position on the continent, and it had a strong central government. It would remain Europe's greatest power until Napoleon's defeat at Waterloo in 1815.

The Holy Roman Empire would continue to exist on paper, but the emperor would have only nominal authority. Four of the electorates—Prussia, Bavaria, Saxony, and Wurttemberg—were made independent, self-governing states owing pro forma allegiance to the emperor; the others were made part of the Austrian empire.

The Peace of Westphalia was the result of the monarchs and ministers gathering together—the first time this had happened in European history. The nations agreed to recognize one another's sovereignty and to create and maintain a balance of power that would prevent future wars. The Peace of Westphalia was thus an important first step toward recognizing that affairs of state could be settled around a conference table rather than on the battlefield.

QUIZ

1. **Most of the fighting in the Thirty Years' War took place in**
    A. France.
    B. the Holy Roman Empire.
    C. Italy.
    D. Spain.

2. **Austria should have expected help from France during the war because both nations were**
    A. Catholic.
    B. Protestant.
    C. ruled by a member of the Hapsburg family.
    D. enemies of England.

3. _____ **emerged from the Thirty Years' War as the dominant power in Europe.**
    A. England
    B. France
    C. Spain
    D. Sweden

4. **Which nation became a unified empire as a result of the Thirty Years' War?**
    A. Austria
    B. France
    C. Germany
    D. Italy

5. **France's primary reason for entering the Thirty Years' War was**
    A. to weaken its hostile neighbors Austria and Spain.
    B. to help its most prominent Catholic ally defeat the Protestants.
    C. to end the threat of Swedish expansion on the continent.
    D. to stimulate an economic recovery at home.

6. **What did the Edict of Restitution state?**
    A. It settled the terms of surrender among the Holy Roman Empire, France, and Switzerland.
    B. It replaced Ferdinand II with Frederich as king of Bohemia.
    C. It banned Protestantism throughout the Holy Roman Empire.
    D. It allowed each elector to decide the official religion of his own state.

7. **What happened in Bohemia as a result of the Battle of White Mountain?**
   A. Catholicism was restored as the state religion.
   B. Catholics emigrated to other nations to escape enforced conversion.
   C. Maximilian of Bavaria was crowned king.
   D. Citizens threw some city officials through the Prague Castle windows.

8. _____ revoked the Letter of Majesty in 1617.
   A. Cardinal Richelieu
   B. Gustav II Adolf
   C. Ferdinand II
   D. Frederich of Bohemia

9. **Although Lutherans were fellow Protestants, Calvinists despised them because**
   A. they had too much in common with Catholics.
   B. they conducted church services in the language spoken by the people.
   C. they maintained their loyalty to the pope.
   D. their approach to religion was too lax for Calvinist taste.

10. **In 1648, the prospects for a unified German nation were dim because the German-speaking states**
    A. lost the friendship of their most powerful ally, Spain.
    B. agreed to the strengthening of the Austrian empire.
    C. had suffered too much damage and lost too many people during the fighting.
    D. refused to consider establishing a policy of religious freedom.

chapter 6

The Age of Monarchy

The period from the Treaty of Westphalia in 1648 to the French Revolution in 1789 was truly the age of the absolute ruler. Powerful monarchs ruled all the nations and principalities of Europe. They believed in the doctrine of the divine right of kings.

Certain conditions were necessary to maintain a strong central monarchy. The monarch must control the aristocracy, ensure the loyalty and obedience of the army, run the administration efficiently from the seat of government, and pursue a clear foreign policy.

In the past, struggles for thrones had been common. Members of royal families had been known to murder one another or engage in civil wars in their desire for power. Once a monarch had power, he or she could never feel secure. One of the best ways to protect the throne was to keep control over the nobles, the most likely and most powerful source of any conspiracy against the monarch.

During the Middle Ages and beyond, armies were made of small, localized units. These troops usually remained loyal to the lord for whom they fought. The seventeenth century saw the birth of the national standing army, which owed its loyalty to the monarch as the head of state. A loyal army would not support an uprising among the common people or the nobility; instead, the monarch would use the army to crush the rebellion.

Ancient Rome had existed as a centrally controlled empire with a vast bureaucracy. In the seventeenth century, European states began to pattern themselves on the Roman model. The civil service was essential to control all the territory outside the capital city. It was responsible for collecting taxes, settling court cases, and so on. No central government could maintain control over the people without having an efficient civil service.

Defending the national borders was an important aspect of maintaining power. No ruler could remain secure on his throne without a clear foreign policy. Monarchs had to maintain defensive alliances and strive to maintain the balance of power among nations; they also had to take steps to avoid being overwhelmed by hostile neighbors.

CHAPTER 6 OBJECTIVES

- Describe the characteristics of a strong monarchy.
- Identify the strong monarchies of Europe in the seventeenth and eighteenth centuries.
- Describe the policies of the monarchs and their chief ministers.
- Explain how England evolved from an absolute to a constitutional monarchy.

Chapter 6 Time Line

- **1643** Louis XIV becomes King of France
- **1649** Charles I of England is executed; English monarchy abolished
- **1653** Oliver Cromwell becomes "Lord Protector" of England
- **1660** Restoration of monarchy in England; Charles II crowned king
- **1661** Mazarin dies; Louis XIV becomes chief minister as well as king
- **1682** Peter I becomes czar of Russia
- **1688** Glorious Revolution; James II deposed; William and Mary become king and queen of Great Britain
- **1689** English Bill of Rights
- **1700** Philip V becomes king of Spain
- **1701** War of Spanish Succession begins

- **1740**   Maria Theresa becomes empress of Austria; Frederick II becomes king of Prussia
- **1762**   Catherine II becomes empress of Russia
- **1780**   Maria Theresa dies; Joseph II becomes emperor of Austria

Louis XIV

In 1643, a five-year-old child was crowned Louis XIV of France. He would reign until his death in 1715. Known to the world as the Sun King, Louis was perhaps the most absolute of the absolute European monarchs of the seventeenth century. He chose the sun for his symbol because it was the source of all light and life on earth.

Like all the monarchs of his era, Louis believed in the divine right of kings. This was not a theory to him, but a reality by which he lived and ruled. Louis considered that he and the state of France were one entity. He had no intention of ceding any of his power to the aristocracy, the Church, or the common people of France.

Domestic Policy

King Louis XIII's chief minister of state, the highly able Cardinal Richelieu, had believed in a strong central monarchy. Jules Mazarin, also a cardinal, succeeded Richelieu in 1642 and became Louis XIV's chief minister. He espoused the same policies as Richelieu; like his predecessor, he discouraged representative institutions. France had no equivalent of the English Parliament. It had a body called the Estates General, which consisted of three groups of deputies representing the hereditary nobility, the clergy, and the commoners. Louis never once convened the Estates General. He and Mazarin preferred to govern without their advice or interference. During Louis' reign, opposition to the king was considered treason; even had the Estates General met, the deputies would have had no power to do anything other than agree with whatever the king wanted. After the death of Mazarin in 1661, Louis served as his own chief minister rather than summon the Estates General.

The reign of Louis XIV saw numerous construction projects. The building of the Canal du Midi (1665–1681), which connected the Mediterranean and the Atlantic, was important for trade and an impressive feat of engineering for the time. The crown also pursued an aggressive tariff policy that discouraged imports and bolstered French luxury industries such as the textile industry. Louis hired architects to oversee the restoration and remodeling of the Louvre and the building of Versailles, the king's "retreat" fourteen miles outside of Paris. An enormous palace with endless corridors of mirrors, marble, and gold leaf, Versailles became a major symbol of the king's absolute power; it also symbolized the dominant role France played in Europe in the seventeenth and eighteenth centuries.

To exercise as much control as possible over the hereditary nobility, Louis XIV required all of them to spend part of each year at Versailles. In the short term, this policy prevented the nobles from hatching any conspiracy against the crown. In the long term, it weakened the all-important bond between estate owners and their tenants. Instead of living on their estates and managing their land and their people, the nobles spent half their time at Versailles; the money that should have been spent on maintaining and improving their estates was wasted on court finery and travel expenses. Louis did not know it, but he was helping to lay the groundwork for the French Revolution. (See Chapter 9.)

Louis XIV also helped to lay the groundwork for the eighteenth-century Enlightenment. The crown was the most important patron of arts and letters in France. Investigation, learning, and publication in the arts and sciences flourished under official state sponsorship, with the establishment of the French academies of letters, science, and the arts. Not since the Renaissance had artists enjoyed such a degree of official protection. This helps to explain why the Enlightenment was centered in France. (See Chapter 8.)

The Fronde was a series of uprisings and rebellions in the Paris-Bordeaux region over the issue of new taxes Mazarin levied on the people to pay for debts run up during the Thirty Years' War. Since the state controlled the army, which had greatly expanded during the war, the rebels were doomed from the start. The Fronde was crushed in 1652.

Foreign Policy

Louis XIV conducted a series of wars in the hope of strengthening France's position in Europe. They included the War of Devolution (1667–1668), the Dutch War (1672–1678), the War of League of Augsburg (1689–1697), and the War of Spanish Succession (1701–1713).

Louis' foreign wars included both successes and failures. He expanded French territory on the northern front, with the annexation of Flanders and Strasbourg. However, he supported the losing side in the power struggle for

England between the Stuarts and the Hanoverians. The worst effect of Louis' wars was that they drained the French treasury of money. This damage to the domestic economy would have serious consequences under Louis' successors.

The most important of Louis' wars was the War of Spanish Succession, which pitted France and Spain against the Netherlands, England, and the Holy Roman Empire. The war began after Louis' grandson was crowned Philip V of Spain in 1700; the idea of a close alliance between France and Spain, or perhaps even a union of the two kingdoms, made the rest of Europe unite in alarm to prevent it. A United Kingdom of Spain and France would be by far the largest nation in Europe, and would disrupt the balance of power. The war was ultimately settled by the Treaty of Utrecht. In exchange for remaining on the throne, Philip V agreed that the crowns of Spain and France would never be united.

England

England had already experienced a century of absolute monarchy under the Tudors. Although Henry VII had taken the English throne by right of conquest, he and his descendants believed in the divine right of kings as much as any hereditary monarch. This belief continued when the Stuart dynasty succeeded the Tudors on the death of Elizabeth I in 1603.

James VI of Scotland ruled England as James I until his death in 1625. An unpopular monarch, James achieved one major accomplishment: he commissioned a new translation of the Bible, to be as scholarly and accurate as possible. The King James Bible, published in 1611, is one of the most influential works in the history of English literature. It inspired generations of English and American writers and statesmen, such as Abraham Lincoln and Winston Churchill, and countless idioms of everyday speech come from its pages. Scholars and historians agree that although more technically accurate English translations of the Bible have been made since, none can rival the beauty, power, and poetry of the King James version.

In 1625, Charles I inherited the throne of England. He was not much more popular than his father James had been, for several reasons. First, Charles's personality was shy, stiff, and rather pompous. Second, the people looked askance on Charles's marriage to French Catholic princess Henrietta Maria; they were concerned that the heirs to the throne might be raised as Catholics. Third, congregations throughout the nation had become divided between high-church and low-church Anglican. High-church Anglicans, of whom Charles was one, favored a ceremonial style of worship that was very similar to the Catholic mass. Low-church Anglicans preferred more Spartan rites and practices that made them more spiritually akin to Presbyterians and Calvinists.

Until this time, Parliament's major purpose had been to grant the monarch any funds necessary to carry out affairs of state such as wars. The request had always been treated as a matter of form. James I had been at odds with Parliament throughout his reign, preferring to rule as an autocrat. Many members of Parliament, resenting the king's lack of respect for their official position, began insisting on a greater say in national policy. They were united in their determination not to allow Charles to rule with the heavy hand his father had shown—especially because many members of the House of Commons were low-church Anglicans or Calvinists and did not look on the king's religious beliefs with favor. Parliament refused to allow the king to raise funds without its permission. Charles agreed to this demand, but as soon as the funds were granted, he disbanded Parliament. The legislative assembly would not meet between 1629 and 1640.

Working with William Laud, the archbishop of Canterbury, Charles tried to impose high Anglican rules and rites throughout Scotland, including a new prayer-book. Scotland, which had been staunchly Presbyterian since the days of the Reformation, showed that is was willing to go to war to defend its religious liberty. Fighting began in 1640 when the Scots marched into England. This in turn forced Charles to convene Parliament to request funds for the war. The representatives immediately realized they were in a position of strength; they passed a series of laws designed to weaken absolutism. The year 1641 saw the imprisonment and execution of Archbishop Laud and an uprising in Ireland. In 1642, Charles I led an armed attack on Parliament, initiating a civil war that lasted until 1649. Oliver Cromwell, a member of the House of Commons, led the Parliamentary forces; thanks largely to Cromwell's considerable military ability, Parliament's troops defeated the monarch's. Later, Cromwell's soldiers conquered both Scotland and Ireland.

Parliament voted to abolish the monarchy, the House of Lords, and Anglicanism as the state religion. In 1649, Charles I was put to death; his teenage sons Charles and James fled the country, eventually finding their way to Holland and safety.

English kings had lost their lives on the battlefield in the past, with the crown going to the victor in battle, but no English monarch before Charles I had ever been condemned to death by due process of law. This marked a major defeat for the European tradition of absolute monarchy and ushered in the modern era of republican government.

Cromwell argued in Parliament for a platform of certain reforms, but his colleagues refused to pass them. By 1653, Cromwell ran out of patience and disbanded the legislature. In 1654, he became the first commoner and the only military dictator ever to rule England, under the title Lord Protector.

Cromwell was a devout Puritan—a sect that practiced an extreme form of Calvinism. Like other British monarchs before him, Cromwell imposed his own religious faith on his kingdom. He closed all theaters and saloons, since Calvinists believed that pastimes such as drinking, gambling, and attending plays were sinful. Cromwell did not go out of his way to persecute Anglicans or Lutherans, but Catholics were forced to practice their faith in secrecy during his reign.

Cromwell ruled England until his death in 1658; this period is called the Interregnum, meaning "between reigns." His son Richard succeeded him, but proved ineffective. It was not long before loyalists restored Charles I's eldest son to the throne he should have inherited on his father's death. With the blessing of Parliament, Charles II was crowed in 1660. His reign is known as the Restoration.

Charles II was an easygoing, tolerant monarch. However, he soon found that Parliament was by no means willing to give up any of the power it had won so recently. As often as not, Parliament opposed the king's attempts to assert his authority. It was clear that in England, the days of absolute monarchy were over.

Since Charles II had no legitimate children, his heir was his brother James, a devout Catholic. A sizable faction in Parliament, dreading the possibility of another Catholic ruler, proposed a bill called the Exclusion Bill. It would bar James or any other Catholic from inheriting the throne. In the argument over the Exclusion Bill, the first British political parties were formed. The Whigs supported the bill and the Tories opposed it. The bill passed the House of Commons but not the House of Lords, and James II succeeded to the throne on his brother's death.

James's harsh anti-Anglican policies made the Whigs and Tories unite against him; when his wife gave birth to an heir to the throne, who would ensure Catholic rule for another generation, they agreed that the monarch must be deposed and replaced. The best candidate appeared to be Mary, James's grown daughter by an earlier marriage. Deputies from Parliament invited Mary and her husband, William of Orange, to rule jointly. They arrived in England in 1688, James fled to France without a shot being fired, and the Glorious Revolution was won.

The most important result of the Glorious Revolution was the passage of the English Bill of Rights. It had two main goals: to unite the people and their monarch once and for all under the same state religion, and to balance the government by giving Parliament certain important rights over the monarch. The Bill of Rights stated that no Catholic could rule England and no British monarch could marry a Catholic. Parliament felt that this step was necessary to avoid any more of the civil wars that had torn the island apart since the days of Queen Mary.

Parliament reinforced its own authority by declaring that it must meet every year. This ensured that the legislative assembly could step in and assume power if the monarch proved irresponsible or incapable. Parliament also assumed other major legislative functions: from this time on, the authority to suspend laws, maintain a standing army, and impose new taxes rested with Parliament, not with the monarch.

In 1707, England and Scotland were officially incorporated as one nation, known as the United Kingdom of Great Britain.

Peter the Great of Russia

Peter Romanov was born in 1672. When Peter was ten, he and his brother Ivan were named dual monarchs of Russia; their older sister Sophia would serve as regent until the boys grew old enough to rule. In 1689, the nobles ousted Sophia from power. On Ivan's sudden death, Peter became Czar Peter I of Russia. Known to history as Peter the Great, he would rule Russia until his death in 1725.

Peter was characterized by genuine intellectual and scientific curiosity. He also had a strong, dominant personality and believed in absolute rule with a very heavy hand. These two qualities of the czar's character had a decisive effect on Russia's development during the early eighteenth century.

Peter was fascinated by European culture. In 1697, he left his homeland to tour Europe in disguise. Given that the czar was six feet, six inches tall—a true giant in an era when people were much smaller than they are today—his disguise fooled no one. However, he enjoyed his ability to speak directly with commoners of all types, and even share their heavy manual labor, as he could not easily have done had he traveled in a more ceremonious style.

When Peter returned to Russia, he made plans to turn it into a modern nation that would take its place beside the great states of Europe. Western influence was soon apparent everywhere in Moscow. At the court and elsewhere, Peter began requiring Western administrative practices and Western efficiency. During Peter's reign, many French, English, and German books were translated into Russian for the first time; Peter himself acquired an impressive personal library. He introduced Western-style dress to replace the traditional Russian costumes; the most famous innovation in personal style was a law against beards, since European fashion dictated a clean-shaven face for a man. Many nobles and gentlemen opposed this law with surprising vigor, for two reasons: first, Orthodox doctrine required believers to wear full beards, and second, a beard was welcome protection against frostbite during the bitter Russian winters. In the end, Peter exempted priests from the no-beard policy.

Peter kept up a constant state of warfare during his reign; the standing army reached a new high of two hundred thousand troops under his rule. By 1721 he had moved Russia's border far to the west, acquiring Estonia, Livonia, and part of Switzerland. In 1703, Peter founded a new capital city at the mouth of the Gulf of Finland, naming it St. Petersburg after himself. Peter would use this beautiful city much as Louis XIV used Versailles; he required the boyars to attend him there during part of every year and forced them to pay for its construction.

Peter the Great died in 1725. Since he named no successor, a period of some chaos ensued. At first, his widow assumed power, ruling as Catherine I; after her death, various factions struggled for power. The situation was resolved in 1762 when Peter II became czar; however, mental and emotional instability made him incapable of ruling. His German wife, Catherine, assumed power when he died suddenly; historians agree that she either murdered him or ordered her followers to do so.

Catherine II, like Peter the Great, was determined to make Russia into a European nation, not surprising given her German origins. She continued Peter's policy of moving the nation's border ever westward. Between 1769 and 1774, Russia gained territory along the Danube River and also a port on the Black Sea.

Catherine absorbed many ideas from the Enlightenment. She introduced Russians to Western music, art, literature, and philosophy. She corresponded with the famed author Voltaire. She founded and supported a number of institutions that would improve society, including a major hospital and a medical school, and led a campaign for inoculation against smallpox. She supported education for girls and young women and opened Russia's first public library. She reformed the legal code to limit the use of torture of prisoners and expanded religious freedoms.

Like other absolute monarchs, Catherine understood the need to protect her position by controlling the aristocracy. She took two major steps to keep the nobles content with their lot. First, she exempted them from taxes. Second, and partly in response to a major peasant uprising, she granted them absolute control over their serfs. With the loss of many important freedoms, including the right to move, the serfs in effect became slave labor. Their status would not improve until the 1860s.

Poland

Poland had been a strong nation-state during the late Middle Ages; a dynastic marriage in 1386 between Princess Jadwiga of Poland and the Grand Duke of Lithuania united the two as the Kingdom of Poland-Lithuania. However, the dynasty died out in 1572, at which point the nobles seized power, granting themselves the right to elect the monarch. The aristocracy proved too powerful for the monarchy, which never recovered enough strength to suppress the nobles. In 1764, Stanislav Poniatowski was elected king; unfortunately for the immediate future of Poland, he was romantically involved with Catherine the Great of Russia, who would use the personal relationship to take over half the kingdom.

By 1772, Russia had annexed Lithuanian territory as far west as the Dvina River. At the same time, Prussia and Austria began taking over Polish territory on their own borders. The Second and Third Partitions of Poland followed in the 1790s, effectively erasing Poland as a nation from the map.

Holy Roman Empire: Austria and Prussia

During the age of monarchy, the Holy Roman Empire as an entity began to pass into history. Its various states began to take shape as independent nation-states, of which the two strongest were Austria and Prussia.

Austria

The Hapsburg family continued to rule in central Europe. In 1711, Charles VI became the latest Hapsburg to be elected Holy Roman Emperor. As time went on with no son being born to inherit the throne of Austria, Charles took steps to prevent the Hapsburg estate from breaking up. He signed the Pragmatic Sanctions, which stated that his eldest daughter, Maria Theresa, would inherit on his death.

When Maria Theresa became empress of Austria in 1740, Frederick of Prussia promptly invaded her territory. The Prussians won the ensuing war and took over the province of Silesia.

Maria Theresa proved to be an enlightened ruler. She centralized her government in Vienna and worked to make the civil service run more efficiently. She made it a matter of domestic policy to bring tax relief to the poorest peasants in the realm.

In 1765, Maria Theresa elevated her son Joseph to the status of a co-ruler. On her death in 1780, he succeeded her as Emperor Joseph II. Like all the Hapsburgs, Joseph believed in his divine right to rule; however, he was a far more benevolent monarch than most. Social reform under Joseph was highly unpopular with the upper classes, who did not welcome notions of equality that weakened their own position atop the structure of power and privilege. (See Chapter 12.)

Prussia

The history of Germany as a nation-state really began in 1640, when Frederick William Hohenzollern became king of Brandenburg-Prussia (later known simply as Prussia). Frederick's main goal was the same as that of all absolute monarchs of his era: to rule over a centrally controlled state. First, he enlarged and strengthened the standing army, ensuring its loyalty to the throne. Second, he achieved control over the junkers—Prussian hereditary nobles—by giving them administrative duties. Third, he began to lay the groundwork for uniting all the territories he had inherited under his sole control.

In 1688, the elector's son became King Frederick I of Prussia. For twenty-five years, he maintained the modern state his father had created. In 1713, his son took over. King Frederick William I continued to streamline the bureaucracy of government and to make it more efficient. Frederick William I also concentrated on the Prussian army, expanding and lavishing money and attention on what soon became a fighting force admired and envied by all Europe. Although the army did not spend much time on the battlefield during this period, it was an intimidating and impressive symbol of the power of the Prussian state.

As the king lay on his deathbed in 1740, he felt apprehensive about his heir. The young man who would rule as Frederick II did not seem to be the stuff of which autocrats were made. As a prince, he spent most of his time reading, composing music, and playing the flute. However, he had always been fascinated by military strategy and would prove a highly effective ruler. He became known to history as Frederick the Great. He took over Silesia, led his nation to victory in the Seven Years' War, occupied West Prussia, and drove both the army and the bureaucracy to greater heights of efficiency and discipline.

Frederick's daring foreign policy was dictated by Prussia's geographical position. Prussia was in the middle of Europe, surrounded on all sides by other nations; this made it vulnerable to invasion at any time. Frederick's solution to this dangerous situation was twofold. First, he built up such an impressive, efficient army that other nations hesitated to attack him. Second, he himself struck aggressive blows to enlarge his territory and intimidate his neighbors.

The blow against Silesia had been carefully calculated. This province was rich in natural resources, which Prussia lacked. Since Maria Theresa was new to the throne, Frederick believed Austria was at its most vulnerable. His gamble paid off in 1745 when he agreed to recognize Maria Theresa as empress and her husband as emperor in exchange for Silesia. The result of this was to elevate Prussia's position among European nations; Prussia and Austria were now considered equally strong German powers.

In the Seven Years' War (1756–1763), Prussia took no part in the fighting over North American colonies. Frederick's goal was to maintain Prussia's position of power in Europe. England allied itself with Prussia, since fighting between Prussia and France meant that France could not concentrate its forces in America. (See Chapter 7.)

Frederick's reign also revealed the influence of the Enlightenment on his thinking. He stressed the importance of merit in the ranks of the civil service, raising the standards for admission. He expanded freedom of speech, promoted education, and reformed the legal system. Although the Prussian state was overwhelmingly Protestant, Frederick did not hinder Catholics from observing their faith. He also developed something of a friendship with Voltaire, entertaining him at court.

By the time Frederick died in 1786, Prussia had become a strong, centralized state. It formed the core of what would become, a hundred years later, a unified Germany.

The Netherlands

The Netherlands became a parliamentary republic after gaining its independence from Hapsburg rule in the Treaty of Westphalia. It consisted of several provinces, each of which sent deputies to the national assembly, the States General, which met in The Hague, at the mouth of the Rhine River on the North Sea. This was also the residence of the hereditary ruler of the Orange family, known as the *stadholder*. In 1688, *stadholder* William of Orange became William I of England, thanks to his marriage to the Stuart princess Mary.

Because the Dutch provinces were small and the population was culturally homogeneous, the provincial deputies of the States General tended to work effectively together rather than bickering. They controlled all foreign-policy decisions, subject to the approval of the provincial legislatures, called "estates."

QUIZ

1. **The Restoration occurred in 1660 when Charles II was crowned king of _____**
   A. England.
   B. France.
   C. Prussia.
   D. Russia.

2. **_____ were the first nation-states to achieve true representative government.**
   A. Prussia and Austria
   B. The Netherlands and Austria
   C. England and the Netherlands
   D. England and Prussia

3. **What was the main reason for the expansion of the Prussian army during this period?**
   A. to extend Prussia's borders by military conquest
   B. to defend the Prussian kingdom from attack
   C. to keep the nobility loyal to the crown
   D. to win foreign wars in the American colonies

4. **The English Bill of Rights was passed as a result of _____**
   A. the Restoration.
   B. the Glorious Revolution.
   C. the English Civil War.
   D. the Exclusion Bill.

5. **Peter the Great's main reason for dictating changes in Russian fashion was**
   A. to modernize Russian society and culture.
   B. to intimidate the boyar class.
   C. to encourage Russians to travel to the West.
   D. to strengthen his personal popularity among his subjects.

6. **Louis XIV required the hereditary nobles to attend him every year at Versailles because**
   A. he wanted to prevent them from conspiring against him.
   B. he wanted to consult them regularly about government policy.
   C. he wanted be able to raise the army on a moment's notice.
   D. he wanted their protection in case of a peasant uprising.

7. **The establishment of _____ helped lead to the Enlightenment.**
   A. the Estates General
   B. the English Bill of Rights
   C. the Whig and Tory parties
   D. the French academies

8. **The War of Spanish Succession was a threat to**
   A. the Spanish colonial empire.
   B. the monarchy of France.
   C. the balance of powers in Europe.
   D. the alliance between Prussia and Austria.

9. **During the Seven Years' War, England allied itself with Prussia in order to defeat**
   A. France.
   B. Russia.
   C. Spain.
   D. Italy.

10. **The main reason for the failure of the Fronde was the opposition of**
    A. the common people.
    B. the nobility.
    C. the clergy.
    D. the army.

chapter 7

The Age of Expansion, Exploration, and Colonization, 1492–1787

The age of monarchy goes hand in hand with the age of exploration and colonization. While European monarchs vied with one another to establish strong nation-states in Europe, they also began sponsoring voyages of exploration beyond the known world. The purposes were fourfold: trade, conquest and expansion, religious conversion, and curiosity. The primary reason for their stupendous success can be summed up in one word: guns.

Europeans had long been trading with Asia, but the overland routes were problematic. Going over land, goods could not be transported any faster than a horse could walk; ships, by contrast, could move much more quickly, and a single ship could carry far more goods than a team of horses. Additionally, the overland routes were dangerous. Traders were constantly vulnerable to robbery and attack, weather caused problems at most times of the year, and geographical features such as mountains created obstacles to a smooth passage. All these factors ate into profits and made the traders look around for water routes to Asia, since transport of goods by water was much easier, more efficient, and less hazardous.

The second motive was conquest and expansion. The story that has unfolded in the previous chapters of this book shows that European nations tended to have an aggressive foreign policy, constantly attacking one another in order to acquire valuable territory and expand their power bases. A larger population meant more revenue for the crown in taxes, more income for the Church in tithes, and more soldiers in the army. Therefore, three of the most power-ful branches of society—the royal court, the clergy, and the military—were united in the desire to explore the seas and lands beyond Europe in the hope of establishing colonies that would make them richer and stronger than their neighbors.

The third motive, religious conversion, was a product of the universal Chris-tian belief that non-Christians were heathens and that it was a Christian's duty to convert them, thus saving their souls from eternal damnation after death. Just as a nation is politically and economically stronger with a larger population, a church is stronger with more believers; therefore, the European churches were eager to send missionaries to Asia, Africa, and the Americas to bring more souls into the fold.

The last motive, and a very powerful one, was a sense of adventure and curi-osity—the urge to find out what lay beyond the horizon and the willingness to take the risk of finding out. This urge has characterized human beings since the beginning of civilization and is responsible for all scientific discovery and technological achievement. Just as the twentieth-century explorations of outer space could not have been accomplished without the fundamental human desire to see and learn about the unknown, the sixteenth- and seventeenth-century voyages of exploration could never have happened if a number of brave souls had not wanted to find out what was on the other side of the ocean.

Although the Chinese had invented gunpowder centuries before, there were no guns in the world that could match what the Europeans had developed by the 1500s. One of the most important axioms to understanding history is that in any conflict, the side with the greater firepower always wins. The Asians had much less sophisticated guns than the Europeans, and the Americans had no guns at all. This is almost certainly the main reason the Europeans were able to impose their will on the peoples of the other continents.

CHAPTER 7 OBJECTIVES

- Identify the motives that led European nations to begin exploring the world beyond Europe.
- Describe where the various European states established trade relations and colonies.
- Identify the major figures of the era and match each person to the geographical area he explored.

Chapter 7 Time Line

- **1487**　Bartholomew Diaz rounds Cape of Good Hope
- **1492**　Spanish-sponsored voyage of Columbus crosses Atlantic; begins cultural exchange
- **1497–99**　Vasco da Gama reaches India
- **1513**　Portuguese reach Southeast Asia
- **1517**　Portuguese reach China
- **1539**　Hernando de Soto explores southeastern North America
- **1565**　Pedro Menendez de Áviles founds St. Augustine on Florida coast
- **1585**　Raleigh establishes English colony on Roanoke Island, Virginia
- **1607**　London Company establishes colony of Jamestown near Chesapeake Bay
- **1620**　*Mayflower* reaches Cape Cod Bay; settlers sign Mayflower Compact
- **1629**　Puritans found Massachusetts Bay Colony by royal charter
- **1776**　British colonies in North America declare independence as United States of America
- **1781**　Great Britain surrenders to United States at Yorktown

Exploration to the East

Europeans had been navigating the South Atlantic and the Mediterranean since ancient times, but it was only in the late fifteenth century that they began to explore the west coast of Africa and to look for ways to reach China and India by water. Europeans had traveled far to the East during the Crusades of the Middle Ages; there had also been solitary travelers like Marco Polo who brought back fabulous tales of sophisticated Eastern civilizations and tangible samples of Eastern luxuries in the form of spices, silks, and porcelain. Such items—especially the spices, which not only improved the taste of food but also helped to preserve it in the age before refrigeration—were highly valued in Europe, commanding high prices because of their scarcity. All the European nations knew there was great profit to be made from overseas trade—if one could establish an easy, efficient, and economical route.

Portuguese Exploration and Trade

Portugal's long stretch of Atlantic coastline and its proximity to Africa placed it in an ideal geographical position to take the lead in these exploratory voyages. With the birth in 1394 of Prince Henry, Portugal also acquired the ideal sponsor for its seagoing ventures.

Prince Henry's passion for ships and the sea, and the skills he acquired in his favorite subject, gave him the nickname Prince Henry the Navigator. Since Henry was not the heir to Portugal's throne, he was free to indulge his time and money on ships and sailing. His fascination with the sea proved enormously profitable for the kingdom.

Henry oversaw and paid for the development of the caravel, a lighter, faster, and more maneuverable sailing ship than those generally used at the time. He sponsored exploratory voyages to West Africa and employed skilled cartographers to record the results. Henry's own considerable skills in navigation were hugely beneficial to the Portuguese fleet.

During the late 1400s, Portuguese explorers made a series of voyages along the west coast of Africa. Their purpose was to gather information and perhaps to set up trading posts; at this time there was no attempt at invasion or conquest. In 1487, one of these voyages stumbled accidentally on the only viable water route to the East.

Captain Bartholomew Diaz and his crew, having ventured almost to the southern tip of Africa, were blown off course during a storm. When the storm ended, Diaz realized that they had rounded Africa's southern tip, which he promptly named Cape of Storms; later it became known as the Cape of Good Hope. This voyage established the viability of sailing to Asia by rounding Africa. (The Suez Canal, which connects the Mediterranean and Red seas and thus provides a much shorter shipping route, was not built until the mid-nineteenth century. See Chapter 14.)

The Portuguese lost no time in fitting out ships for a trade expedition to Asia. In 1498, Vasco da Gama became the first European to reach India by sea. He learned two facts of major importance on this first encounter. First, the Indians showed no interest in the European goods Da Gama offered to barter for their spices; they wanted money. Second, Arab traders already had control of a thriving spice trade in the area. Da Gama understood that the Portuguese would have to drive the Arabs out if their own trade ambitions were to succeed.

When Da Gama returned to Europe and sold a shipload of Indian pepper for sixty times the price he paid for it, it was clear that the thunderstorm that sent Diaz's ship off course had been a great stroke of economic good fortune for Portugal.

As a small nation with a small population, Portugal was interested not in conquest but in trade. At this point in history, the Portuguese made no attempt to invade or colonize African or Asian nations. Their goals were commercial: to establish permanent trading posts with small staffs and to make money. Their first trading post in the area was in Calicut at the southern tip of India. In 1510, they managed to oust the Arab traders and establish their own presence in Malacca (on the Malay peninsula) and Goa (on India's west coast). Arab traders would continue to operate in the area, but on a smaller scale; they were especially successful in continuing their trade with Venice, to which their ships had easy access via the Adriatic Sea.

During the 1540s, Portugal became the first European nation to make direct contact by sea with Japan, and by the 1550s the Portuguese had set up trading posts in China and throughout the Southeast Asian islands. In addition to purchasing Asian goods for export to Europe, the Portuguese made a handsome profit by carrying goods between Asian nations that traded with one another, such as China and Japan.

Dutch Trade

Like Portugal, the Netherlands was a small nation; without the large armies of the great powers like France, it had concentrated on economy rather than foreign policy. By the turn of the seventeenth century, the Dutch had developed Europe's most substantial sailing fleet.

The first Dutch voyage to the East took place in 1595; it returned more than two years later with a cargo that made huge profits, showing the Dutch that shipping trade in this area was financially viable.

It was not long before the Dutch gained the upper hand over the Portuguese in trade with the East. The Dutch had larger ships; in addition, they did not carry guns, which left more room for cargo. They also had superior trade goods to offer the Indians and Chinese in exchange for their wares.

In 1602, the Dutch East India Company was founded. It sold shares of stock and offered the investors a regular return on the profits. As the Portuguese had done before them, the Dutch earned a large profit not only on trade between Asia and Europe but also by serving as carriers of goods in the lively inter-Asian trade.

On the European mainland, Spain was trying to subdue the Netherlands; since Portugal and Spain were allies, this gave the Dutch the excuse to attack Portuguese ships and strongholds in the East. By the mid-seventeenth century, when Spain finally recognized Dutch independence, the Dutch had ousted the Portuguese from all their trading posts in the Indian Ocean, Indonesia, and the China seas.

Exploration to the West

Europeans were unaware of the existence of the Americas and the Pacific Ocean when they first considered sailing westward to reach the East. When they reached the western hemisphere at the end of the fifteenth century, they began a new era of colonization and cultural exchange.

Spanish and Portuguese Exploration

The race for American colonies and the continuing cultural exchange between the Americas and Europe began in 1492, when Christopher Columbus arrived in the Caribbean with a fleet of three ships. Columbus, an Italian sponsored by the Spanish monarchy, had sailed forth looking for the elusive trade route to India and China. He reasoned that since the world was spherical, one should be able to reach the East by sailing west. There was only one flaw in his theory; the existence of the Americas and the Pacific Ocean lay between Europe and Asia.

In his four voyages to the Caribbean, Columbus claimed Cuba, Hispaniola, Antigua, and the Bahamas for Spain, establishing a base of operations for the Spanish explorers who followed him. The islands are called the "West Indies" because Columbus never realized that he had not in fact reached India; the misnomer "Indians" has stuck to the earliest inhabitants of the Americas ever since.

When Columbus returned safely to Spain from his first voyage, bringing with him gold nuggets, Caribbean plants, and several Taino people, word spread throughout Europe. Many other explorers were curious to see the "new world," and the monarchs of Europe realized that by sponsoring explorers, they could establish colonies and expand their power bases abroad. Missionaries were also pleased at the discovery that there were whole societies of people they could try to convert to Christianity.

In 1500, the Portuguese landed in South America where they would establish a vast, profitable colony called Brazil. In 1513, Vasco Nuñez de Balboa sailed to Panama, crossed the isthmus, and became the first European to see the Pacific Ocean. In 1519, Ferdinand Magellan of Portugal sailed all the way around South America and continued on to the west. Magellan died in the Philippines, but thirty-five of his crew returned safely, having circled the globe. This voyage established that it was indeed possible to reach Asia by sailing west.

Between 1519 and 1531, the Spaniards defeated the mighty Aztec and Inca armies of Mexico and Peru. The great wealth they seized fired the imaginations of explorers such as Juan Ponce de Leon and Hernando de Soto, who sailed to North America in search of similar wealth. These men are known to history by the romantic name of *conquistadors*, a word that celebrates their adventurous spirit and undoubted bravery while minimizing the fact that they were motivated by greed and behaved brutally to those whose lands they invaded.

The conquistadors explored the Southeast and Southwest of North America, failing to find any evidence of gold. None of them realized at the time that the wealth of North America was in its natural resources: timber, fruit, vegetables, a mild seasonal climate, and fertile land.

In 1565, Pedro Menendez de Áviles established the first permanent European colony in North America when he founded the city of St. Augustine, Florida. The Spaniards began to settle Texas in the late 1600s and California in the mid-1700s. At one time, Spain claimed almost two-thirds of what is now the United States.

By the 1770s Spain was reaping an enormous profit from its colonies. The Spaniards had organized their territory into the viceroyalties of New Spain and Peru, which were broken down into smaller, locally administered units. Spain controlled the wealth of the colonial gold and silver mines, with the crown taking a one-fifth share of the profits. In addition, the colonists were banned from trading with any nations besides Spain.

Naturally, the Spaniards and Portuguese exploited the native populations for the purposes of labor. Conditions were little better than chattel slavery at first; like all people in positions of economic power throughout history, the masters and owners paid the workers as little as possible and curtailed their freedoms as much as they could. Under political and religious pressures from Europe, and thanks in large part to the protests of the influential Catholic missionary Bartolomeo de las Casas, working conditions eventually improved somewhat.

European invasion was catastrophic for the native populations of Latin America. Their empires were destroyed, their cultures all but obliterated, and their people enslaved in backbreaking, dangerous jobs in mines and plantation fields. The American population dropped drastically after the invasion; many were killed in armed conflict, but the vast majority succumbed to European diseases like smallpox. Never having been exposed to these diseases, the Americans had no natural resistance.

With the native workforce dying by the thousands, the Spaniards had to find another source of labor. This was the beginning of the slave trade between Africa and the Americas; it would continue for nearly three hundred years.

The European Impact on Latin America

- **1492**   Columbus claims Cuba, Hispaniola (later Haiti/Dominican Republic), and Bahamas for Spain

- **1493**   Columbus claims Antigua for Spain

- **1494**   Spaniards begin rule of Jamaica

- **1498**   Columbus discovers Venezuela

- **1500**   Pedro Alvarez Cabral of Portugal arrives on coast of Brazil; by 1540 area develops into large-scale exporter of sugar

- **1501**   Spanish reach Panama

- **1510**   Vasco Nuñez de Balboa returns to Panama

1519   Pedro Arias Dávila founds Panama City; Panama becomes part of viceroyalty of New Granada after 1739

1519   Hernán Cortez invades Tenochtitlan (present-day Mexico City) and captures from Aztecs by 1521

1524   Spaniards invade Guatemala (heart of the Maya civilization) and Costa Rica; establish Spanish Kingdom of Guatemala

1532   Francisco Pizarro conquers Incas in Ecuador and Peru; founds Lima in 1535

1535   Cortez proclaims viceroyalty of New Spain (includes Mexico and parts of what will eventually become U.S.A.)

1536   Pedro de Mendoza founds Buenos Aires

1536   Spaniards found city of Valparaiso

1537   Spaniards enter Paraguay

1538   Spanish establish Sucré in present-day Bolivia, then called Upper Peru

1538   Spaniards establish colony of New Granada, which includes Bogotá

1541   Spaniards found Santiago, Chile

1544   Viceroyalty of Peru is established; includes Buenos Aires, Chile, Ecuador, Colombia

1545   Spanish establish Potosí in present-day Bolivia, then called Upper Peru; this area becomes important for silver mining, later tin

1550   Spaniards found city of Concepción, Chile

1620s British annex Barbados, colonize Bahamas

1632   British settle Antigua

1655   British take Jamaica from Spain

1697   Haiti ceded from Spain to France

1763   British take over Dominica

1776   Viceroyalty of La Plata is established; includes Argentina, Bolivia, Paraguay, and Uruguay

French Exploration

The French began their voyages to America for business reasons: they wanted to expand the fur trade. Giovanni da Verrazano in 1524 and Jacques Cartier in 1535 were the first Frenchmen to explore any part of North America. It took until 1603 for the French to establish their first American colony, when a party of fur traders traveled west to Canada. Samuel de Champlain went with the party as mapmaker. He mapped the St. Lawrence River and the Atlantic coast. Champlain founded the towns of Port Royal and Quebec. He established friendly relations with the Algonquin and Huron Indians; this friendship led to an important alliance of forces during the French and Indian War.

In 1615, Champlain became the first European to see the Great Lakes. This area became the hub of the French fur-trading industry. As the French prospered, they explored farther south. They settled parts of Ohio and sailed down the Mississippi to the Gulf of Mexico, where René-Robert Cavelier, Sieur de la Salle founded the colony of Louisiana.

English Exploration

The earliest English voyages to the west were made in search of a trade route to Asia; the elusive Northwest Passage. In 1497, John Cabot landed on the coast of Maine, becoming the first European since Leif Erikson (a Norseman who had reached the coast of Canada about five hundred years earlier) to see North America. It was Cabot's voyage that assured Europeans that they had stumbled across a new continent: America was clearly not Asia.

Cabot never returned from a second voyage. His son Sebastian followed him in 1508, reaching the entrance to Hudson Bay. In 1509 Henry Hudson found the mouth of the Hudson River and followed it north to Albany before he realized it led north, not west. On a second voyage, Hudson drove his crew farther and farther west through a network of islands north of Canada. Terrified for their lives in the unknown, frigid waters, Hudson's crew marooned him and turned the ship back east toward safety.

England's interest in acquiring colonies arose when Elizabeth I realized that Spain and France were establishing a foothold in the Americas. During the 1560s, English pirate ships began venturing into the Atlantic to capture Spanish cargoes (see Chapter 4). Cousins John Hawkins and Francis Drake were especially successful; Drake became the first Englishman to sail around the globe, and he was knighted on his return to England in 1580. This gesture on the queen's part was one of the sparks that set off the great naval battle with the Spanish Armada in 1588 (see Chapter 4).

England joined the North American land grab by sending Sir Walter Raleigh west in 1584 to claim a large territory that included the present-day states of Virginia, West Virginia, Maryland, and the Carolinas. Raleigh named the territory Virginia, in honor of Elizabeth, the Virgin Queen.

Raleigh and his companions established a town on Roanoke Island, off present-day North Carolina. A second group of settlers sailed west for Roanoke the following year, led by John White, who immediately returned to England for supplies. When White sailed back to the colony in 1590, he found no trace of the settlement he had left behind. No one knows to this day what became of the settlers of Roanoke.

This failure did not discourage the English from trying. Their first success was the Chesapeake Bay colony of Jamestown, founded in 1606. By 1638, England had founded seven colonies along the Atlantic coast. As the American population grew, the colonies began to expand westward, carrying out the commands of their royal charters.

Conflict

Conflict broke out between the British and French when each side wanted to stop the other from expanding its colonial territory. Both the French and the British claimed the Ohio River valley. The French built Fort Duquesne where the Allegheny and Monongahela rivers meet to form the Ohio. The British governor of Virginia appointed nineteen-year-old George Washington to deliver a letter warning the French to leave British territory. The French laughed in Washington's face, and when British troops attacked them, the French won the first encounter. This took place in 1754. The end to conflict was only temporary. It soon broke out again in what would be known as the French and Indian War.

In Europe, Britain and Prussia banded together against France and Austria. Soon Sweden, Russia, and various small, independent states in central Europe joined the war on the French side. The goal of this alliance was to invade and defeat Prussia. This aspect of the French and Indian War, fought on the European continent, is called the Seven Years' War; it lasted from 1756 to 1763. Together, the two wars are often referred to as the Great War for Empire.

In the end, Prussia was able to hold its ground against invasion and conquest, thanks to the strength of its British ally.

Results

Fighting in the colonies ended in 1761. Representatives of France and Britain signed the Treaty of Paris in 1763. France had lost much of its fleet in the fighting, and it gave up almost all its North American possessions. Canada and all holdings east of the Mississippi River (except New Orleans) were ceded to Britain, and all territory west of the Mississippi was ceded to Spain. This would prevent an immediate British takeover of the entire continent.

Britain had also gained a prize of enormous value in natural resources, as well as a prosperous colonial economy. However, Britain had spent vast sums of money on the war and now needed to tax the colonies to pay for it. In the end, of course, this British attempt to force the colonists to bear the burden of the war debt led to the colonies' declaration of independence from Britain and the creation of the United States of America. Britain surrendered to the US army in 1789 and withdrew from North America, maintaining only its connection with Canada, which would become an independent nation in 1867.

QUIZ

1. **The term *Northwest Passage* refers to**
   A. the overland route that traders traveled between Europe and Asia.
   B. Ferdinand Magellan's voyage around the world.
   C. the English Channel that separates England from France.
   D. a trade route that would lead west from Europe to Asia by water.

2. **_____ is an important historical figure because his voyage west initiated a major cultural exchange between Europe and the Americas.**
   A. Jacques Cartier
   B. Christopher Columbus
   C. Hernando de Soto
   D. Sir Walter Raleigh

3. **Which European nation was the first to establish colonies in North America?**
   A. England
   B. France
   C. Portugal
   D. Spain

4. Their _____ enabled the Dutch to supplant the Portuguese in Asian trade.
   A. larger ships
   B. stronger military
   C. more-enlightened monarch
   D. earlier success

5. Spanish explorers were initially disappointed with North America because they failed to find
   A. fertile land.
   B. Indians.
   C. gold.
   D. fresh water.

6. In 1754, war broke out between the British and French over
   A. control of the fur trade.
   B. treatment of the Indians.
   C. religious differences.
   D. territorial expansion.

7. _____ was the first man to claim North American territory for England.
   A. Sebastian Cabot
   B. Henry Hudson
   C. Sir Walter Raleigh
   D. John White

8. The 1497 voyage of _____ assured Europeans they had found not "the Indies," but a new continent.
   A. John Cabot
   B. Christopher Columbus
   C. Giovanni da Verrazano
   D. Pedro Menendez de Áviles

9. Portugal was in an ideal position to explore the African coast because
   A. it wanted to build up its colonial empire.
   B. it was the most powerful nation in Europe.
   C. it was geographically close to Africa.
   D. it could always count on support from Spain.

10. **Portugal's most important goal on its voyages to Asia was**
    A. establishing trade relations.
    B. annexing territory.
    C. military conquest.
    D. converting the Asians to Christianity.

PART I EXAM

1. _____ briefly became a dominant European power during the Thirty Years' War.
   A. England
   B. Italy
   C. Russia
   D. Sweden

2. What was Spain's motive in sponsoring the first voyage of Christopher Columbus?
   A. to acquire a monopoly over North America's natural resources
   B. to establish a viable transoceanic trade route to Asia
   C. to convert the American and Caribbean populations to Catholicism
   D. to expand its power base by establishing settled colonies

3. The Holy Roman Empire is best described as
   A. an absolute monarchy run by a highly efficient, centrally controlled bureaucracy.
   B. a group of city-states united by a common language, a common religious faith, and a shared cultural heritage.
   C. a collection of independent principalities and free cities owing allegiance to one titular monarch.
   D. a constitutional monarchy with an emperor as the head of state and a representative assembly that carried out the will of the people.

4. _____ was France's original motive for sponsoring exploratory voyages to North America.
   A. Establishing settled colonies
   B. Expanding its power base
   C. Improving profits from trade
   D. Converting the native population

5. Which was the main cause of Russia's lack of a prosperous mercantile middle class?
   A. Russia was the only European nation to worship in the Orthodox faith.
   B. Travel was too difficult and Russians lived too far apart from one another.
   C. The Russian princes and czars were constantly trying to finance wars.
   D. Russia had no natural rivers, which were necessary as trade routes.

6. **The strong hereditary monarchs of the sixteenth and seventeenth centuries believed that the _____ constituted the greatest potential threat to their own authority.**
   A. military
   B. clergy
   C. nobility
   D. common people

7. **During the early Renaissance, humanists studied more Latin than Greek because**
   A. ancient Greek was the language of all educated Europeans, especially the clergy.
   B. ancient Roman scholars had written more accurately about the sciences.
   C. Greek texts dealt with forbidden topics such as polytheism.
   D. Latin texts were more readily available and easier to read and understand.

8. **Which best describes the status of the Holy Roman Empire at the end of the Thirty Years' War?**
   A. It was ready to establish a representative government.
   B. It was well along the road to becoming a unified nation-state.
   C. It was substantially weakened from the devastation of combat.
   D. It had become the dominant power in Europe.

9. **_____ chose the sun for a personal symbol to suggest that, like the sun, the monarch was the source of life and light to the subjects.**
   A. Elizabeth I
   B. Frederick the Great
   C. Louis XIV
   D. Peter the Great

10. **Many Russian boyars and hereditary princes served in the military because**
    A. the monarch offered them landed estates in exchange for their service.
    B. they were required to do so by the laws of the country.
    C. the military was more like a gentleman's club than a fighting force.
    D. it was the only opportunity they had to travel long distances.

11. _____ supports the thesis that the Thirty Years' War was fundamentally political and territorial, rather than religious.
    A. France did not ally itself with the Holy Roman Emperor.
    B. Sweden invaded the Holy Roman Empire when Ferdinand signed the Edict of Restitution.
    C. Catholics in the empire supported the Hapsburg ruler Ferdinand II.
    D. Frederich of Bohemia led a Protestant army against Maximilian of Bavaria.

12. _____ is considered the single event or action of the Church that sparked the Protestant Reformation.
    A. The granting of indulgences in exchange for financial contributions
    B. The interrogation policies of the Roman Inquisition
    C. The insistence on conducting Church business and services in Latin
    D. The lack of education demonstrated by many parish priests

13. The Medici family of Renaissance Florence is known for its involvement in all these areas except
    A. the arts.
    B. the sciences.
    C. banking and high finance.
    D. politics.

14. The round-the-world voyage of _____ established the fact that one could reach the east by sailing west.
    A. Christopher Columbus
    B. Giovanni da Verrazano
    C. Sebastian Cabot
    D. Ferdinand Magellan

15. Which best explains or defines the principle of the divine right of kings?
    A. The monarch has the authority to rule because he or she is a Christian of the same faith as the people.
    B. The monarch's authority comes directly from God; thus he or she has absolute authority within the realm.
    C. The monarch is a literal and figurative descendant of God.
    D. The monarch maintains his or her authority because of the cooperation and support of the Church.

16. **Why did early Russian princes and czars emphasize the expansion of the military?**
    A. because Russia had no natural features to protect it from invasion
    B. as a means of keeping the peasants and commoners under control
    C. as part of a plan to invade and conquer Poland and eastern Europe
    D. as part of a plan to invade Mongolia and southern Asia

17. **Which figure was most instrumental in bringing about the Protestant Reformation?**
    A. John Calvin
    B. John Knox
    C. Martin Luther
    D. Thomas Cranmer

18. **_____ eventually entered the Thirty Years' War with the purpose of weakening its long-standing enemy, Austria.**
    A. Britain
    B. France
    C. Poland
    D. Sweden

19. **The most serious consequence of the French wars under Louis XIV was that**
    A. France lost a great deal of valuable territory to its hostile neighbors.
    B. France endangered an important alliance with Britain.
    C. the French treasury was drained by the high costs of war.
    D. the French alliance with Spain was permanently broken.

20. **_____ was the first European nation to develop recognizable equivalents of modern-day political parties.**
    A. Britain
    B. France
    C. Prussia
    D. Spain

21. **What role did the wealthy middle class play in the fifteenth-century revival of the arts in Italy?**
    A. sponsored major architectural and artistic works, thus providing artists with a livelihood
    B. encouraged experimentation with new techniques of painting and sculpture
    C. granted hereditary titles of nobility to artists, scholars, and writers
    D. provided scholarships for artists to study at major European universities

22. **Britain provoked its North American colonies to declare their independence by**
    A. taxing them to pay for the costs of the French and Indian War.
    B. refusing to allow them any local autonomy.
    C. conducting diplomacy with the French colonies that was hostile to their interests.
    D. revoking their various royal charters.

23. **Martin Luther argued against conducting services in Latin because**
    A. he had never learned to read or understand Latin.
    B. the common people did not speak or understand Latin.
    C. the Bible was written in Hebrew and Greek, not Latin.
    D. many parish priests had little understanding or knowledge of Latin.

24. **Peter the Great's affinity for Western European culture led him to do all of the following except**
    A. build a new Russian capital city as far west as possible in his realm.
    B. correspond with key figures of the French Enlightenment.
    C. introduce European fashions in dress to Russian society.
    D. reorganize the Russian bureaucracy along Western lines.

25. **What advantage(s) did Russia gain from the expansion of the empire during the fifteenth and sixteenth centuries?**
    A. a major cultural exchange with Western Europe
    B. the spread of the Orthodox faith
    C. an efficient, centrally controlled bureaucracy
    D. greater tax revenues and greater military strength

26. **As a result of the Thirty Years' War, _____ was established as a unified empire under Hapsburg rule.**
    A. Austria
    B. Italy
    C. the Netherlands
    D. Spain

27. **The original and primary purpose of the Council of Florence was to**
    A. plan and establish seminaries throughout Europe for the training of Catholic priests.
    B. eliminate the Avignon papacy so that there would only be one pope, in Rome.
    C. reunite the Orthodox and Roman Catholic churches.
    D. facilitate an exchange of ideas and information between Eastern and Western European scholars and clergy.

28. **The major goal of Prussian foreign policy during the eighteenth century was**
    A. to defend the kingdom from the powerful armies of other nations.
    B. to unite as much German-speaking territory as possible under one rule.
    C. to establish a power base in the Americas.
    D. to maintain a balance of power with other European nations.

29. **The Act of Supremacy, passed by Parliament in 1534,**
    A. granted Henry VIII an annulment of his marriage to Catherine of Aragon.
    B. established that church services in England would henceforth be conducted in English, not Latin.
    C. revoked all papal authority in English affairs of church and state.
    D. stated that Henry VIII's marriage to Anne Boleyn was valid and their children were legitimate.

30. **_____ won independence from Hapsburg rule at the end of the Thirty Years' War.**
    A. Spain
    B. France
    C. the Netherlands
    D. England

31. **In the early modern period, the story of _____ is characterized by frequent violent, sometimes murderous, rivalries among members of the royal family.**
    A. England
    B. France
    C. Italy
    D. Russia

32. **_____ was probably the major cause of the downfall of Ivan IV of Russia.**
    A. Conspiracy among the boyars
    B. Mental instability and physical illness
    C. Treachery within his family
    D. Repeated military failures

33. The kingdom of _____, which gained near-complete indepen-
    dence in 1648, would eventually become the core of a unified German nation.
    A. Bavaria
    B. Bohemia
    C. Prussia
    D. Saxony

34. Most victims of the Black Plague died in urban areas because
    A. urban areas suffered more from air pollution.
    B. there were fewer doctors and clergymen in cities.
    C. most Europeans at that time lived in cities.
    D. urban conditions were crowded and unsanitary.

35. Pope Paul III summoned the Council of Trent in 1545 with the purpose of
    A. translating the Latin Bible into all the modern European languages.
    B. creating a detailed plan for the reform of the Catholic Church.
    C. devising ways to dismantle the newly established Protestant denominations.
    D. establishing Inquisitions in the Catholic nations of Spain, Italy, and France.

36. The drawback to the huge military buildups that characterized the age of mon-
    archy was
    A. the creation of a social class that might rise against the monarch.
    B. the huge expense to the national treasury.
    C. the fostering of an institution in which nobles and commoners might serve
       as equals.
    D. the need for military families to support themselves without their fathers or
       husbands.

37. During the strict Puritan rule of _____, all the London theaters
    and saloons were closed.
    A. Charles I
    B. Oliver Cromwell
    C. Charles II
    D. James II

38. The _____ held sway in the Russian principalities until they were finally driven out in 1480.
    A. Chinese
    B. Poles
    C. Swedes
    D. Tatars

39. Which important principle of European politics is illustrated by the peace treaty agreed upon at the end of the Thirty Years' War?
    A. the balance of power
    B. free trade
    C. human rights
    D. hereditary rule

40. _____ led immediately to a rise in literacy throughout Europe.
    A. The invention of the pendulum clock
    B. The proof that the planets moved around the sun
    C. The process of printing with movable type
    D. The establishment of a public school system

41. England's victory over the Spanish Armada was due to the superiority of its
    A. navy.
    B. army.
    C. diplomacy.
    D. bureaucracy.

42. The basic purpose of the English Bill of Rights was
    A. to unite England, Scotland, Ireland, and Wales in an official ceremony.
    B. to set forth individual rights of all British citizens.
    C. to force British Catholics to convert to Protestantism or leave the country.
    D. to establish once and for all that Britain was a Protestant nation.

43. Which best describes the major tenet of Calvinism?
    A. God predetermines everything that happens on earth.
    B. Human beings are saved by the power of genuine faith alone.
    C. Human beings are saved if they carry out good works throughout their lives.
    D. Communion with God takes place in an individual's heart and mind.

44. **The major factor in the defeat of the Fronde was the opposition of**
    A. other European nations.
    B. the bourgeoisie.
    C. the national army.
    D. the press and the intellectuals.

45. **Which best describes the main tenet of Renaissance humanism?**
    A. The creations and inventions of human beings are more important and valuable than what exists in nature.
    B. Human beings are unique, divinely created individuals with individual ideas about the great questions of philosophy.
    C. Every human being is born free and equal and is entitled to protect his or her life and liberty.
    D. The ordinary worker, as the producer of human necessities, is the most valuable member of society.

46. **All these actions of Catherine II of Russia might be described as those of an enlightened monarch, except**
    A. the introduction of works of Western music, art, and philosophy to Russia.
    B. the founding of schools for girls and young women.
    C. the granting of absolute control over their serfs to the nobility.
    D. the campaign for inoculation against smallpox.

47. **Between 1380 and 1613, the status of the Russian government depended almost entirely on**
    A. the success or failure of the annual harvest.
    B. the personality and abilities of the prince or czar.
    C. relations between the ruler and the Orthodox Church.
    D. the size of the military force.

48. **Over the course of the seventeenth century, Britain established itself as**
    A. an absolute monarchy.
    B. a popular democracy.
    C. a constitutional monarchy.
    D. a military dictatorship.

49. **The Thirty Years' War began with an act of Lutheran violence toward Catholic officials in** _____
   A. Austria.
   B. Bohemia.
   C. Geneva.
   D. Prussia.

50. **What was the purpose of the Ninety-Five Theses?**
   A. to found a new Christian religious denomination
   B. to arouse support for the cause of Catholic reform
   C. to provide an alternative to the harsh doctrines of Calvinism
   D. to raise funds for the translation of the Bible into German

Part II

Seventeenth-Century Scientific Revolution to 1900

chapter **8**

The Scientific Revolution and the Enlightenment, 1543–1789

The Scientific Revolution and the Enlightenment came about as direct, although not immediate, results of the Renaissance and Reformation. During the Renaissance, many ancient Greek and Latin texts came to light and were seriously studied for the first time in centuries. Scholars learned of ancient discoveries in mathematics, astronomy, and philosophy that had been suppressed or dismissed by the Church. The Renaissance also encouraged individual scholars to question the Church's teachings. The perfection of the printing press made the widespread dissemination of old and new knowledge possible. Finally, the Reformation loosened the stranglehold on thought that Christianity had maintained for centuries.

During the Scientific Revolution, direct observations of nature gave people a new way of understanding the world. The Church saw the Scientific Revolution as a threat for two reasons: it changed *what* people thought and, more important, *how* they thought. The increase in human knowledge of the workings of the universe that occurred during the Scientific Revolution was the product of experimentation—of scientists making observations, taking notes, studying their data, and developing theories and conclusions based on what they perceived with their five senses. The Church was naturally hostile to a process that threatened its own supremacy over what people thought. Church officials did not want to change the centuries-old system in which their own scholars and teachers interpreted the world in accordance with their faith, and insisted that the people accept this interpretation rather than thinking about the matter for themselves.

The great thinkers—called *philosophes*—of the Enlightenment applied this same scientific process of critical thinking to social and political problems. They believed in the perfectibility of humanity and society; their goal was a peaceful, prosperous world in which ignorance, greed, and tyranny had no place. For nearly a century, the *philosophes* wrote, argued, debated, and taught that all people were born free and equal, and that individuals should be able to make their way in the world as reasonable beings with a right to decide how and where they wished to live. In the end, they brought about, at least in part, the new world they had imagined; their teachings led directly to major revolutions in British North America and in France.

CHAPTER 8 OBJECTIVES

- Explain the causes of the Scientific Revolution.
- Identify the major achievements and discoveries of the Scientific Revolution.
- Define the Enlightenment and its major causes and effects.
- Identify the major figures of the Scientific Revolution and the Enlightenment and match each person to his or her accomplishments in science, mathematics, literature, and philosophy.

Chapter 8 Time Line

1543   Copernicus argues in *De Revolutionibus* that planets move around the sun

1577   Tycho Brahe proves that comets are astral bodies

1609   Johannes Kepler discovers that planets move in elliptical orbits

- **1610** Galileo observes moons of Jupiter
- **1633** Roman Inquisition forces Galileo to recant
- **1637** Descartes publishes work on analytic geometry
- **1654** Christiaan Huygens invents the pendulum clock
- **1687** Newton publishes *Principia Mathematica*
- **1748** Montesquieu publishes *L'Esprit des lois*
- **1759** Voltaire publishes *Candide*
- **1762** Rousseau publishes *Contract social*
- **1776** American Revolution begins
- **1789** French Revolution

The Scientific Revolution

The ancients, first in the Middle East and then in Classical Greece and Rome, had made great strides in mathematics and the sciences. However, during the Christian era, any scientific teachings that conflicted with the Bible were rigorously suppressed and denounced as heresy.

During the Middle Ages, scientists theorized without having the means of testing their ideas by experimentation. By the seventeenth century this was no longer the case. The invention of the telescope, for example, made it possible to see the heavens up close and observe how the planets moved through space. By the same token, printing had spread throughout Europe beginning in the 1400s, so it was much easier to publicize and share new knowledge than it had been in medieval times. It made possible a true scientific community of scholars who knew one another, corresponded, and shared and discussed their ideas.

The era is known as the Scientific Revolution for two reasons. The first is the major discoveries in astronomy, physics, and mathematics that took place at this time. The second is a shift in thinking that was both the cause and the result of the Scientific Revolution. In the past, people had believed that what happened in the universe was the result of divine whims that were beyond human understanding; now they saw the universe as a machine that worked according to fixed laws that human beings could discover and understand. However, the Scientific Revolution did not do away with human faith in God;

rather, it suggested that God had created the universe and set it in motion according to the laws the scientists had observed. God was considered similar to a watchmaker, who designed and built a watch, wound it up, and left it to run on its own.

As new discoveries followed one another, science became the hobby of many people of leisure. These rich people, including monarchs such as Catherine the Great of Russia, helped the Scientific Revolution in two ways. First, their interest in science and mechanics lent an air of respectability to experimentation and discovery. Second, they were reliable sources of patronage and sponsorship, providing financial support, influence with the powerful, and welcome interest and enthusiasm to many scholars.

Major Figures of the Scientific Revolution

The Scientific Revolution was an international phenomenon; scholars from all over Europe took part in it. This chapter describes the most important figures of the era.

Copernicus

Nicolaus Copernicus was born in 1473 in Torun, Poland. He learned astronomy from the books he read as a student in Italy. Books of the time agreed that the Earth was at the center of the universe and that the other heavenly bodies, including the sun, traveled around it. In ancient times, both Ptolemy and Aristotle had arrived at this view by observing the heavens. Despite Aristotle's status as a pagan from the Classical era, the Church fathers had always accepted his view of astronomy because it allowed them to teach that humankind, God's supreme creation, had its proper place in the center of the universe.

Copernicus, however, came to believe that Aristotle and Ptolemy were wrong. He suggested that the sun, not the Earth, was at the center of the universe, with the planets orbiting it. It seemed to Copernicus that since the Earth and its moon were spherical, the orbits of the planets should be circular; however, he realized that from the point of view of the Earth, the orbits could not be perfect circles. In 1543, Copernicus published his thoughts and discoveries in a book called *De Revolutionibus*, known in English as *On the Revolutions of the Heavenly Spheres*. He died the same year.

Brahe

The next great European astronomer was Tycho Brahe. Born in 1546 to a noble family in what was then Danish territory, Brahe was fortunate in having as his patron a king who provided him with a fully fitted observatory. This enabled him to conduct direct experiments in astronomy—the first in Europe for many centuries. While Copernicus' theories had been more or less guesses, Brahe's observations told him that while the sun and moon traveled around the Earth, the other planets orbited the sun. Like Copernicus, he could not understand why the planets' apparently circular orbits were not regular.

Kepler

Brahe's assistant, the brilliant Johannes Kepler, took discoveries of the heavens one step further. Born in 1571 in the free city of Weil der Stadt, Kepler used mathematics and direct observation to show that the orbits of the planets were ellipses, not circles. As soon as he replaced the idea of circles with that of ellipses, the orbital paths became regular. Kepler also proved that the planets orbited the sun at different speeds. His greatest work was *On the Motion of Mars*, published in 1609; it soon appeared on the Holy Office's *Index of Forbidden Books*.

Astronomy took a giant leap forward with the discovery of the telescope, first patented in the Netherlands in 1608–1609. Scientists had realized during the 1300s that a glass lens could magnify an object seen through it; they had been using this knowledge ever since to manufacture eyeglasses and magnifying glasses. However, these were only intended to improve people's vision for everyday purposes such as reading. No one had thought to apply the same idea to achieving a close-up view of such faraway objects as the stars.

Galileo

Mathematics and engineering professor Galileo Galilei of Pisa was the first to make extensive use of the telescope to study the planets. With this new invention—at that time no more than a plain narrow tube a little over a yard long, with concave and convex lenses inside—he was able to see things in the heavens that had simply not been visible to his predecessors.

Looking through his telescope in 1610, Galileo realized immediately that Jupiter had its own moons in orbit around it, just as the Earth had a moon. This discovery alone proved that Earth was not the center of the universe around which all other objects orbited. When Galileo published his new knowledge of the heavens, Kepler and most of Europe's intellectuals, including the Jesuit astronomers, eagerly accepted them.

Through his telescope, Galileo saw the rings around Saturn, although he did not understand what they were. He observed that, contrary to Aristotle's assertion that all heavenly bodies were perfect, smooth spheres, the surface of the Earth's moon was craggy and irregular. Since the Church had accepted Aristotle's theory of the universe, this meant that Galileo was well on his way to making an enemy of one of Europe's most powerful institutions.

In 1632, Galileo published *Dialogue on the Two Great Systems of the World*. Written in the form of an imaginary dialogue between Copernicus and Ptolemy, this work discussed theories about planetary orbits and tides. A lifelong and devout Catholic, Galileo dedicated the *Dialogue* to Pope Urban VIII. It was clear that he anticipated no trouble from the Church because of his writing; he had carefully refrained from discussing certain forbidden topics, such as the work of Kepler.

To Galileo's surprise, Urban VIII summoned him to Rome to appear before the Inquisition on the charge of defying the Holy Office's policy against writing about Copernican theory. Galileo produced documentary proof of his assertion that he was permitted to write speculatively about Copernican astronomy. Despite this evidence, the Inquisition refused to face the public mockery that would have resulted from making a mistake over a figure so internationally famous as Galileo. The Holy Office therefore sentenced Galileo to deny the validity of his own discoveries, then placed him under custody of the liberal archbishop of Siena, who encouraged him to continue working and writing. In effect, Galileo remained under house arrest until his death in 1642. He was free to study, experiment, and write, although it proved difficult (though not impossible) to find publishers in the face of a Holy Office ban on anything he might produce.

Within the next few years Galileo's works spread throughout Europe in various translations and editions. His last book, *The Two New Sciences*, discussed the structure of matter, the strength of materials, and the laws governing natural motion. He discovered the laws of falling bodies and the mathematical formula we use to describe acceleration.

Defending his own writings in his later personal correspondence, Galileo argued that God had given human beings the ability to observe and reason. What people could see and understand with their five senses must be the truth; for instance, that planets moved around the sun. He argued that if this appeared to conflict with the scriptures, then human understanding of the scriptures must be at fault.

Newton

The year of Galileo's death saw the birth of Isaac Newton in rural Lincolnshire, England. Newton attended Cambridge University and studied the works of Galileo and Kepler. Newton revolutionized scientific thinking in Europe with his discovery of the principle of gravity—the single, constant force in the universe that attracted objects to one another. Newton realized that it was gravity that attracted the planets to the sun and the moons to the planets; gravity was what kept each body in a regular orbit at a constant distance from the larger mass around which it revolved. Newton's work explained how gravity could be calculated mathematically; he was the first scientist to apply calculus to astronomy.

The importance of Newton's discovery of the principle of gravity cannot be underestimated. It revolutionized European thinking, proving once and for all that the people could understand the way their own world worked. Before Newton, Europeans had understood the universe as operating by divine whims that they could not hope to understand; after Newton, they understood it as operating by fixed, comprehensible laws. For the first time, an understanding of the world could be based on human reason and experience, not on faith.

Like Galileo and those who had gone before him, Newton believed that his scientific theories were perfectly compatible with Church teaching. In his view, the law of gravity was a divine creation, and he was doing honor to God by revealing his divine plan. Unfortunately, the Church could not accept this view; as it had always done, it reacted to independent intellectual endeavor with suspicion and hostility. In a sense, the Church was right to recognize the threat posed by scientific discovery. Since science proved that the Church had been teaching an inaccurate and false theory of the structure of the universe, *all* Church teaching was called into question. The Scientific Revolution permanently weakened the place the Church held in popular regard.

The Enlightenment (The Age of Reason)

In the wake of the Scientific Revolution came the Enlightenment, a period of intellectual achievement that lasted for approximately a century, from the English Revolution in 1689 to the French Revolution in 1789. The Enlightenment is also called the Age of Reason. This movement was a natural consequence of the Scientific Revolution, which had introduced a new thought process to the West. During the Age of Reason, intellectuals applied that new way of thinking to social and political questions. They argued against political and religious tyranny, against a fixed hierarchy of social ranks, against censorship, and against chattel slavery. They argued for freedom—freedom of individual thought, freedom of the press and the arts, freedom to have a say in one's own government, and freedom to rise in the world according to merit rather than the accident of birth and rank.

The Enlightenment was centered in France—specifically in Paris—for a variety of reasons. First, France was the dominant power in Europe because of its victory in the Thirty Years' War (see Chapter 5). Second, French was the common language of educated Europeans in the eighteenth century, just as Latin had been during the Renaissance. Third, the establishment of the French academies of arts, sciences, and letters had given a degree of official approval and sponsorship to intellectuals, although this was also true in other nations, and censorship still operated in France. Enlightenment thinkers viewed Britain as the ideal society; although it had many problems yet to overcome, Britain was a constitutional monarchy with a relatively representative government and relative religious tolerance, and therefore a haven from tyranny. Last and not least, France had a central geographical location on the European continent; the less restrictive conditions in Britain might make it appear a natural center for an intellectual movement, but it was an island on the other side of the English Channel.

The thinkers of the Enlightenment were men (and some women) of all European nations: Britain, Germany, France, Poland, and Italy. They achieved fame in various fields: there were poets, playwrights, political thinkers, nonfiction writers, scientists, novelists, philosophers, and economists. They were collectively known as *philosophes*—a French word that can perhaps best be translated as "critical thinkers." What united the *philosophes* as one group was this critical way of thinking—the habit of applying the same reasoning process to the problems and questions of their age. They came to a variety of conclusions—there were in fact some fierce disagreements among them—but all used the same method to arrive at them.

The Enlightenment marked a break with the past in two major ways. First, the Middle Ages and the period that followed had generally been a time of pessimism, or at best resignation. Many medieval Church officials and even scholars had believed the world would end in 1500; people made the best of life on earth only in the hope of achieving something better after death. By contrast, the Enlightenment was an era of optimism, in which the great intellectuals believed in the perfectibility of humankind. The *philosophes* believed that reasoning and knowledge could solve the problems of society, if properly applied. They believed that a world of peace, prosperity, and earthly happiness could truly be achieved. Their ideas about political theory were based on notions of individual liberty, which they and their followers expressed in the French Declaration of the Rights of Man (see Chapter 9) and the American Declaration of Independence and Bill of Rights.

Second, human society had always accepted that human beings were God's creation; people had always dedicated their endeavors to the glory of God and had prayed for God's assistance when going into battle or danger. This attitude even persisted during the Scientific Revolution. During the Enlightenment, the *philosophes* began openly questioning the relevance, if not the existence, of God. They focused on human achievement as the product of a particular individual's merit, and honored that person rather than God.

Major Thinkers of the Enlightenment

The *philosophes* of the Enlightenment were such a large and varied group that this book can only cover a few of the most prominent.

Montesquieu

Charles-Louis Secondat, Baron de Montesquieu, was born in 1689 in the Gironde region of southwestern France. His two most famous works are the *Persian Letters* (1721) and *L'Esprit des lois*, or *The Spirit of Laws* (1748).

Many scholars consider the *Persian Letters* as the book that began the Enlightenment. It is in the form of a collection of letters written by two fictional Persian travelers in Europe. The travelers observe and comment on French society, government, and customs, and also discuss conditions at the Persian court they have left behind. Montesquieu used this format to make some pointed, although veiled, criticisms of the despotism that prevailed at this time in France. He scoffed at the vanity and pride that the hereditary nobles took in their social position, noting that it came not from intelligence or virtue but from the accident of birth. Montesquieu published the *Persian Letters* anonymously in the Netherlands, a common course for authors to pursue at that time if they thought their ideas would stir up trouble with the authorities. The book was a great success, going through several editions in a single year.

The Spirit of Laws is a work of serious political theory; unlike *Persian Letters*, it does not make its points under the guise of fiction. This was the first book to advocate a balanced government made of different branches—executive, legislative, and judicial—each of which had some power over the others. Montesquieu believed this was the best way to avoid the autocracy that he felt was corrupt and harmful to society. The work also examined the roles of major social institutions such as the Church, which lost no time placing it on the *Index of Forbidden Books*. However, it was widely read and highly influential; fifty years after the book's appearance, the government of the United States was organized along the lines suggested by Montesquieu.

Voltaire

Born in Paris in 1694, François-Marie Arouet was educated by the Jesuits and determined early on to pursue a career in writing. Around 1718, he coined the pen name "Voltaire," by which he was known for the rest of his long and productive life.

One of Voltaire's most important concerns was freedom of religion. During a three-year stay in England in the 1720s, he observed what he considered an ideal society, one that supported its artists and men of letters while allowing its citizens to worship as they saw fit. By praising England enthusiastically in his *Letters on England* (1733), Voltaire implied severe criticism of the very different conditions in France; as a consequence, the book was banned in his own country. Voltaire was twice imprisoned in the Bastille for his writings; after the second prison term, he moved to the Swiss border area, where it would be easy to flee if the state pursued him in the future.

Voltaire published throughout his lifetime, both fiction and nonfiction, and kept up a voluminous correspondence with all the great thinkers of his age. His best-known work is the short novel *Candide* (1759), which lampoons many of the worst aspects of European society: government, military life, and religion. The novel concludes that "one must cultivate one's garden"—in other words, what is most important is to use one's intellectual and philosophical skills to solve real, practical problems in a realistic and practical way.

Voltaire lived to the great age of eighty-four, not quite long enough to witness the French Revolution (see Chapter 9) but long enough to see himself crowned as the elder statesman of the Enlightenment.

Rousseau

Jean-Jacques Rousseau, born in 1712 in Geneva, Switzerland, was in many ways the odd man out among the *philosophes*. As his thinking developed over time, he quarreled violently with almost all of them. Concentrating on man's emotional side rather than his reasoning powers, Rousseau believed passionately in the importance of each person as a unique individual. His works insist that the emotional makeup of a person is just as important as the intellectual; therefore, he has often been considered the father of the Romantic movement in the arts (see Chapter 11).

In *The Social Contract* (1762), Rousseau described his ideal society. He believed that social structure was inherently evil because, as he could see for himself, it created false ideas of inequality. He saw people born into one social rank, and thus condemned to stay in it regardless of natural merits or faults. Rousseau believed that without an imposed social structure, human beings would follow their nature and would relate to one another in benevolence rather than self-interest. This notion of the "noble savage" seemed ludicrous to many of the other *philosophes*, who believed that education was the key to a better society.

Diderot

Denis Diderot was born in 1713 in the town of Langres in northeastern France. Like Voltaire, he received a good education under the Jesuits. He was able to turn his hand to any number of intellectual tasks, including editing, translating, and writing both fiction and nonfiction.

Diderot's most important contribution to the legacy of the Enlightenment is the *Encyclopédie*. The project came about when he accepted a commission to translate *Chambers' Cyclopedia* into French. Diderot decided to publish his own encyclopedia, which grew over time to seventeen volumes of text (published 1751–1765) and eleven volumes of engraved illustrations, completed in 1773. Until 1758, mathematician Jean Baptiste d'Alembert worked with Diderot as coeditor; when D'Alembert withdrew, succumbing to pressure from powerful vested interests who did not want to see the work published, Diderot carried on alone.

As its name suggests, the *Encyclopédie* was an attempt to sum up all human knowledge in one place. It included articles by all the greatest thinkers and writers of the age (including Voltaire, Rousseau, and Diderot himself) on a variety of topics: science, technology, crafts, mathematics, art, religion, music, and history. The purpose of the *Encyclopédie* was to enlighten the ignorant—to provide ordinary people with information that everyone, as a sentient being in the world, should know. The *philosophes* believed strongly in the value of education; they saw ignorance as their enemy. They believed that educating the common people was one of the most basic and important ways to improve society.

QUIZ

1. **The Scientific Revolution and the Enlightenment share which of the following?**
   A. the approval and support of the Church
   B. the design of new systems of government
   C. the process of critical thinking and experimentation
   D. the invention of new solutions to major social problems

2. **_____ is an important historical figure because he realized that the planets moved in regular elliptical orbits around the sun.**
   A. Tycho Brahe
   B. Nicolaus Copernicus
   C. Galileo Galilei
   D. Johannes Kepler

3. **One important reason France was the center of the Enlightenment was that**
   A. it was the largest centrally located nation in Europe.
   B. it had a more despotic government than any other European nation.
   C. its people spoke the language common to all educated people of the time.
   D. it did not allow censorship of the press.

4. **What argument did Galileo make in support of his discoveries about the planets when the Church refused to accept them?**
   A. that what could be observed by the human eye must be the truth
   B. that Church fathers had no right to make pronouncements about astronomy
   C. that other intellectuals and scientists agreed with his findings
   D. that he had used the finest scientific instruments of the day

5. **Church officials were hostile to the discoveries of the Scientific Revolution because**
   A. the discoveries were not the result of proper experimentation and study.
   B. the scientists who made the discoveries were all Protestants.
   C. they objected to the scientists' expressed disbelief in God.
   D. these discoveries contradicted and disproved what the Church had always taught.

6. **The term *philosophe* is best translated as** _____
   A. scholar.
   B. critical thinker.
   C. student.
   D. intellectual.

7. **Which statement is true of all the *philosophes* of the Enlightenment?**
   A. They were all French.
   B. They all supported and agreed with one another.
   C. They all shared a common way of thinking.
   D. They were all knowledgeable about mathematics and science.

8. **Rousseau has been called the father of the Romantic movement because**
   A. he imagined a government operating under a system of checks and balances.
   B. he believed in the supreme importance of each human being's individual personality and emotions.
   C. he wrote clever satires on the society of his day.
   D. he conceived the idea of a multivolume French encyclopedia of knowledge.

9. **Which best describes the *Encyclopédie*?**
   A. a satire of French government and society
   B. a compendium of historical and scientific facts, dates, and important events
   C. a compilation of information on scientific, mechanical, artistic, and historical topics
   D. an illustrated guide to the lives of France's most famous citizens

10. **Which best describes what the *philosophes* hoped and believed the future might hold for humankind?**
    A. They believed that society might become peaceful, prosperous, and happy.
    B. They believed that the world would end in a great war among all nations.
    C. They believed that there was no possibility that society would ever improve.
    D. They believed that society would succumb to despotism.

chapter **9**

The French Revolution and the Napoleonic Wars, 1789–1815

The French Revolution had a number of direct causes. First, the eighteenth-century Enlightenment gave birth to new ideas about the equality of man (see Chapter 8). Second, the Glorious Revolution in Britain proved that a limited monarchy was a workable system (see Chapter 6), and the American Revolution provided a unique example of a republican government founded on the idea, if not the practical reality, that its citizens were equal under the law. Third, unchecked spending by the French government caused rising prices, higher taxes, and food shortages, which led to popular demonstrations and demands for reform.

It was the combination of all these things that made the French Revolution happen when it did. When the government raised taxes to pay for war debts, the people might have grumbled and paid them—but the Enlightenment had created the new idea that if people were created equal to one another, the aristocrats should share the tax burden of the commoners.

Like all absolute monarchies, the French monarchy was inherently conservative. The king genuinely believed that he ruled by divine right and that in his person he represented all branches of the government; therefore, he did not even want advice from his ministers, much less any demands from the people.

The French Revolution was entirely unlike the English one that had taken place exactly a century before. The British Parliament had been a functioning legislative assembly for centuries; it was organized and powerful enough to subordinate the monarch and take competent charge of the realm. The French, on the other hand, had no legislative assembly worthy of the name; their attempts to establish one failed repeatedly. Both nations found themselves under military dictatorship for a time, but Oliver Cromwell's goals and ideas bore no resemblance to those of Napoleon Bonaparte.

The Napoleonic era, named for its most prominent figure, was characterized by Bonaparte's attempt to take over all of Europe—something that had not occurred since the days of the Roman Empire. Napoleon fell from power as swiftly and spectacularly as he rose to it, for a variety of reasons. First, France's success in taking over other nations made it the common enemy of all Europe; as in previous historical situations, a nation that upset the balance of power would soon cause other nations to unite against it. Second, the new French nationalism that resulted from the Revolution inspired the people of other nations to the same emotion; national pride was a major motivating factor in military victories over Napoleon. Third, so many French soldiers had died in Napoleon's early wars that the French army was largely made up of foreigners by the end of the era; German and Polish soldiers felt no particular personal loyalty to the emperor, and none at all to France. Fourth, Napoleon could not be both an emperor and a general at the same time; with his attention divided between leading the army and running the government, neither could be expected to operate efficiently or effectively.

The Congress of Vienna broke new ground in its attempt to establish an international peacekeeping organization of European states. This attempt succeeded in one way: the nineteenth century was almost without wars among the major powers of Europe. However, its leaders had a more conservative bent than the mass of Europeans, and some of the provisions of the Congress would lead directly to the national uprisings that characterized the 1800s.

CHAPTER 9 OBJECTIVES

- Describe the steps that led to the end of the monarchy in France.
- Explain how the various legislative assemblies gave way to the empire.
- Describe the rise and fall of Napoleon.
- Discuss the results of the Congress of Vienna.

Chapter 9 Time Line

- 1788   Estates General meet for the first time since 1614; Tennis Court Oath
- 1789   **14 July** People of Paris storm the Bastille

  August Declaration of the Rights of Man and of the Citizen is written
- 1793   Louis XVI and Marie Antoinette executed
- 1804   Napoleon declares himself emperor of the French
- 1808–1814   Peninsular War
- 1812   Russians defeat French; French retreat from Moscow
- 1814   Napoleon abdicates and is exiled to Elba
- 1815   Battle of Waterloo; final defeat of Napoleon
- 1815   Congress of Vienna

Major Causes of the French Revolution

Royal policies were a major cause of the French economic crisis of the late 1700s. Foreign and domestic policies both proved ruinous to the stability of the realm.

The Economy

By 1789, France's economy was in turmoil. Ministers had raised taxes to pay for foreign wars, some of which were being fought across the Atlantic. Since aristocrats and the clergy were tax-exempt, the entire burden fell on the classes least able to afford it: the peasants, artisans, and bourgeoisie. This caused great popular resentment. Royal extravagance and a poor grain harvest further damaged the economy.

During the French and Indian War (see Chapter 7), France spent large sums to send troops and supplies across the Atlantic. After losing the war, France immediately began improving the army and rebuilding the navy—an expensive project. In 1778, France entered the American Revolution as an ally of the colonists. By the time of the American victory in 1783, France had spent more than a billion *livres* on the military.

From 1783 to 1788, the government survived by borrowing money; the king's ministers attempted to reform the tax laws so that the wealthy landowners would have to contribute something, but the attempt failed to become law. In 1787 and 1788, a cycle of drought and then fierce hailstorms and flooding destroyed most of the nation's grain crop; this led to soaring prices, high unemployment, and conditions of near-famine by the spring of 1789. Throughout the countryside, people went on rampages, breaking into storehouses and stealing everything edible.

The Monarchy

The most important obstacle to reform in French society was the conservative nature of the monarchy. An absolute monarch, being in a position of power, had no incentive to reform society. Both Louis XIV and Louis XV believed that they ruled by divine right and that their judgment should never be questioned. Instead of embracing a system of checks and balances and a government with multiple branches of authority, the king of France believed that in his own person, he was the government—courts, legislature, and executive. *L'etat, c'est moi* (the government and I are one entity)—Louis XIV may never actually have said this, but he lived and believed it and passed the belief on to his successors.

Louis XIV died in 1715, when his heir was a five-year-old child. The Duc d'Orléans ruled France until 1723, when the king reached legal adulthood at age thirteen. Although Ivan the Terrible had taken firm hold on power in Russia at the same age, Louis XV showed no great desire to end the regency; his tutor and chief minister ruled the nation in fact, if not in name, for another seventeen years. Once Louis took over the actual business of governing in 1740, he relied heavily on the advice of his closest ministers. Their inconsistent advice led France into costly wars, with no plan for paying off the war debts besides raising taxes on the poorest classes of society, which could least afford them.

Louis XVI succeeded his grandfather Louis XV in 1774. At a time when France needed a strong, practical leader, Louis was timid and weak. His marriage to Austrian princess Marie Antoinette did nothing to strengthen his position with his subjects, as Austria and France were old enemies. His dismissal of many of the experienced government ministers certainly proved a mistake. Some of these men had attempted to reform the tax system by establishing a tax on the landed aristocracy; this chance of reform was gone when the ministers were dismissed from office.

Louis XVI and his ministers, unable to find any way to solve the problems on their own, called the Estates General to a meeting at Versailles. This was the first time the nation's only assembly had met since 1614.

The Estates General

The Estates General was a large group of officials divided into three categories by social status. The First Estate was made of clergymen, the Second Estate of hereditary nobles, and the Third Estate of commoners.

The First Estate

Members of the First Estate had two things in common: they were all employed by the Catholic Church, and they were all therefore exempt from paying taxes. Apart from that, however, they were a diverse group of men, from wealthy aristocrats to poor commoners. High-ranking bishops and cardinals lived in style and luxury, while parish priests suffered nearly as much from poverty and hunger as the peasants in their congregations. These poorer priests had a great deal of sympathy with the members of the Third Estate.

The Second Estate

The Second Estate was made up of the hereditary nobility. Like the clergy, the French nobility was tax-exempt. These aristocrats owned most of the land that did not belong to the Church or the state. Only members of the Second Estate were eligible for high government office. Many were nearly bankrupt because of the custom of the times that allowed noblemen to live on credit—to run up enormous debts that tradesmen had little power to compel them to pay. It was quite common for a French aristocrat of the time to have an empty purse but still eat well and dress expensively.

The Third Estate

The Third Estate included all French subjects who were neither aristocrats nor clergymen—a much larger group than the First or Second Estate. This group included a much greater variety of people—peasants, artists, intellectuals, and members of the French middle class, or *bourgeoisie*. Like the clergy, some members of the Third Estate were very wealthy, others very poor. The most crucial difference was that members of the Third Estate had to pay taxes. In spite of representing the greatest number of people, the Third Estate had the least power and influence over national policy.

Members of the Estates General did not vote individually; each estate received one vote on any question that arose in debate. This of course meant that the Third Estate was usually outvoted by two to one; the clergy and aristocracy were hardly likely to vote to help shoulder the tax burden or to make any other changes to a system that protected their privileges. However, some members of the Third Estate realized that the time for change might have arrived. There were important bonds between many members of the First and Third Estates. First, many of the clergy were commoners, not nobles. Second, many of them were badly off financially; like members of the Third Estate, they were aware of the desperate need for reform.

Toward a New Government

On May 2, 1789, Louis XVI met the deputies of the Estates General. His refusal to listen to the Third Estate's objection to the voting system created a stalemate at the outset. Over the next several weeks, members of the Third Estate urged the poorer deputies of the First Estate to join them in their fight for reform. Finally, on June 17, these deputies met on an unused tennis court near the palace (the king had ordered the doors of the usual meeting rooms locked). The deputies, calling themselves the National Assembly, together swore what became known as the Tennis Court Oath, vowing to remain united (thus preventing possible conspiracy, desertion in the ranks, and betrayal) until they had established a new government.

The National Assembly presented a list of demands to the king. On June 23, Louis XVI agreed to accept only those reforms that were most palatable to the Second Estate—individual liberty, freedom of the press, and a degree of tax reform. He did not accept such provisions as equal eligibility for office or a sweeping reform of the social hierarchy. When the National Assembly expressed the intention to carry out its reforms without his consent, the king gave in. Members of the First and Second Estates who had remained loyal to the old order joined the National Assembly.

Naturally, the people of Paris were gathering every day to hear and discuss the news from Versailles, only fourteen miles away from the capital. Although reform was on the way, it was not happening soon enough to satisfy them.

When the Parisians learned that the king had dismissed minister Jacques Necker, they had had enough of waiting. Because Necker was a liberal who had always favored reform, his dismissal sent a clear signal to the people that the king was not going to help them or take care of them. On the morning of July 13, the people of Paris rose up against all authority; they took to the streets in fury, breaking into shops and stealing the goods, especially guns and ammunition.

The main reason the people of Paris were so successful in their uprising was that the forces of law and order were on their side. Control of the army and the police is essential for success in taking power. The palace guards of the Louvre and all the soldiers quartered in Paris, who suffered as much as anyone else from the scarcity of food and the inflation, threw in their lot with the commoners.

On the fourteenth of July, the people marched on the Bastille. Built as a fortress in 1370, this massive structure had served as a state prison under Louis XIV. In 1789 it was nearly empty of prisoners, but it was not long since Voltaire, the symbolic figurehead of the Enlightenment and one who had always criticized the old regime, had been imprisoned there on two occasions. This made the Bastille a hated symbol of tyranny and injustice in the eyes of the students and intellectuals; commoners who had never heard of Voltaire still considered the prison a symbol of oppression. In addition to the symbolic value of destroying it, the Parisians wanted the weapons that were stored inside.

By early afternoon on what has since been known as Bastille Day, the prison had given way. The Parisians freed all remaining prisoners, commandeered the store of weapons and ammunition, and took brutal revenge on the chief magistrate and governor. They hustled them into the streets, turned the angry mob loose to almost literally tear them to pieces, then rammed their severed heads onto sharp pikes and paraded them through the streets in triumph.

News of the riots in Paris soon reached the nearby towns. Mob rule took over France as the common people forced mayors and other officials to abandon their offices. Throughout the countryside, peasants looted and set fire to the chateaux of their hated aristocratic landlords, often murdering them in the process.

Louis XVI summoned troops from Flanders to Versailles, hoping that this show of strength would make his subjects back down from their demands. The troops arrived at the end of September. On October 5, the women of Paris had had enough of seeing their children starve. They marched on Versailles, armed with a motley collection of sticks and kitchen knives. When they reached the palace, they shoved their way in past the guards and servants, demanding to be taken into the presence of the king.

Louis might have refused to give in to an angry mob of women, but there was a small army at their backs—thousands of members of the National Guard, fully armed, had followed the women from Paris. Louis and his Flemish troops were not proof against this small army. Louis agreed to provide bread for the people of Paris and to return to the capital as a prisoner of the National Guard. Waving the new French flag of red, white, and blue—the tricolor—the soldiers escorted the royal family to the long-abandoned palace of the Tuileries on October 6. The monarchy had been supplanted by the National Assembly.

The king and queen had no doubt about the future. They believed that the French people would no longer accept a monarchy, and therefore there would be no place for them in the new society. They worked out an escape plan. Dressed in old clothing, Louis walked out of the Tuileries one June night in 1791, boarded a waiting coach, and set out on the road to Austria, where he hoped his brother-in-law would provide shelter and perhaps troops willing to back his restoration to the throne. In a small town along the road where the coach stopped briefly, someone recognized the king in spite of his disguise. Louis was stopped in Varennes and taken back to Paris. Many members of the hereditary nobility left France around this time as well; the months of mob violence convinced them that they would soon have to pay with their lives for their ancestors' centuries of privilege. Hundreds of them fled to England, while others crossed the border into Austria, where they plotted to return to France and restore the monarchy.

The Declaration of the Rights of Man and of the Citizen

During the period of rioting and unrest, the National Assembly had begun work on a document that would set forth the rights and privileges of all French citizens. This document, known as the Declaration of the Rights of Man and of the Citizen, bore some resemblance to the American Declaration of Independence. It included a preamble and seventeen articles that called for a society based on equal treatment for all; freedom of speech, of the press, and of religion; the right to own property and to resist oppression; and the supremacy of just and reasonable laws that would treat all citizens equally. All of these were important ideas of the Enlightenment. The king had signed the Declaration, although unwillingly.

The National Assembly had intended for Louis to rule as a constitutional monarch, with limited legislative powers and a major ceremonial role. The king's attempted escape made them change their minds. It appeared that Louis could not be trusted to play the role they had imagined for him. It seemed more likely that he would try to bring back an absolute monarchy if he were allowed his freedom.

The First Republic

In October 1791, the National Assembly was replaced by the Legislative Assembly. The deputies had agreed that no one who had served in the National Assembly would be eligible for the elections, so though the new assembly was made up of many talented and able men, none was experienced at legislation. Most of the new deputies favored either a constitutional monarchy or a republic. The king's attempted escape, and news of the schemes of the departed aristocrats, swung the balance of feeling in the assembly toward a republic.

In the fall, Parisians voted for the men who would represent them in the new government, which was called the National Convention. This legislative body comprised 750 deputies, many of whom had served in the National or Legislative assemblies. Their first tasks were to write a new constitution for France and to decide the fate of the royal family. Since most of the deputies were democratic in their political convictions, they felt no sentiment in favor of the monarch. They believed that "Citizen Louis Capet" was a traitor to the Revolution and should be executed. This attitude prevailed over the conservatives, who argued for mercy. After a brief trial in which the king behaved with dignity, he was condemned to death and executed in January 1793. By December, nearly two hundred more would take the same journey to the scaffold.

Many members of the National Convention belonged to one of two informal clubs for deputies and intellectuals who shared a political philosophy: the radical Jacobins or the more moderate Girondins. The working people of Paris, called *sansculottes* (literally "without breeches"; breeches were tight-fitting trousers worn by men of the leisure class, while the workers wore comfortable loose-fitting trousers), supported the Jacobins, whose price-fixing and food rationing put an immediate end to the worst of the food shortages. The Jacobins soon found themselves gaining power in the Convention; the Girondins lost all political power when a mob of *sansculottes* attacked them in their meeting place. In effect, this brought about one-party rule in France.

The Terror

By June 1793, the Committee of Public Safety, established by the National Convention and headed by Maximilien Robespierre, had acquired complete authority over the government and thus over the people. A lawyer, Robespierre had been one of the deputies of the Third Estate who went to Versailles in 1789. As a Jacobin, he had favored the king's execution.

Under the Committee's rule, France underwent a period of violence known to history as the Terror. During this period, anyone denounced as an enemy of the state was imprisoned, hastily tried, and taken to the guillotine for execution. Crimes against the state included plotting, speaking, or writing anything that criticized the Revolution. In most cases an accusation was enough—no concrete evidence was necessary—and private conversations were as much of a crime as public statements. Anyone who showed sympathy for an "enemy of the state" could also be imprisoned and executed.

Many of the aristocrats of France who had not already fled to safety were guillotined, Queen Marie Antoinette among them. Fortunately, this disgraceful episode was short-lived. By March 1794, public sentiment turned against the Terror as the people realized that executing the innocent did nothing to preserve the Republic. Ironically, Robespierre was among the last to be guillotined.

With the end of the Terror came the downfall of the Committee. The National Convention had become the common enemy of all the factions—royalists, Jacobins, and moderates. It was clear that the Convention would have to give way to some strong central authority more capable of taking control. When the deputies of the Convention realized in October 1794 that it was only a matter of time before the Parisians rose up against them, they appealed for help to the army, then under the command of Napoleon Bonaparte.

The Rise of Napoleon

Born in Ajaccio, Corsica, in 1769, Napoleon had been educated at a French military academy. His extraordinary ability in mathematics and geography made him excellent officer material. In 1794, Captain Bonaparte led a successful attack against the Austrians that led to his immediate promotion to the rank of general. Charged with controlling the mob in Paris in 1794, Napoleon decided to threaten it with grapeshot—clusters of small musket-balls fired from cannons at point-blank range. The ensuing incident, known to history as a "whiff of grapeshot," wounded and killed many people and effectively ended the threat against the Convention. This efficient handling of the emergency marked Napoleon as a figure of major importance in France. He was soon leading the army to victorious campaigns in Italy and Austria. Despite a failed campaign in Egypt, he returned to Paris in 1799 to loud popular acclaim.

By the time of Napoleon's return, the Convention had given way to the Directory—yet another attempt at creating a strong, functional legislature. The Directory had five hundred deputies, of which two-thirds were elected or appointed from among the Convention members and the rest elected by the local assemblies of France. The Directory was a muddle just as the Convention had been; it had no strong leader and no internal agreement about how to shape a new government. Many ideas that had ruined the Convention returned in the Directory. It took all political rights away from members of the Second Estate who had returned to France after the Terror. It arrested and deported hundreds of members of the old First Estate. Rather than permitting religious freedom, it tried to do away with religion altogether by suppressing the Catholic Church. The Directory found itself unable to agree on provisions for a constitution, and its leaders soon realized they would have to try again to form a workable legislative assembly.

Because Napoleon was the acknowledged head of the military forces, the Directory turned to him again for help in controlling the mobs of Paris as it tried to form a new government. Over November 9 and 10, the Directory fell and was replaced by a body of three consuls, one of whom was Napoleon. He quickly became First Consul, the only one with any real power.

Napoleon Rules France

Napoleon had spent his youth and all his adult life in the military, which was famed for its organization, its clear rules, and its chain of command. He began his rule of France by organizing its government along these lines, from the local to the national level. Under Napoleon, France acquired its first national bank and public school system. Napoleon also improved the division of France into administrative *départments* (similar to British or American counties) and reestablished the Catholic Church by concordat with the pope in 1801. The concordat reorganized the Church in France administratively and gave the government greater control over it. To Napoleon, this was strictly a practical matter; he had no religious convictions of his own, but he perceived that their Catholic faith and heritage was too important to his subjects to jettison.

The Convention had attempted to write a new law code as early as 1793. Using its work as a basis, Napoleon revised and finalized what became known as the Code Napoleon or Napoleonic Code, which went into effect in 1804. The Code Napoleon set forth the basic rights of the citizens and clarified the fact that in the Republic, the laws would apply equally to all.

In August 1802, in an election of sorts, Napoleon was chosen First Consul for life. He was now a military dictator in all but name. It did not take long before he demanded another vote, this time over whether he could pass his title on to his sons. In 1804, Napoleon declared himself hereditary emperor of the French for life. In effect, France had exchanged one absolute ruler for another.

Napoleon's Military Career

From 1800 to 1809, Napoleon was spectacularly successful on the battlefield. During this period he pursued the same military strategy in every case: to identify and attack the enemy's weak point, and never to be forced on the defensive.

In 1805 Napoleon was on the march against Austria, which had formed an alliance with Russia in the hopes of securing the Rhine River and the Black Forest against future French invasions. The Austrians fought the French all through September and October while they waited for Russian reinforcements to arrive. With the goal of severing the link between the troops and their supply lines, Napoleon anticipated every move of the Austrian generals. The Austrians surrendered on October 20. Napoleon then marched his army east to meet the Russians under General Kutuzov. The armies met at Austerlitz, a town about fifty miles north of Vienna. The French defeated the Russians and the war ended in the Treaty of Pressburg. This treaty finally abolished the Holy Roman Empire, replacing it with the French-controlled Confederation of the Rhine. This was the high point of Napoleon's military career.

In 1808, France found itself at war with Spain. First the French invaded and subdued Portugal, then moved into Spain to overthrow its monarchy. Napoleon wanted an alliance with Spain, and thus wanted to replace the hereditary monarch with someone he could trust. His army imprisoned the ruling Bourbon family and installed Joseph Bonaparte, Napoleon's brother, as king. This provoked the Spanish to rise up in a burst of angry nationalism against the invaders. Napoleon, who had expected to take over Spain easily, was unprepared for this response.

Britain soon entered the war on the side of Spain and Portugal. The Duke of Wellington, head of the British army, found himself in command of a combination of Spanish, British, and Portuguese troops. Wellington, unlike Napoleon, preferred to fight on the defensive. This meant a long war of attrition.

Meanwhile, Napoleon had decided to invade Russia over disagreements with Czar Alexander I. With the French army fighting on the Iberian Peninsula, Napoleon gathered an army from territories controlled by France. By June 1812, some 650,000 troops—Germans, Poles, Austrians, and Italians—had marched to the Russian border.

Crossing the barren plains of Russia in intense summer heat took a terrible toll on the Grand Army. The land provided no shade trees, no crops, and few sources of fresh water. Unable to scavenge much to eat or drink, the soldiers began falling dead by the side of the road. Eventually they began killing and eating their own horses.

In September the armies met at Borodino. Napoleon again defeated Kutuzov, but at the price of fifty thousand casualties, none of whom could be replaced because France had come geographically too far from its sources of supply.

Kutuzov ordered his troops to retreat toward Moscow. He knew that when winter arrived, the French would have to surrender. When the Russians reached the capital, they evacuated and burned it. When the French arrived, they found no food and little shelter. By October, Napoleon acknowledge that the French would have to return to the West. The Grand Army began the long retreat—only to realize the Russians had turned and were pursuing them. Thousands of Grand Army soldiers died in the retreat. The remnants of the army crossed the border in December.

Meanwhile, the Peninsular War was clearly lost. Facing enormous military defeat on two fronts, Napoleon abdicated in 1814.

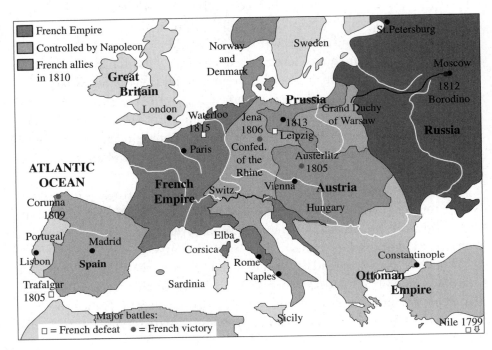

The Napoleonic Wars

The End of the Napoleonic Era

Louis XVI's brother now became king of France, ruling under the name Louis XVIII (when Louis XVI was executed in 1793, the crown prince had automatically become Louis XVII, but the child disappeared; historians believe he died in prison during the Terror). The government decided to banish Napoleon to the small Mediterranean island of Elba. They promised him a budget with which to govern Elba, but it was never paid. Therefore Napoleon was unable to carry out his plan to organize Elba's administration, rebuild its roads, and in other ways repeat on this smaller scale what he had done in France. Bored with enforced idleness on Elba, he had little to look forward to but the mail, which brought him letters from old soldiers pleading with him to return to France and take over the reins of government. In 1815, Napoleon persuaded himself that he must save France. He quietly took ship with seven hundred soldiers, arms, and money. Docking in Cannes and marching north, Napoleon's army was soon strengthened by the addition of a French infantry battalion encountered on the road.

When the news of Napoleon's escape reached the leaders of Europe, they reacted swiftly and in concert. They chose Wellington to command the allied forces—British, German, Dutch, and Belgian troops—with the Prussian army under General Blücher standing by to help him. Facing two armies about ninety miles apart, one in Belgium and the other in Germany, Napoleon decided to attack from the center to keep them separate while eliminating each army in turn.

Wellington prepared for the attack by positioning his men on the high ground above the fields of the town of Waterloo. On June 18, Napoleon's troops were ready to attack. Meanwhile, General Blücher was leading the Prussian troops into position.

After a long day of fighting, the French were defeated. This last battle ended the Napoleonic era and finished Napoleon's public career. "Meeting one's Waterloo" is still today an idiom that signifies failure. The British declared Napoleon a prisoner of war and banished him to the South Atlantic island of St. Helena, where he died in obscurity in 1821.

The Congress of Vienna

The leaders of Europe met in Vienna in September 1814 to restore the balance of power that had been so drastically upset by the conquests of Napoleon. The work of the Congress of Vienna was briefly interrupted when Napoleon returned from Elba, but the leaders resumed work after the Battle of Waterloo and completed their task by June 1815.

Each nation was represented at the Congress of Vienna by a monarch or a prominent military or political figure, as follows:

- Austria—foreign minister Prince Klemens von Metternich
- Britain—foreign secretary Viscount Castlereagh; Duke of Wellington
- France—foreign minister Charles Talleyrand
- Prussia—chancellor Prince Karl August von Hardenberg
- Russia—Czar Alexander I

The leaders had two main goals. First, they wanted to restore the balance of power in Europe by redrawing or restoring boundary lines. All territory acquired by France under Napoleon was either restored to independence or given to one of the four major powers—Austria, Britain, Prussia, and Russia. Second, the Congress was concerned not only with restoring the balance of power, but also maintaining it for the future. At the end of the Thirty Years' War, France had emerged as the most powerful nation; at the end of the Napoleonic Wars, it was clear that some other strong nation must be created as a check on any future French threat of European domination. This led the Congress to agree on the desirability of unifying the German states into one centrally governed nation. By 1819, nearly forty German states had formed the German Confederation, temporarily under the presidency of Austria.

Another aspect of maintaining the balance of power over the long term was the establishment of the Quadruple Alliance. This group, formed of representatives of the Great Powers, agreed that it would meet as often as necessary over the next twenty years to see that the terms of the peace were carried out and to discuss any matters of international concern that might arise. The members of the Quadruple Alliance believed in three principles: legitimacy, compensation, and containment.

Legitimacy

European ideas of the divine right of kings and the special qualities of royal families were very slow to die; the men of the Quadruple Alliance were not democrats, nor did they espouse republican ideals. They strongly believed that royal power properly belonged in the hands of legitimate monarchs. Napoleon stood outside this category because he was not of royal blood and also because he had seized power during a revolution rather than accepting it in an orderly transfer of authority.

Compensation

The leaders agreed that nations that had suffered from Napoleon's invasions and power grabs should be compensated. To their way of thinking, this meant giving territory rather than money to the victors. As part of the final peace settlement, five nations were given new territory: Austria, Denmark, Prussia, Russia, and Sweden. (Britain was on the winning side but was given no compensation since it had never been invaded.) Most of the Italian provinces were divided among these nations.

Containment

The third principle was that of containment: of arranging matters in a way that would prevent, or at least discourage, future French aggression on the continent. Strengthening the union of the German states was the major step taken toward checking French aggression.

The Quadruple Alliance was the first European attempt to create an international peacekeeping organization. It failed in the long run; its first meeting was also its last. However, its goals were important because they showed the trend that diplomacy was taking in history. Peace conferences after major international wars would occur again in the twentieth century, and serious international peacekeeping efforts would also be undertaken again.

QUIZ

1. **The people of Paris succeeded in overtaking the Bastille because**
   A. they had planned the attack with great care.
   B. they knew of the existence of the Declaration of the Rights of Man.
   C. they were outraged over the dismissal of Jacques Necker.
   D. the National Guard did nothing to stop them.

2. **The Legislative Assembly decided against establishing a constitutional monarchy because**
   A. the king refused to rule jointly with the legislature.
   B. the radical and republican deputies outnumbered the monarchists.
   C. Louis XVI proved by his attempted escape that he could not be trusted.
   D. the people of Paris were determined that the king should be executed.

3. **An alliance with _____ made it possible for the Third Estate to establish a new government.**
   A. Louis XVI
   B. Maximilien Robespierre
   C. poor members of the First Estate
   D. members of the Second Estate

4. **All members of the First Estate were**
    A. common working people.
    B. clergymen.
    C. hereditary nobles.
    D. soldiers in the regular army.

5. **The women of Paris marched on Versailles in 1789 to**
    A. burn down the palace.
    B. arrest and imprison the royal family.
    C. steal whatever they could find.
    D. demand an end to the food shortage.

6. **Napoleon signed a concordat with the pope and restored the Catholic Church in France because**
    A. he was a devout Catholic.
    B. he was afraid of the power of the pope.
    C. he believed that a traditional form of worship was important to the people.
    D. he wanted to maintain the French clergy in a position of power.

7. **The Declaration of the Rights of Man and of the Citizen guaranteed** _____
    A. individual rights and freedoms to the people of France.
    B. a specific form of government.
    C. an end to the hereditary monarchy.
    D. the establishment of a new Fourth Estate.

8. **Which group of people was the most politically conservative?**
    A. the First Estate
    B. the Second Estate
    C. the Third Estate
    D. the armed forces

9. **Napoleon's 1812 invasion of Russia failed primarily because**
    A. the French army could not withstand the Russian winter.
    B. his army was poorly and unwisely commanded.
    C. he did not have enough troops to defeat the Russians.
    D. the Russian army was better trained than the French.

10. **Why did the delegates to the Congress of Vienna recommend German unification?**
    A. because Prussia had played a significant role in defeating Napoleon
    B. because Britain and Prussia were allies
    C. because a united Germany would balance France as a strong central nation
    D. because there had been too much warfare among the German states

The Industrial Revolution, 1750–1914

The tale of modern European history can be seen as a series of revolutions. The Protestant Reformation was truly a revolution in Christian worship. The Scientific Revolution gave birth to a completely new way of thinking about the universe. The French Revolution attempted to establish a government along the lines of Enlightenment ideals. And the Industrial Revolution brought manufacturing into the modern era of mass production and consumption.

The Scientific Revolution, of course, was a major prerequisite of the Industrial Revolution. It created a climate of fascination with mechanics, physics, and technology without which the engineering achievements of the Industrial Revolution could never have taken place.

The Industrial Revolution began in Britain long before it developed on the European continent. This was due to a variety of factors, including Britain's stable government and society and its lack of direct involvement in the Napoleonic Wars. British engineers and inventors developed most of the technology that would make the Industrial Revolution possible.

The Industrial Revolution arrived on the European continent around 1830; it took root first in the nations that already had the mercantile mind-set and the natural resources to make it happen. As the nineteenth century rolled on, the nation-states began altering and developing their banking systems, the source of finance that made industrial growth possible. In addition, governments soon saw from Britain's example that by industrializing, they would make money on a vast scale; therefore, they supported laws and regulations that favored industrial development.

The Industrial Revolution also saw a major change in society; for the first time, individual workers realized that they had the power to improve their own working conditions. This did not happen overnight and it was met with fierce resistance from the owners and managers, but slowly the workers of Europe began to achieve recognition as a class with its own power and its own rights.

CHAPTER 10 OBJECTIVES

- Identify the causes and effects of the Industrial Revolution.
- Explain why the Industrial Revolution occurred first in Britain and only much later on the continent.
- Identify the major figures of the era and match each person to his accomplishments in science and engineering.

Chapter 10 Time Line

- **1733** John Kay invents the flying shuttle
- **1763** James Watt improves the steam engine (invented 1698)
- **1764** James Hargreaves invents the spinning jenny
- **1769** Richard Arkwright invents the water frame
- **1779** Samuel Crompton perfects the "spinning mule"
- **1787** Edmund Cartwright patents the steam-powered loom
- **1825** Railroad steam engine demonstrated
- **1830** Opening of Liverpool and Manchester Railway; German states establish *Zollverein*
- **1833** British factory legislation

The Industrial Revolution Begins in Britain

The Industrial Revolution began in Britain for two main reasons; one was its geographical makeup and the other was its society.

Geography

The island of Great Britain was crisscrossed by a network of canals and rivers; therefore, it was relatively cheap and easy to transport goods. The climate was temperate enough for travel and outdoor work year-round, except in the very coldest weeks of winter, and there were no major geographical obstacles to transportation, such as mountain ranges or vast deserts. Britain also had vast resources of coal, which was a main element of industry until late in the twentieth century.

Due to its geographical isolation from the European continent, Britain was largely unaffected by the Napoleonic Wars that consumed Europe from the end of the eighteenth century to 1815. Although Britain sent troops to the continent and British troops played a major role in Napoleon's defeat on the battlefield, France did not invade Britain, and its government and economy were not shaken up by the wars.

Society

From the Glorious Revolution in 1689 to the beginning of World War I in 1914, Britain was a very stable society. The constitutional monarchy functioned well, the banking system was prosperous, and the population was thrifty. Men and women who owned their own small businesses—taverns, stores, mills, or farms—tended to invest their profits back into the business. In addition, men who owned small businesses could vote; this connected the interests of industry to those of government.

Changes in Farming

The British agricultural industry adopted Dutch methods of crop rotation, fertilization, and diversification. The term *crop rotation* refers to planting a field with a different crop each year—for example, wheat the first year, rye the second, and potatoes the third. Each crop drew different nutrients and minerals from the soil; therefore, rotating the crops allowed the soil to replenish its own resources. Diversification worked well for the same reason. Planting a variety of crops made the best possible use of the soil. It also cut down on poor harvests; if the wheat crop failed, for example, the potato crop might still thrive.

In 1701, Jethro Tull perfected a seed drill that could be harnessed to a horse. As the horse walked down the field, the drill sowed the seeds neatly and uniformly. Previously, the farmer had had to do his own sowing by walking down his rows and casting handfuls of seeds as he walked. The seed drill sped up the process and made it more efficient. Food production increased 300 percent over the course of the eighteenth century in Britain. Many people credit Tull's seed drill and other pioneering agricultural ideas with a major part in this change.

Probably because of the increase in food production, the British population would double between 1780 and 1851.

Because innovations in farming made large-scale farms more economically profitable than small ones, landowners began the process of enclosure—fencing in large tracts of privately owned land. Traditionally, the British had always permitted subsistence farming on any open fields, regardless of who owned the land. This made it possible for villagers to raise crops and feed their families. With the changes in agricultural methods, however, landowners joined in the enclosure movement, thus consolidating their fields for large-scale farming. Enclosure forced many villagers to move to the cities looking for work for wages. This large-scale urban migration, of course, provided the factories with a steady supply of workers. In this way, agriculture played its own major role in the overall manufacturing economy.

Changes in the Textile Industry

Britain's textile industry—both cotton and wool—was a major part of its economy. Sheep grazed the grasslands that covered the nation. For generations, their wool had been sheared, spun into yarn, and woven into cloth. Before the eighteenth century, this work had been done largely by hand.

Major changes in the textile industry began in 1733, when John Kay invented the flying shuttle. In 1764, James Hargreaves followed with the spinning jenny. Together, these inventions made the spinning and weaving process much faster and more efficient. More changes came later in the century: In 1779, the spinning mule combined the capabilities of the spinning jenny with the power of an invention called the water frame. When Edmund Cartwright perfected the first steam-powered loom in 1787, the weaving and spinning process took another giant step toward mass production.

Steam is probably the single most important word for an understanding of the Industrial Revolution. Europeans had understood the power of fire for many generations, and wood had served well as fuel. At the same time, although timber was a renewable resource, trees were slow to grow and had to be planted. Britain, once heavily forested, had used up most of its timber by the 1700s. Coal was another source of power, and coal was abundant, but it was also buried deep below the ground, and getting it out was difficult, expensive, and time-consuming. (In time, coal became so necessary to British productivity that a major coal-mining industry developed.) Steam had the advantages of being accessible, free, and available as long as the rivers had water in them.

Thomas Savery developed Britain's first steam engine just before 1700. In 1705, Thomas Newcomen improved Savery's design. In 1763, James Watt improved the Newcomen engine. By the late eighteenth century, all the mills and factories in Britain were steam-powered. It was steam power that made the first railway locomotive possible; later, coal powered the engines.

In 1830, the Liverpool and Manchester Railway opened. This development marked a major change in European lives. Until this time, nothing could move over land faster than a person could walk or a horse could run. Now, people could travel rapidly; journeys that had once taken seven or eight days could now be completed in a few hours. The railway proved popular and profitable, and within fifty years British workers had laid track and were driving engines all over the country. By 1880, technology had progressed so much that the trains were moving at three times their 1830 speed.

The main reason for building the railway, of course, was not for passenger travel but for freight. The railway made it possible for large quantities of goods to be transported quickly and efficiently over land for the first time in history. This reduced shipping costs, which in turn created larger markets and greater demand for goods; as demand rose, production increased. Owners were making enough profits to expand their businesses, building more factories and hiring more workers.

The Industrial Revolution on the Continent

The European continent lagged behind Britain in industrial development for several reasons. First, the French Revolution and the Napoleonic Wars had caused a major upheaval in France, Austria, Spain, and Russia; no nation can pay much attention to its domestic economy when it is embroiled in war. Second, the European powers distrusted one another; the Congress of Vienna did not do away with important political and territorial rivalries. Third, tariffs restricted free trade among European nations; this in turn restricted markets for goods. Last, the men of Britain's thriving mercantile middle class had a certain amount of political influence because they could vote for their representatives in the House of Commons. Representative governments like this were still very rare on the European continent; hence the continental middle class, which supported industrialization, had much less power and influence.

The Industrial Revolution on the continent began in Belgium. This small nation at the northeastern corner of France was, like Britain, rich in the coal that was necessary for industrialization. Geographically, Belgium and Britain were separated only by the narrow band of the English Channel, and British production techniques found their way across with relative ease, despite British attempts to keep their mechanical secrets for their own profit. The Cockerill family settled in Belgium around 1800 and began to build spinning equipment and machinery. By 1830 they had created a major manufacturing industry. Naturally, their success inspired imitators, and Belgium soon had a thriving economy.

From Belgium, industry slowly spread throughout Europe. National borders shifted throughout the nineteenth century, so industrial development is best thought of in regional rather than national terms. Industrialization depended largely on the location of natural resources. Technologies were changed in areas where the resources did not match the British model. For example, the Mediterranean region was not rich in coal; therefore, French and Italian factories tended to rely on waterwheels and water turbines. Additionally, the sheep of southeastern Europe were not the same types that thrived in Britain. Their wool had a finer texture and could not be spun and woven on the same kind of equipment used in the British mills. The engineers of Spain and France showed their ingenuity by modifying the machinery to suit the needs of their raw materials.

The railway was also slower to develop in Europe than in Britain. By 1848, however, several major railways crisscrossed Europe, particularly in Germany, northern France, and Austria. By 1870, most of the continent—even the less accessible regions such as southern Italy—was linked by railways. It was possible to travel all the way to Russia by train.

The governments of Europe had originally hoped that extending the railways would bring industrialization to areas that were less far along technologically. By midcentury, they had become well aware of the enormous profits to be made in mass production of goods. However, the railway proved an ineffective means of stimulating industry; its greatest usefulness was in linking the areas that were already industrialized, which was a great aid in shipping and international trade.

By 1860, Britain's industry was entirely modernized. On the continent, Belgium, France, and Switzerland had made the most progress toward mass production. However, things would change in the second half of the century. Generally speaking, the nations of northern central Europe had the most industrialized economies and those in southeastern Europe the least, with Spain, France, and Italy occupying a position somewhere in between.

Industry affected the German economy more than that of any other nation. By the outbreak of the First World War in 1914, Germany had surpassed the rest of continental Europe in production. In 1890, Britain had produced twice as much steel and mined twice as much coal as Germany; by 1914, Germany's output of both coal and steel was double the British amount.

Industries differed in different nations depending on their manufacturing traditions and on the raw materials available to them. Major coal-mining industries sprang up in central France, in Belgium, and near the major cities of Krakow, Leipzig, Hanover, and Vienna. In Italy, Milan was a major center for textile production and engineering.

Labor Relations

The Industrial Revolution changed the manner of production. It did away with the model that had existed in Europe for centuries and replaced it with a new one. Workers learned that their place in the scheme of industry was quite different from what it had been before.

In the past, work had been done at a slow pace and largely by hand, with tools that were not mechanized; for example, people had woven cloth on looms for centuries, but the weaving was done by hand. Items were produced one at a time, in much smaller quantities. The pressure to turn goods out ever-faster and make ever-higher profits was not there. Workers considered themselves artisans because of their level of individual effort and the unique qualities of their products.

With the arrival of the factories, all of this changed. The process of manufacturing changed so that dozens of workers labored together in the process. Goods were made as cheaply as possible. Taking time to make something perfect was discouraged because it was not cost-effective. The important thing was to produce great quantities of goods as quickly as possible.

Artisans rightly saw the Industrial Revolution as the end of their own era. At the same time, industrial workers felt that they were caught in a trap. The owners and managers were concerned mainly with the company's profits. They had no incentive to establish safety regulations or to treat workers well, since this would cost time and money. Britain's large working-class population meant that factory and mill hands could easily be replaced if they were injured or if they quit. Therefore, owners spent as little as possible on their workers and demanded as much as they could get away with. The modern concept of the weekend did not exist; the workweek lasted six days, with Sunday, the Christian Sabbath, being the only day of rest. A workday generally lasted from 6:00 in the morning until 8:00 at night, with perhaps twenty minutes for lunch. Women and children were hired in great numbers because they earned less than men, and since wages for all were kept at starvation levels, all members of the family had to contribute. Parents put their children out to work at age five or six.

Machinery was dangerous to operate at the best of times, and the long hours made for tired workers who were sometimes too exhausted to move as quickly and carefully as was necessary for safety. Many workers were severely injured by the machines they operated—in such cases, compensation depended entirely on the generosity of the owner. Workers were also exposed to dangerous levels of industrial pollution, constantly inhaling chemicals, smoke, and lint. Mine workers faced the worst danger of all, that of being buried alive if the underground tunnels collapsed.

Realizing that factory conditions were neither reasonably safe nor humane, and that an entire social underclass was being created, the government began to pay attention. Liberals provided undeniable evidence that the owners would not pay their workers fairly or provide decent working conditions unless they were forced. Government regulation of industry seemed to be the only way to guarantee that workers would be treated fairly.

Many politicians were influenced by the writings of two social and political thinkers: social reformer Jeremy Bentham and economic theorist John Stuart Mill. Both men argued that if one person's situation was bad, the entire community was that much weaker; if one person's situation improved, the entire community was that much stronger. Therefore, what was bad for one individual was automatically bad for everyone; conversely, the good of the individual would inevitably lead to the good of the community. According to Bentham and Mill, it was in everyone's economic interest to treat others fairly and ethically. This way of thinking suggested that owners and workers had a mutual interest in maintaining cordial relations: that a factory in which workers and owners were both content with their situation would be more profitable.

Eventually, workers realized that while one individual worker had no bargaining power, 150 workers together could shut down a factory simply by going on strike—walking off the job so that the factory would sit idle. Since workers were the means of production, the profits of the factory depended entirely on their labor. Once workers realized that together they were strong, trade unions began to arise. This did not happen until the last half of the nineteenth century.

Owners were bitterly opposed to trade unions. First, they believed that no one had any right to tell them how to run their own businesses. Second, they were well aware of the bargaining strength of united workers, and they were afraid of it. Owners usually argued that workers' demands were too high. They painted a picture of union workers as lazy people who wanted a luxurious standard of living without effort. History shows that this picture is grossly distorted. Workers have always argued for reasonable hours, reasonable safety conditions, and wages that would allow them to support their families in reasonable comfort. Of course, owners were prone to consider any decrease in their profits "unreasonable"—and higher wages, shorter hours, and improvements to lighting and safety came out of the profits.

Trade unions became legal in Britain in 1871, in France in 1884, and in Germany after 1890. They were generally organized by the type of skilled worker. With the coming of the twentieth century, unskilled workers began to form unions as well.

The Industrial Revolution changed the European economy. As the nations industrialized, their per capita income rose. In northern Europe, the average person quadrupled his or her income between 1830 and 1910; even in the Balkans, the least industrialized region of Europe, individual income more than doubled.

The Industrial Revolution also spurred a rise in international trade. The nineteenth century was a major period of expansion for several European nations, as they colonized Africa and built empires see Chapter 14. Imperialism had a twofold effect on the rise of industry. First, it created new markets for goods manufactured in Europe. Second, it provided industrial nations with new repositories of the natural resources that were necessary to keep their factories running.

QUIZ

1. **What effect did industrialization have on a nation's economy?**
   A. It created heavy debts because of expenditures on machinery and new plants.
   B. It caused a sharp rise in the per capita income.
   C. It created greater tax revenues for the central government.
   D. It enabled people to begin buying on credit on a regular basis.

2. **Which best describes the social philosophy of John Stuart Mill and Jeremy Bentham?**
   A. Individuals should always do what they think is best for themselves.
   B. Individuals should always do what they think is best for others.
   C. If one person's situation improves, the whole community is that much better off.
   D. If one person's situation deteriorates, the rest will gain from that person's loss.

3. **The pioneering achievements of Jethro Tull in agriculture allowed farmers to _____ much more efficiently.**
   A. rotate their crops
   B. diversify their crops
   C. fertilize their fields
   D. sow their seed

4. **Which nation was producing the greatest amount of coal by the 1914 outbreak of World War I?**
   A. Britain
   B. Germany
   C. France
   D. Russia

5. **How did the Napoleonic Wars affect industrialization in Britain?**
   A. They slowed down the process.
   B. They did not affect the process.
   C. They sped up the process.
   D. They made the process a waste of time.

6. The _____ industry was the mainstay of the British economy.
   A. textile
   B. publishing
   C. mining
   D. service

7. _____ power was crucial to the Industrial Revolution in countries where coal was scarce.
   A. Electric
   B. Fire
   C. Solar
   D. Steam

8. Industrial development in Europe depended most on which factor?
   A. availability of natural resources
   B. availability of workers
   C. proximity to the railroad
   D. topography and climate

9. Why did Britain not rely on timber as a source of fuel for its factories?
   A. It was too time-consuming to cut and haul it.
   B. It had largely been used up by the time of the Industrial Revolution.
   C. It was not a renewable or cheap resource.
   D. It was not as readily accessible as coal.

10. The most important source of power for a wage worker in a factory was
   A. membership in a trade union.
   B. the ability to vote in parliamentary elections.
   C. ownership of stock in the company he or she worked for.
   D. the ability to rise in the company through promotion.

chapter 11

European Revolutions, 1815–1849

The nineteenth century in Europe is often described as a century of peace, with no major wars breaking out between 1815 and 1914. This picture is somewhat distorted; there was a great deal of violence in Europe during this century. However, it was a new kind of war: this was the century of the popular uprising. Where most wars in the past had been fought *between* nations, this century saw a series of revolutions fought *within* nations, in which the people rose up and demanded their independence.

Slowly and gradually, Europeans had been moving toward a more inclusive and egalitarian society. The rise in literacy and education that had begun with the Reformation and continued through the Enlightenment had removed some of the barriers separating the aristocrats from the commoners. Ordinary people had come to believe that they had the same rights as aristocrats—such as the right to some voice in their own government and the right to own property—and they began to rise up in massive numbers and fight for their rights. Examples of constitutional governments in Britain, France, and the United States led to loud calls for written constitutions in many European nations.

By the nineteenth century, ideas of liberty and equality had spread through-out Europe and gone some way toward creating a new force—nationalism. The seeds for the nationalist movement were sown at the Congress of Vienna, when the leaders redrew the map, marking national boundaries without respect for ethnic, linguistic, or cultural divisions in the population. For instance, the people of Italy once again found themselves under the rule of Germans and Austrians.

One wave of revolutions took place in 1830 and another in 1848. These revolutions can be understood as a struggle between the forces of liberalism and conservatism, the two mainstream political movements of the day. Liberal-ism, which supported representative forms of government, triumphed in the nineteenth century, although several conservative governments were still in power in 1914.

CHAPTER 11 OBJECTIVES

- Name and describe the major political movements of the early to mid-nineteenth century.
- Trace the political history of the great powers of Europe to 1848.
- Discuss the popular uprisings from 1815 to 1848 and describe their results.
- Define the Romantic movement in the arts and name the key figures.

Chapter 11 Time Line

- 1818   Congress of Europe meets
- 1830   Charles X of France abdicates; Louis Philippe becomes king
- 1830–1831   Belgium becomes an independent nation
- 1832   Reform Act
- 1837   Queen Victoria is crowned
- 1848   *Communist Manifesto* published; revolutions in France and other nations
- 1853–1856   Crimean War

Political Parties and Struggles

Politically, the nineteenth century can be defined as the age of "-isms." These were political movements, ways of thinking that crossed national borders. They were not formal political parties but political philosophies that could be found in several European nation-states.

Most influential Europeans espoused one of two political philosophies; today we would call these the "mainstream" political trends of the era. These were conservatism and liberalism—words that, in nineteenth-century Europe, meant something quite different from their contemporary American definitions.

Conservatism

Conservatives can be defined by their distrust of the people. They did not accept Enlightenment ideas about equality; rather, they believed that a strong executive—preferably a hereditary monarch—should run the government, with some participation by the wealthiest citizens, especially the hereditary nobles. The conservatives opposed freedom of the press, believing that the monarch was the best judge of what should and should not be published. Merchants, aristocrats, and clergy, especially high-ranking clergy, were usually conservative.

The conservatives did not want to return to the days of autocracy or despotism along the lines of Louis XIV. Instead, their ideal was an absolute but benevolent monarch, one who used his or her powers for the good of the people and who worked with other monarchs to maintain a balance of power among nations.

Liberalism

The most important difference between nineteenth-century liberals and conservatives was that liberals looked ahead toward an age of representative government, while conservatives looked backward to an age of absolute monarchy.

Liberals disapproved of absolute monarchy because history had shown them that too many monarchs were arbitrary, tyrannical, weak, or incompetent. They were, however, willing to accept a hereditary constitutional monarchy. An ideal liberal government would have a written constitution, perhaps a constitutional monarch, an elected legislative assembly, and separation among the government's branches. This last was important because it would prevent the executive from becoming a tyrant; the legislative and/or judicial branches would step in to protect the people.

The liberals supported individual rights such as the right to private property, freedom of speech, and freedom of the press. They even supported the right to vote, although they believed it should be limited to men who owned property; property owners were generally better-educated and thus, according to the liberal view, deserving of more rights and privileges.

Neither conservatives nor liberals imagined a place in the political system for the lower classes. Although the workers, farmers, and common people comprised the majority of the population of Europe, they lacked what both conservatives and liberals believed to be the main qualifications for participation in government: high social position, wealth, property, and education. Conservatives believed that a benevolent monarch could be trusted to take proper care of the nation's workers because it was his or her duty as the servant of the state; liberals urged the legislative assemblies of Europe to specific action on workers' rights, such as regulation of factories.

Nationalism

Nationalism is similar to patriotism. It refers to the pride a person takes in his or her nation and culture.

During the nineteenth century, the people of Europe began to identify themselves more with their native countries than had ever been the case in the past. Formerly, people had thought of themselves as belonging to a particular family, town, village, or perhaps even a province. Some monarchs, such as Elizabeth I of England, had attracted a high degree of personal popularity. However, since borders constantly shifted in Europe, relatively few people thought of themselves as being citizens of a nation.

With the Enlightenment and the coming of the nineteenth century, a gradual shift in thinking became apparent. Europeans began to think of themselves as Frenchmen, Spaniards, or Britons. Even in places like Italy that were still not unified nations, the people took pride in their common language, their shared history, and their unique national culture. The revolutions of the nineteenth century encouraged nationalism by defining national borders and making them permanent. By 1900, nationalism was deeply rooted all over Europe—at least among the educated classes.

Nationalism was a unifying force in culturally homogeneous nations like France, where the vast majority of the population spoke the same language and worshiped in the same church. However, in a diverse empire like Austria-Hungary, which included a variety of ethnic groups and religions, it could be explosive. Nationalism could make citizens react adversely to a monarch or leader who was born outside the country's borders. In the twentieth century, it would be one of the forces that led to both world wars. Nationalism is also the main reason for the conflict that continues to exist in the United Kingdom between Ireland and England. (See Part 3.)

Socialism

Socialism is a form of government in which the good of the whole is more important than the rights of the individual. In a socialist state, the government is in charge of major institutions such as education and health care. In a socialist economy, the state owns and controls the businesses and can establish prices. In a capitalist economy, all businesses and industries are privately owned, and the laws of supply and demand set the prices. Socialism was to thrust deep roots into European soil; by the end of the twentieth century, most European nations would have mixed economies, with major elements of socialism as well as capitalism.

One interesting but short-lived form of socialism developed early in the nineteenth century. Utopian Socialism was based on the Greek word *utopia*, meaning "nowhere": a utopia was an ideal society in which there was no conflict, which of course exists nowhere. However, in the nineteenth century, hopeful philosophers believed in the possibility of a real utopia. They envisioned self-sufficient communities in which everything was jointly owned. Followers of Robert Owen in England and Charles Fourier in France founded a number of small utopian communities, but none lasted very long. It seemed that for human beings, private property was desirable and a certain degree of conflict was inevitable.

Marxism

The political philosophy known as Marxism is based on the *Communist Manifesto* (1848), written jointly by Prussians Karl Marx and Friedrich Engels. They argued that the history of Europe was the history of the struggle for supremacy between classes. First the aristocrats had ruled, next the monarchs had seized dictatorial powers, and in the nineteenth century the middle class was growing stronger. Finally, wrote Marx and Engels, it would be the turn of the proletariat, or the working class, which would have to use violence to take over society.

In *Das Kapital* (1867–1894), Marx wrote that all goods should be priced according to the amount of work that went into them. The worker who produced goods, Marx argued, was a far more valuable member of society than the owner, who produced nothing.

Naturally, the wealthy dismissed Marx's arguments as the ravings of a madman. For many centuries, a small percentage of Europeans—the upper class— had possessed and enjoyed most of the money, while the vast majority—the working class—possessed and enjoyed almost none of it. This was the settled order of society and it had always been so. Marx's suggestion that workers should enjoy the profits of their own labor was truly revolutionary.

Marx's ideas angered political thinkers across the spectrum. Conservatives opposed him because he suggested overturning a social order that they wanted to maintain at all costs. Liberals opposed him because he did not believe in the rule of the few or even of the educated; he was much more democratic. Nationalists scorned him because he insisted that one's country of origin counted for nothing; what mattered was whether or not one worked for a living. Capitalists despised him because he insisted that workers, not owners or management, should enjoy the profits and run the industries themselves.

Nation-States in the Nineteenth Century: The Great Powers and the Holy Alliance

In the wake of the French Revolution, the more conservative among the Great Powers were united in their feeling that future popular uprisings should be suppressed. In September 1815, just after the Congress of Vienna, the three most conservative Great Powers—Austria, Prussia, and Russia—formed what became known as the Holy Alliance. Leaders of these three nations agreed to assist one another in stamping out any attempt to threaten what they saw as the peace and stability of the new European map of 1815. As conservative monarchies, they viewed popular rebellions and insurrections as serious threats to political stability. As it turned out, the three nations would frequently have to send troops to put down such rebellions. Their superior military strength led them to success in most cases, but ultimately the tide of history was against them.

Austria

Officially founded in 1804 although it had existed as a monarchy for some time before that (see Chapter 12), the Austrian Empire found itself threatened by the forces of nationalism. The empire was not culturally homogeneous, but instead was made of several ethnic groups, each of which fought for independence and self-rule in the nineteenth century.

Hungarians and Italians both rebelled against the empire in 1848 and 1849. In each case, the goal was independence from the empire. Austria went so far as to grant Hungary a separate constitution, but then revoked it. When Hungary retaliated by declaring independence, Austria called on its Russian ally for military aid and defeated Hungary in 1849.

The Austrian army forcibly put down the Italian uprising in July of 1848. It also intervened to destroy the newly created Roman Republic, formed when the pope was forced into exile for political reasons. France, which agreed with Austria on the undesirability of Italian unification, marched into Rome and occupied it until 1870. (See Chapter 12.)

Britain

Britain began the nineteenth century much farther along the road toward republicanism than any continental European nation; it already had a constitutional monarchy and a powerful legislative assembly. However, there was plenty of discontent among the working class, as social reforms to date had not improved factory conditions. The Industrial Revolution had certainly provided employment for many, but such employment was little better than industrial serfdom. (See Chapter 10.)

Although Ireland was represented in Parliament, the Catholic Irish (the vast majority of the population) were barred from office by a law that restricted membership in Parliament to Anglicans. During the 1820s, the Tory majority in Parliament passed two major bills repealing religious restrictions on eligibility for office. These bills were by no means popular with the balance of Englishmen, and in the elections of 1830 the Whigs gained the majority. They passed the Reform Act of 1832, which adjusted the number of seats per borough, giving the larger populations in urban boroughs more representatives. The Whigs also passed labor laws that barred women and children from working in the extremely dangerous and unhealthy conditions in Britain's coal mines. The liberals hoped that this would enable children to attend school and women to take care of their families.

England still had laws that restricted suffrage to men who owned a certain amount of property. In the 1830s, only about ninety thousand of England's 6 million adult men could vote. In 1867, the Conservative (formerly Tory) leadership in Parliament passed a reform bill that extended suffrage to most homeowners and renters. This immediately doubled the number of eligible voters.

In 1849, Prime Minister Robert Peel repealed the Corn Laws, which had maintained high import duties on grain. Benjamin Disraeli, prime minister in 1867 and from 1874 to 1880, saw a number of domestic reforms through Parliament. In 1875, the Public Health Act and the Artisans' Dwelling Act helped urban workers by improving sanitation and providing public housing for those in need.

Late in the nineteenth century, the Whigs and Radicals combined forces and formed the Liberal party. Its leader was William Gladstone, who served as prime minister both before and after Disraeli's second term in office. Gladstone oversaw these numerous important social reforms:

- promotion in the military governed solely by merit, not social rank
- reform of the civil service
- introduction of compulsory free public education
- introduction of the secret ballot
- extension of voting rights to farm workers
- second redistribution of seats in Parliament to make representation proportional

France

Under Louis XVIII, who became king of France in 1814 upon the abdication of Napoleon, France made some progress toward becoming a constitutional monarchy, including the establishment of a legislative assembly similar to the British Parliament or the U.S. Congress. However, there were many political parties in France at this time, and all of them felt that Louis XVIII's moderate policies did not concede enough in the proper direction. Everyone wanted to shift government from its centrist position, but none of the factions could agree. Republicans wanted to abolish the monarchy, while radicals wanted to establish full-blown socialism. On the opposite side, the royalists wanted a return to a seventeenth-century style of absolute monarchy. In other words, one group wanted the legislature to have control; one group wanted the people to have control; and one group wanted the monarch to have control.

In 1824, Charles X succeeded Louis XVIII. Charles was a conservative, with an old-fashioned belief in the monarch's divine right to rule. When the 1828 elections shifted the balance of power in the legislature toward the liberals, Charles tried to come to terms with their very different philosophy of governing. However, he was unable to see himself as the constitutional monarch the liberals wanted him to be. In 1830, Charles dismissed the legislature, established censorship of the press, and revoked voting rights for certain categories of citizens.

The people reacted furiously. With the National Guard on their side, they started firing on the army in the streets of Paris, building barricades from sandbags and any sturdy objects they could find. Nearly nineteen hundred people died during these violent demonstrations. Charles, realizing that his people would never tolerate an absolute monarch, but unwilling to compromise, abdicated. He was the last hereditary monarch to rule France.

The legislature selected Louis Philippe as the new constitutional monarch; he was the great-great-grandson of the Duc d'Orleans, who had served as regent during the early years of the reign of Louis XV (see Chapter 9). Known as the "Citizen King," Louis Philippe ruled as a moderate liberal until 1848. He restored freedom of the press and revoked Charles's restrictions on voting rights.

During the two decades of Louis Philippe's reign, discontent developed among the social and economic classes of the nation. The bourgeoisie prospered under the new regime, but little of the profits reached the pockets of the working class. Socialists and radical republicans seized on this discontent to arouse support for their cause. When they were barred from holding public meetings in 1848, they staged a repeat of the 1830 revolution; the people mounted the barricades in the streets and fired on the army. Once again, the people succeeded in forcing the king to abdicate.

However, the various factions could not agree on what kind of new government to establish. The liberals, radicals, and socialists had much in common but could not compromise on matters where they disagreed. The socialists favored a Marxist system in which the workers would own government-supervised factories and share equally in the profits. The liberals considered this system far too radical but agreed to implement some national workshops as a temporary measure to bring down the high unemployment. The workshops were highly successful with the laborers; more than 120,000 had joined by April, with more on the waiting list. However, the 1848 elections returned a National Assembly with a moderate-to-conservative majority. These deputies immediately closed the workshops, which resulted in a return to violent protests in the streets of Paris. More than three thousand people died during the June Days of 1848.

In the end, the National Assembly created a constitution for a new French republic. The constitution called for a strong president, a unicameral legislature, and voting rights for all adult men. When elections were held, Louis Napoleon Bonaparte became the first president of the Second Republic of France.

Like his more famous uncle, Louis Napoleon wanted more power than he could have in a republican system of government. In 1851, he forced the legislature to extend his term for another ten years. When a national vote showed that the vast majority of the people approved his actions, he had himself declared Emperor Napoleon III. (The title "Napoleon II" had been given to the son of Napoleon I, although he never ruled.) This was the end of the Second Republic.

Napoleon III ruled as a despot, but in some ways a benevolent one. He suppressed any attempt of the legislature to exercise its powers, and he tolerated no demonstrations or opposition from the people. However, he instituted a number of projects that vastly improved the domestic economy, such as major public-works projects, the construction of a national railroad, and numerous treaties that eased and encouraged trade. From about 1860, his politics grew more liberal and reformist. In 1870 he approved a new constitution; although it called for a hereditary monarchy, it also established a democratic parliament.

Napoleon's downfall, like that of his uncle, came about because of failures in his foreign policy. A failure to check the spread of Prussian power culminated in 1870 in France's defeat in the Franco-Prussian War. The emperor's reign ended abruptly with the proclamation of the Third French Republic. The new National Assembly negotiated the peace with Prussia, including the surrender of Alsace and Lorraine. This treaty was highly unpopular in France, especially in Paris, where radicals soon declared Paris' independence from France and established a new government of their own, the Paris Commune. The Commune did not last long; it turned out to be no match for the national army and was obliterated at the cost of twenty thousand lives.

By 1875 the National Assembly accepted that it would be impossible to restore the monarchy in any form. The deputies devised a new legislative structure modeled after the U.S. Congress. The lower house was popularly elected, the upper house chosen by the political parties, and the president elected by members of both houses.

A famous incident occurred in 1894 when the military courts found Captain Alfred Dreyfus guilty of treason. The evidence was weak at best, and the case dragged on for years, with prominent liberals such as novelist Emile Zola speaking out on Dreyfus's behalf. In the end, it was proved that Dreyfus had been convicted on the basis of forged documents. The military courts refused to reverse their verdict; however, the president of France pardoned Dreyfus and a civil court overrode the military verdict. This incident served to unite liberals, socialists, and republicans for some time to come.

Prussia

The prevailing sentiment in Prussia was conservative and anti-nationalist. However, Prussian liberals rebelled against the government, demanding one with greater representation. This time the liberal forces won a victory. In 1848, Frederick William IV was forced to summon a new legislative assembly, the National Parliament of the German Confederation, and agree to a new constitution.

This was a moment of triumph for the liberals, but internal disagreements weakened and divided them. The king soon disbanded the assembly and replaced the constitution with a more conservative version. In Prussia as elsewhere in Europe, the liberals and socialists, who should have been natural allies against the conservatives, could not agree on what they wanted. Their differences prevented German unification at this stage. When the liberals formed a parliament in Frankfurt and asked the king to rule a united Germany as a constitutional monarch, he refused. With no executive, and with parties that were constantly at odds, the parliament broke up in 1849. In a little over twenty years, Germany would become a unified nation for the first time. (See Chapter 13.)

Russia

Although Russian society had a liberal element, autocracy was far too firmly entrenched to give way to any notions of republicanism. Russia did not experience a genuine public uprising until 1905. Although this was put down, it sowed the seeds of the Bolshevik Revolution of 1917. (See Chapter 16.)

The Minor Nations and States

Events played out in the minor nations and states of Europe in much the same way as in the Great Powers.

Belgium

Belgium had been made a part of the Netherlands in 1815 at the Congress of Vienna and was clearly discontented with this situation. As a nation that was becoming wealthy due to its participation in the Industrial Revolution, Belgium did not want to be a part of a larger empire. In 1830, Belgium rebelled against the Netherlands; with French and British support, it regained its independence in 1831.

Greece

Greece had been under the rule of the Ottoman Empire since 1453. In 1821, the Greeks rebelled against the occupying Turkish forces. With aid from Russia, France, and Britain, the Greeks were able to drive the Turks out and declare independence in 1827. In this one case, the Holy Alliance aided the rebels because the occupying force was Turkish rather than European; European nations had always been willing to unite against invasions from the Ottoman Empire. Although Turkey had one foot in Europe, the Ottoman Empire was Muslim and Europeans had regarded it as a heathen, enemy culture since the days of the Crusades.

There were so many conflicting political factions in Greece that the Greeks agreed they were not ready for self-government; they accepted the proposal of the Great Powers to establish a monarchy. Seventeen-year-old Prince Otto of Bavaria agreed to accept the Greek throne, ruling as Otto I.

Otto I proved an unpopular ruler. First, he was a foreigner, and nationalism was strong in Greece; the people did not welcome a non-Greek ruler. Second, he was politically conservative, unwilling to accept the Greeks' insistence on a written constitution. In 1843, the feelings against Otto finally boiled over in a *coup d'etat*. At this point the king conceded many of his subjects' demands, and government in Greece became more liberal, including parliamentary elections.

Italy

Most of the Italian states had been divided among the Great Powers at the Congress of Vienna. In 1821, there were popular uprisings in Naples and Piedmont; however, troops of the Holy Alliance nations eventually crushed these attempts to establish constitutional government. Further rebellions took place in Parma and Modena in 1831. These also were unsuccessful, as was a rebellion in the Papal States, which was put down by French troops. Austrian troops occupied much of Italy until 1838. Italian unification would take place during the 1860s. (See Chapter 13.)

Poland

In 1830, it was not possible to find a nation called "Poland" on the European political map. Poland had been carved up and divided among Austria, Russia, and Prussia in the late 1700s (see Chapter 6). However, nationalism was strong among the ethnic Poles, and it was only a matter of time before they rose up against their foreign rulers.

Polish rebellion against Czar Nicholas I broke out in the Kingdom of Poland—a region centered around Warsaw—in 1830. The Poles won the first skirmishes and achieved a short-lived independence, which was crushed by the Russian troops in 1831. This was followed by a campaign of "Russification" under the czar, who revoked many Polish rights and privileges in an attempt to replace Polish language and customs with Russian ones. Despite further sporadic uprisings in Krakow, Warsaw, and elsewhere, Poland would not regain its independence until 1918.

Spain

Because Spain had always been the most conservative of all European nations, liberals and socialists had far less support there than elsewhere. The Spanish middle class, far less extensive and powerful than in other nations, did urge reform to the best of its limited ability. In 1820, the army led a rebellion against Ferdinand VII, forcing him to agree to Spain's first written constitution. However, French troops eventually came to the king's aid, suppressing the rebellion and murdering most of the rebels.

Between 1869 and 1874, the Cortés (legislative assembly) attempted to establish a constitutional monarchy and gain acceptance of a liberal constitution. This was achieved in 1875. However, the Spanish idea of a constitutional monarchy was far more conservative than the ideas prevailing in Britain or France. The real power in Spain would long remain where it had always rested—in the hands of the great landowners, the Church, and the army.

The Romantic Movement

The nineteenth century saw the birth of a major movement in literature and the arts. This movement is called Romanticism. Writers, musicians, and artists of the Romantic era celebrated their own individuality in their novels, poetry, symphonies, songs, and paintings.

Romanticism was something of a revolt against the Classical or Neoclassical era that had begun in the late 1700s and lasted through about 1815. This had been an era of rigidly controlled artistic forms, such as the sonata in music.

Where the Classical era concentrated on form, the Romantic era concentrated on content. As an outgrowth of the Enlightenment, Classical music and art celebrated reason; as an outgrowth of nationalism, Romantic music and art celebrated emotion. It was a glorification of the artist as a creative individual, an era in which each artist cast aside fixed rules and consciously placed his or her individual stamp on his or her work.

In literature, Romanticism lasted from about 1830 to 1850. Johann Wolfgang von Goethe of Frankfurt and Jean-Jacques Rousseau of Geneva were early influences on the Romantic writers, who included E. T. A. Hoffmann (Prussia); Alexander Pushkin (Russia); Samuel Taylor Coleridge, Charlotte and Emily Brönte, and Mary Shelley (Britain); and Victor Hugo (France).

In music, the Romantic movement lasted from about 1830 to about 1900. The great Romantic composers are often included under the misleading label "classical music"; in fact, the Classical era in music lasted only from about 1750 to 1820. Classical composers begin and end with Franz Josef Haydn, Wolfgang Amadeus Mozart, and Ludwig van Beethoven; the last is considered a bridge to the Romantic era in music. Major Romantic composers include Franz Schubert of Austria; Robert Schumann, Johannes Brahms, Felix Mendelssohn, and Richard Wagner of Germany; Frédéric Chopin of Poland; Pyotr Ilyich Tchaikovsky of Russia; Hector Berlioz of France; and Giuseppe Verdi of Italy.

QUIZ

1. _____ would be the most likely group to accept rule by a constitutional monarchy working with an elected legislature.
   A. Conservatives
   B. Socialists
   C. Liberals
   D. Marxists

2. The fall of Louis Napoleon, or Napoleon III, came about because of
   A. the Paris Commune.
   B. the Franco-Prussian War.
   C. the Revolution of 1830.
   D. the Revolution of 1848.

3. _____ is an important historical figure because he first suggested that the heretofore lowly worker was the most valuable member of society.
   A. Benjamin Disraeli
   B. William Gladstone
   C. Karl Marx
   D. Alfred Dreyfus

4. The Holy Alliance aided the rebels in Greece because
   A. the purpose of the Alliance was to support nationalism.
   B. the Alliance wanted to push the Turks out of Europe.
   C. the members of the Alliance planned to divide Greece among themselves.
   D. the Greeks had always come to the aid of Alliance members.

5. The political trend in Britain in the nineteenth century is best described as
   A. conservative.
   B. repressive.
   C. communist.
   D. reformist.

6. Which best describes the main reason for the political turmoil in France during this period?
   A. the lack of a written constitution
   B. a series of incompetent monarchs
   C. disagreement among the political factions
   D. defeat in the Franco-Prussian War

7. _____ rebelled unsuccessfully against the czar in 1830–1831.
   A. Austria
   B. Greece
   C. Poland
   D. Russia

8. Reform in Britain during the nineteenth century came about primarily because of the support of which group?
   A. liberals
   B. conservatives
   C. nationalists
   D. Romantics

9. The writings of Karl Marx and Friedrich Engels aroused the opposition of all these groups except
   A. capitalists.
   B. Communists.
   C. liberals.
   D. nationalists.

10. In which nation-state would nationalism be most likely to cause political and social instability?
    A. an empire with an ethnically diverse population
    B. a heavily industrialized nation with a large population of workers
    C. a nation-state whose people shared a common cultural and linguistic heritage
    D. a state that practiced religious toleration

Empires of Eastern Europe: Austria-Hungary and Russia to 1914

Austria and Russia, the two great empires of Eastern Europe, shared certain important characteristics during this period of history. Both were members of the Holy Alliance, which had been established to preserve traditional monarchies like their own. Both were large, unwieldy landmasses (although Russia was much larger) and thus somewhat difficult to control. Both had large standing armies. Both suffered as a result of the Napoleonic Wars. Neither showed any willingness to establish any type of popular representation in government.

Although liberal conditions prevailed in Austria, the monarchy was conservative at heart. Emperor Joseph II did not dream of ruling as a constitutional monarch, nor of sharing his powers with other branches of a government. As a representative of the Hapsburgs, a family that had ruled European kingdoms for centuries, Joseph believed that he was the person best fitted to rule his own realm. Traditions of divine right, family honor, and class superiority all affected his thinking. However, Joseph's actual policies were enlightened and benevolent; his subjects enjoyed many rights and freedoms that were unusual for the time.

Russia continued to develop along political and social lines that differed greatly from those prevalent in the nations of Western Europe. Because a Russian czar was an absolute ruler of the old style, the welfare of Russian society was heavily dependent on his personality—a factor that was less weighty in nations like France, where others exercised some restraints on the monarch's power. As had been the case in France, unlimited autocracy would eventually lead to revolution in Russia.

CHAPTER 12 OBJECTIVES

- Describe conditions in Austria under Joseph II.
- Explain how the Kingdom of Austria became the Austro-Hungarian Empire.
- Describe political and social conditions in Russia during the nineteenth century.
- Describe the causes and effects of the 1905 Russian Revolution.

Chapter 12 Time Line

- **1804**   Austrian Empire founded
- **1815**   Congress of Vienna
- **1825**   Nicholas I becomes czar of Russia
- **1853**   Crimean War begins
- **1861**   Emancipation of serfs in Russia
- **1867**   Creation of dual monarchy of Austria-Hungary
- **1905**   Russo-Japanese War; First Russian Revolution
- **1908**   Austria-Hungary annexes Bosnia

Austria: From Kingdom to Empire

Austria was a kingdom within the Holy Roman Empire in 1780, when Joseph II Hapsburg assumed full power. Before that date he had ruled jointly with Empress Maria Theresa, his mother. (See Chapter 6.)

Both Maria Theresa and Joseph were enlightened monarchs, more forward-looking in their policies than most other European rulers. For example, they abolished judicial use of torture in 1776. They also cut back on the ostentatious spending that was a feature of most European courts, as exemplified by Versailles. Joseph especially preferred a simpler style of living. He often described himself as "first servant of the state." However, being the "first servant" did not make Joseph less of an autocrat. The difference between him and a monarch like Peter the Great or Louis XIV (see Chapter 6) was that Joseph intended to be a benevolent despot. He believed that it was his duty to oversee his subjects just as a loving father would care for his family. Just as the father considered himself the wisest and most mature individual in the home, thus deserving of total authority, Joseph II believed his royal birth made him the person best fitted to run his own kingdom.

The Hapsburgs were generous patrons of the arts. Vienna, Austria's largest and most important city, was perhaps the most cosmopolitan city in Europe in the late 1700s. Vienna saw the birth of the Rococo style of architecture, which was lighter and more fanciful than the Baroque style that had preceded it. Rococo buildings were easily recognized for their elaborate decoration, carvings, and trim; interiors were spacious and airy, furniture was delicate in shape and weight, and color schemes were light and pretty. Vienna was the center of the musical world, with composers Christoph Willibald Gluck, Franz Josef Haydn, and Wolfgang Amadeus Mozart all being major figures who enjoyed court patronage. Ludwig van Beethoven also spent much of his musical life in Vienna.

Maria Theresa and Joseph were both inclined toward social reform. When Joseph assumed full power in 1780, he quickly relaxed censorship, causing an immediate rise in the number of published books. In 1781, he abolished serfdom throughout Austria; he also took charge of the Austrian civil service, reorganizing it into an efficiently functioning bureaucracy.

Joseph II was a Roman Catholic like all the Hapsburgs before him; however, unlike many of his predecessors, he understood the importance of tolerance in creating a stable realm. In 1781, Joseph issued the Toleration Edicts, which expanded civil rights for Protestants, Orthodox Catholics, and Jews throughout Austria (although social customs continued to pressure Austria's Jewish citizens to assimilate). Joseph closed numerous monasteries throughout the empire and used their funds to reorganize and improve the Church organization, bringing it under the authority of the government. In a true union of church and state, the clergy became civil servants, their salaries paid by the government. Joseph also instituted a mandatory level of education for priests.

Among his other social reforms, Joseph founded Austria's General Hospital—the first of its kind in Europe—and one of Europe's first free public school systems. He passed agricultural reforms that made conditions much easier for individual small farmers. It was no wonder that ordinary Austrians, particularly those of the poorer classes, came to regard Joseph as their defender and protector.

Given his liberal social policies, it is not surprising that Joseph aroused strong opposition from the Austrian nobility. The aristocrats did not welcome his attempts to establish a certain measure of equality in society; they preferred to keep their special privileges and status for themselves. The Church hierarchy did not offer Joseph much support either, resenting what they perceived as interference. In 1790, Joseph reluctantly revoked numerous reforms in the Hungarian region, realizing how unpopular they were with the powerful classes.

Upon his death in 1790, Joseph II was succeeded by his brother, who would rule as Leopold II. Leopold had ruled Tuscany as its Grand Duke since 1765. He shared the reforming instincts of his mother and brother but had generally instituted new programs more slowly and cautiously. Leopold restored certain features of pre-Josephine Austria, particularly as regarded special privileges for the landlords of great estates.

Francis II succeeded his father Leopold II on the latter's death in 1792. By this time, the French Revolution had made all hereditary monarchs rather apprehensive. Francis was more openly conservative than either his father or his uncle; however, he did not undo the progress that had been made toward modernization. In fact, he oversaw the passage of advanced, enlightened criminal and civil law codes in 1803 and 1811.

Francis was distracted from domestic programs by a 1792 declaration of war from France. The fighting lasted off and on for nearly twenty years, with Austria coming off the worse throughout. In 1792, France's primary goal was to subdue Belgium and the Rhine region; it did not issue direct threats against Austria until 1800.

The Kingdom of Austria officially became the Austrian Empire in 1804, the year in which Napoleon declared himself emperor of the French. Many hereditary European rulers took this as a personal affront, since Napoleon was not of royal blood and therefore, in their eyes, had no right to assume such a title. Francis's claim to the title "Emperor of Austria" was largely a symbolic gesture, intended as a reminder of the long-standing status of the Hapsburgs as Holy Roman emperors and kings. Francis's assumption of the title did not change Austria's type of government, nor its national borders.

In 1805, Napoleon and the Grand Army marched into Vienna; later that year they won a major victory at the town of Austerlitz. As part of the treaty that ended this stage of the fighting, Austria gained the territory of Salzburg; in return, however, it gave up its rights to other territories, and Francis II finally, officially, and permanently dissolved the Holy Roman Empire (which had existed only as a formality since the days of the Thirty Years' War).

By 1810 Austria had practically been reduced to the status of a French satellite, and in 1812 Napoleon commandeered thirty thousand Austrians to serve in the Grand Army in its march on Russia. Naturally, Austrians were deeply hostile toward France and its rule; they felt no incentive to serve Napoleon. The fact that the Grand Army had comparatively few French troops is one reason for its downfall in Russia. By 1912, it was composed largely of German, Italian, Polish, Czech, and Austrian soldiers from countries Napoleon had subdued.

The Congress of Vienna made the Austrian Empire a unified, contiguous landmass for the first time in its history. This new Austrian Empire included Hungary, Transylvania, Croatia, the Czech states of Bohemia and Moravia, and the Italian states of Lombardy and Venetia. Austria was also given the responsibility of overseeing the confederation of German states created at the Congress.

Because the Austrian Empire was not culturally homogeneous, the force of nationalism created political and social instability. Too many small ethnic groups within the empire wanted self-determination. Both the Italians and the Hungarians rose up in 1848. Although both rebellions were crushed by virtue of the Austrian state's military superiority, it was only a matter of time before some measure of independence would become a fact. In 1867, Austria and Hungary formally declared a dual monarchy; from that time, it was known as the Austro-Hungarian Empire. Emperor Franz Joseph of Austria would rule both kingdoms, and joint ministries oversaw the foreign affairs and finances of both kingdoms, but Hungary had a separate constitution and a separate legislature.

Having gained its own independence, Hungary now found itself in the same position as Austria: it was a large nation with a diverse population. Hungary granted Croatia a measure of self-determination in 1878. In Austria, ethnic Germans in Bohemia and Moravia were satisfied with the status quo, since Austria was officially a German-speaking nation, but ethnic Czechs in the region demanded greater independence.

Discussion among the Great Powers in 1878 led to Austria's making the Balkan nation of Bosnia into a protectorate. In 1908, in a move to protect Austrian control of certain trade routes, the empire officially annexed the protectorate. Bosnia's large and vocal Serbian population immediately began trying to regain Bosnian independence. This strong Serbian nationalism would contribute largely to the outbreak of World War I in 1914 (see Chapter 15).

The Russian Empire

If Austrian monarchs were conservative, Russian monarchs were far more so. The Russian government had been autocratic from the time the nation first drove the Tatars from power, and it would remain that way in the nineteenth century despite the passage of some degree of social reform. Liberalism was strong among Russian intellectuals, but they had little influence or power compared to the nobles, military officers, and high-ranking clergy, who were mainly conservative.

By 1818, serfs in the Baltic provinces had been emancipated. Alexander I then ordered his aides to draw up a plan for abolishing serfdom throughout Russia, but the idea was so unpopular that he abandoned it by 1820. However, the serfs did achieve some rights and privileges in the 1820s and 1830s: a measure of self-government, village schools, and health clinics. As was so often the case in Russia, all these reforms were chaotic in their administration, however neat they appeared on paper. Serfs in the Baltic were given no land, so in fact they gained only the freedom to move.

Alexander's brothers, Constantine and Nicholas, were each in a position to succeed him. Constantine, the elder of the two, had no desire to rule. He renounced his position in the line of succession in 1822, leaving Nicholas to become czar in 1825. Nicholas I soon proved himself an old-style autocrat, very different from his generally liberal brother Alexander I. Nicholas believed in Russian nationalism, Orthodox Christianity, keeping the lower classes in what he regarded as their proper place, and the rule of the absolute monarch throughout Europe. Under his rule, only the nobility could attend secondary schools and universities, and the civil rights of religious and ethnic minorities within Russia were curtailed. In foreign affairs, Nicholas supported any monarch facing a popular uprising.

Both Alexander I and Nicholas I oversaw major territorial expansion. Russia had completed its westward march with the partitions of Poland, but it continued to expand to the south, reaching the Aral Sea in 1853 and as far south as the Afghanistan border in 1885. Russia also expanded south on its eastern border, taking over territory on the Pacific that allowed it to establish the port city of Vladivostok; for the first time Russia gained access to the East by water. The completion of the Trans-Siberian Railroad in 1904 made overland travel from Vladivostok to Moscow possible. These two developments were extremely important for trade.

In 1853, war broke out in the Crimea, a region controlled by the Ottoman Turks on the coast of the Black Sea. Nicholas I started the war with two goals. First, he wanted to take over Turkish-controlled provinces along the southern reaches of the Danube River. Second, he wanted to seize control of certain "Christian shrines" within the Ottoman Empire. The Russian invasion of the Crimea aroused the opposition of Britain and France, who had their own Mediterranean interests to protect. Historians agree that the Crimean War was disastrously mismanaged on all sides, particularly by the British commanders. Russia concluded a peace treaty with the Turks in 1856, but it did not last. Russia and Turkey were at war again by 1877.

Nicholas I died before the Crimean War was over. His son and successor Alexander II would rule until 1881. Alexander understood that the age of the autocratic ruler was over; he was determined to emancipate the serfs. This was a long and complex process. Since serfs owned no land, the government would have to provide it for them at the start. Changes to the judicial system and to local government would be needed. In addition, landowners argued that emancipation would deprive them of valuable property; Alexander and his aides would have to find a way to compensate them for the loss. In 1861, the serfs were officially freed from bondage.

Although Alexander ruled as a moderate, many liberals in Russian society felt that his reforms did not go far enough. During the 1870s, violent demonstrations became common as students and other liberals tried to gain support for their political cause. This period of unrest ended abruptly in 1881 when a bomb hurled by an anarchist in a crowd exploded at the czar's feet. Severely wounded, Alexander died later that day.

Alexander III succeeded his father, Alexander II. He reacted to his father's assassination by suppressing all liberal tendencies in society, rather than giving in to liberal demands. His policies included strengthening the central bureaucracy, extending the powers of the police, and revoking freedom of the press.

The year 1905 was pivotal for Russia. The country lost the Russo-Japanese War, in which Japan flatly put a stop to Russian expansion into China. It was also the year of a major popular uprising that would eventually culminate in the Bolshevik Revolution of 1917.

The 1905 revolution had several contributing causes. First, liberal, Marxist, and socialist ideas had traveled eastward to Russia, whose intellectuals and workers had enthusiastically espoused them. Second, the government had instituted widespread industrialization in Russia without understanding the consequences to either the peasants or the workers. Third, a severe famine in 1891 had taken its toll on the people.

Workers throughout Russia went on strike in 1905, establishing soviets—the word means "workers' councils"—everywhere. These bodies, intended to serve as local governments, were based on the Marxist ideal of turning society over to the rule of the workers. They did not last, but would return in 1917. Peasants also rose up in fury over social conditions, especially the issue of land ownership. All of these issues would play into the Bolshevik Revolution and the end of the empire in 1917.

QUIZ

1. **What was the major effect of the Russo-Japanese War of 1905?**
   A. The serfs of Russia gained their independence.
   B. Russia established a port on its eastern border.
   C. Russia's expansion into China was halted.
   D. Russia annexed Japan.

2. **The Russian _____ strongly opposed Alexander I's plan to emancipate the serfs.**
   A. nobility
   B. civil service
   C. legislature
   D. military

3. **What was the effect of Austria's Toleration Edicts of 1781?**
   A. the suppression of nationalism within the empire
   B. the establishment of universal free public education
   C. government regulation of wages and worker safety in the factories
   D. expanded civil rights for religious minorities

4. **What was one reason for Vienna's status as Europe's most cosmopolitan city in the late 1700s?**
   A. opposition from the clergy
   B. royal patronage and support of the arts
   C. the excellence of the Austrian education system
   D. the establishment of the General Hospital

5. **France declared war on Austria in 1792 with the purpose of**
   A. recruiting soldiers for the Grand Army.
   B. securing its alliance against Russia.
   C. conquering Belgium and the Rhine region.
   D. creating a joint Austro-French kingdom.

6. **What effect did the Congress of Vienna have on Austria?**
   A. It transformed Austria into the dual monarchy of Austria-Hungary.
   B. It unified Austria into one contiguous landmass.
   C. It placed Austria under the authority of the Confederation of the Rhine.
   D. It imposed liberal policies upon Austrian subjects.

7. **Which best describes the trend or pattern of government in Russia during the nineteenth century?**
   A. Liberal czars alternated with reactionary ones.
   B. Reactionary czars ruled throughout the era.
   C. Liberal czars ruled throughout the era.
   D. Government gradually became more democratic.

8. **All these factors helped bring about the outbreak of the 1905 Revolution except**
   A. the spread of liberal and Marxist ideas.
   B. the reactionary policies of the czar.
   C. the effect of industrialization on the peasants.
   D. the emancipation of the serfs.

9. _____ joined the Turks in opposition to Russia during the Crimean War.
   A. Britain and France
   B. Austria and France
   C. Austria
   D. Poland

10. Which aspect of Joseph II's reign demonstrates his conservative views?
    A. establishment of a General Hospital and public school system
    B. passage of the Toleration Edicts
    C. belief in the monarch's fitness to rule absolutely
    D. patronage of the arts

German and Italian Unification, 1815–1871

The spirit of nationalism led to the unifications of two of Europe's largest ethnic and cultural populations—the Italians and the Germans—in the late nineteenth century. Masterminded in both cases by shrewd ministers of state—Cavour in Italy and Bismarck in Prussia—the unification process in both cases happened surprisingly quickly and smoothly. However, each nation would proceed very differently once unification was accomplished.

Unlike Germany, Italy had a previous history as a unified nation. Italy had been the center of the Roman Empire and had continued to exist under one central government until the sixth century A.D. The Italians had a shared language, an ancient shared history of ruling the known world, and a common culture. This made Italy a natural breeding ground for nationalism.

Once unification was completed in 1861, however, complications ensued. First, the Church refused to go along with unification, perceiving it as a threat to ecclesiastical authority. This rift between the pope and the heads of the Italian state would not be resolved for many years, and it made them into enemies, thus depriving the people of one of their most important common bonds—their shared faith. Second, a rift developed between the northern and southern regions of the country. The northern provinces were prosperous and had gone some way toward industrialization, while the south remained poor and rural. Most men of authority in the new government—the king, the prime minister, the provincial governors, and a large majority of the high-ranking military officers and civil servants—came from the north, which caused resentment in the south.

As Piedmont became the core of Italy, Prussia was to become the core of Germany. The foundations for Prussian supremacy had been laid as early as 1640 and continued under Prime Minister Otto von Bismarck. Bismarck used his considerable diplomatic skills to provoke France into declaring war on Prussia, which caused the southern German states to rally to Prussia's support. An easy German victory led to unification in 1871. The new German Empire, ruled by the king of Prussia (now kaiser of Germany), established its headquarters in the Prussian capital city, Berlin. A bicameral legislature, with a popularly elected lower house and an upper house of hereditary German princes, satisfied the goals of both upper and middle classes.

CHAPTER 13 OBJECTIVES

- Locate the unified nations of Italy and Germany on a map of Europe in 1871.
- Explain the steps in the process of unification for Germany and Italy.
- Identify the major figures of German and Italian unification and match each one to his political and/or military accomplishments.

Chapter 13 Time Line

- **1852** Camillo di Cavour becomes prime minister of Sardinia
- **1859** Sardinia receives Lombardy; other northern Italian states unite with Sardinia
- **1860** Garibaldi invades Sicily, then liberates Sicily and Naples; southern Italian region unites with northern
- **1861** Italy is declared a unified nation; king of Sardinia is crowned Victor Immanuel II of Italy
- **1862** Bismarck becomes prime minister of Prussia
- **1866** Prussia defeats Austria

- **1867**   Prussia annexes various German states into North German Confederation
- **1870**   Papal States become part of unified Italy
- **1870–1871**   Franco-Prussian War
- **1871**   German Empire declared; Wilhelm I of Prussia crowned emperor

The Unification of Italy

Although it had ruled the Mediterranean region and much of Western Europe in the days of ancient Rome, Italy had not existed as a unified nation-state since the sixth century. In modern Europe, *Italy* was a geographical term that signified the Italian peninsula, and the word *Italian* referred to the people who lived there and spoke that language. The people of the numerous Italian states were regionally divided to some degree; the fertile north had evolved into a prosperous industrial society, while the wine-producing south was largely poor and rural. However, the people were culturally homogeneous, sharing a common language, a common history, and a common religion. Italy was thus a natural breeding ground for nationalism and unification.

The Congress of Vienna had divided Italy among the victors of the Napoleonic Wars as follows:

Italian State	Ruled By
Papal States	Pope
Naples and Sicily	Bourbon monarch
Lombardy, Venice, Tyrol	Austria-Hungary
Parma, Modena, other states	Hapsburg monarchs

Nationalist forces in Italy rebelled against their foreign rulers. This happened in Parma and Modena in 1831, where the uprisings were crushed, and again in 1848 with the same result. Republican forces fomented a revolt against the pope, declaring the Republic of Rome in 1848. Since France and Austria were united in the desire to maintain a divided and weak Italy, they worked together to put down the rebellions. French troops occupied Rome until 1870.

In 1852, Count Camillo di Cavour become prime minister of Sardinia, a kingdom that included both the island of Sardinia and the Piedmont region of northern Italy. Like almost all successful ministers in European history, Cavour was crafty, clever, and entirely practical in his outlook. He used national alliances to achieve his goal of uniting the rest of Italy to Sardinia.

At Cavour's urging, Sardinia fought on the side of the British and French in the Crimean War. Having thus formed a friendship with France, Cavour joined Napoleon III in an attack on Austria. As a result, Lombardy and Sardinia were united in 1859. Later that year, most of the rest of northern Italy joined the union of Italian states.

In 1860, the fiery republican Giuseppe Garibaldi led an invasion of his followers, the Red Shirts, into the kingdom of Sicily, ostensibly to join a popular uprising. With covert assistance from Cavour, Garibaldi liberated both Sicily and Naples. Although Cavour was a monarchist and Garibaldi was a republican, they found common ground in their desire to unify their people.

Garibaldi believed that the natural next step was to march into Rome, but Cavour felt it was better to hold off rather than make an enemy of the pope. Therefore, he sent Sardinian troops to maintain peace in the Papal States. Next, with Garibaldi's full support, he held an election throughout the states of southern Italy to decide whether the people were ready to join the northern states and Sardinia as a unified nation. The nation was officially united in 1861; the king of Sardinia was crowned Victor Emmanuel II of Italy later that year.

The Papal States—a sizable region surrounding Rome—remained the only holdout. Italian unification would rob the pope of his authority as a head of state; he would be marginalized, as head of the Church only. The 1860 unification reduced the Papal States to the city of Rome and the area immediately surrounding it.

The new Italian government was closely based on the Sardinian model. The king of Sardinia became the king of Italy. The new Italian parliament, meeting in 1860, was officially referred to as "the eighth session of the Sardinian Parliament." The vote was limited to men over the age of twenty-four who were literate and owned property—a total of about 8 percent of all Italian men in that age group.

The administrative structure and tax codes of the old Kingdom of Sardinia were extended to apply to the entire nation. Cavour felt that, for the moment, it was best to present a unified nation to the rest of Europe. Debate and factionalism might have destroyed the unity that he had worked so hard to achieve. Internal debate, he felt, could come later. This decision caused a rift between the northern and southern regions of Italy, as the south resented the dominance of leaders from Piedmont in the north. Most of the army's high-ranking officers were from Piedmont, most of the provincial governors were from Piedmont, and more than half the top positions in the civil service were held by men from Piedmont or its neighboring provinces Lombardy and Venetia. A further divisive factor came from the Vatican; Pope Pius IX retaliated for the reduction of his authority by encouraging the foundation of Catholic political parties whose goal was to undermine the new Italian state.

When France declared war on Prussia in 1870, occupying French troops abandoned Rome. This left the pope undefended, and the Italian army immediately marched in to complete the unification process. Rome, once the center and apex of Classical civilization, had enormous symbolic importance to the Italians, and it was immediately named the new Italian capital city. This did not

The Unification of Italy

end the hostility between the Church and the Italian state; if anything, it grew more intense. It would not be resolved until Prime Minister Benito Mussolini signed an agreement naming the Vatican an independent city-state in 1929. (See Chapter 17.)

The Unification of Germany

In 1862, Wilhelm I of Prussia appointed Otto von Bismarck prime minister. Bismarck's name has become closely identified with the term *Realpolitik*, or "the politics of realism." Like Richelieu of France and Cavour of Italy, Bismarck was a very able man, both pragmatic and determined. Bismarck's focus was on a united Germany with a strong monarch.

Bismarck's belief in a strong monarchy made him a political conservative, and in the 1860s he was faced with a hostile liberal majority in Parliament. Therefore, Bismarck directed the nation's attention to foreign affairs. This would allow him to maintain control of the domestic policy, since civilian populations always accepted special government controls and restrictions during wartime.

Prussia and Austria together fought Denmark over control of the duchies of Schleswig and Holstein; the result was joint Prussian-Austrian rule of the duchies. In 1866, Bismarck led a successful war against Austria, which quickly gave up its share in the affairs of Schleswig and Holstein. Prussia had now formed what would be the nucleus of a united Germany.

In 1867, as a result of Bismarck's diplomacy, Prussia annexed three more states and the free city of Frankfurt, thereby bringing all the German-speaking states north of the Main River under Prussian control.

The opportunity for the final step in German unification arrived in 1870. Bismarck decided to go to war with France, believing that the other German states would come to Prussia's aid. He changed the wording of a press release so that it gave the appearance of a deliberate insult from the Prussian king to the French emperor. On reading the statement, Napoleon III immediately declared war on Prussia. As Bismarck had calculated, the southern German states allied themselves with Prussia against their common enemy, France.

The war can accurately be describe as "Franco-German" rather than "Franco-Prussian" because many German states besides Prussia played a major role in defeating the French. The efficiency and superior strategy of the German military brought the French to a speedy surrender. The peace treaty gave Germany control of Alsace and Lorraine, and provided for a compensatory payment to Prussia of 5 billion francs. Although Prussia had provoked the war, France had technically been the aggressor, and at any rate was on the losing side. This peace settlement created deep resentment in France; this resentment would become an issue during and after the First World War (see Chapter 15).

On January 18, 1871, Wilhelm I of Prussia was officially crowned emperor of Germany. In a final insult to the French, the Germans held the ceremony in the Hall of Mirrors at Versailles.

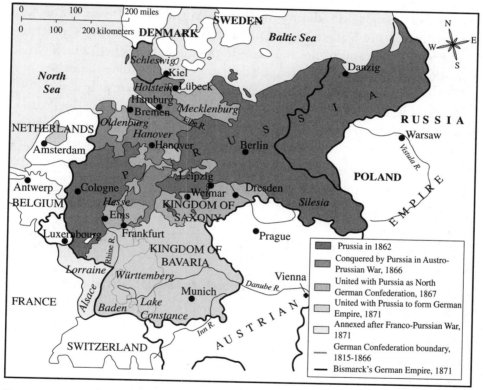

The Unification of Germany

The legislative assembly of the new German Empire was similar to the British Parliament; it was bicameral, with a Federal Council (Bundesrat) of hereditary nobles and an Imperial Diet (Reichstag) of popularly elected representatives. All men age twenty-five and older had the right to vote for their representatives in the Reichstag. The princes in the Bundesrat, of course, inherited their seats, just as the British peers inherited their places in the House of Lords. Both the Bundesrat and the Reichstag had to pass any given bill in order for it to become German law. The king of Prussia became the emperor, or kaiser (from the Latin *caesar*), of Germany. Although Wilhelm I found such a pompous title silly and personally embarrassing, it was a source of pride among his subjects. The imperial title suggested a connection between the German Empire and the Holy Roman Empire, although in fact the Holy Roman emperors had ended up as the ruling family of Austria, not Prussia.

Nationalism was a major force in the creation of the German Empire. Both the nobles and the common people supported unification; troops were strongly motivated by nationalism during the Franco-Prussian War. It was nationalism that motivated the leaders to press Bismarck to demand heavy reparations from France at the end of the war, despite the minister's belief (which would be justified by future events) that the demand was vengeful and unwise.

Prussia had worked toward control of a unified German state since 1640; unsurprisingly, it became the most powerful province in Germany. The Prussian king became the hereditary German emperor; Prussian generals were in charge of the German army; the efficient Prussian bureaucracy administered the civil service; and the Prussian capital, Berlin, became the capital of Germany.

QUIZ

1. **Which region of Italy had the greatest power and influence after unification?**
   A. the islands
   B. the mountain provinces
   C. the northern provinces
   D. the southern provinces

2. **Pius IX refused to support Italian unification mainly because the new government**
   A. robbed him of his status as a head of state.
   B. abolished Catholicism throughout Italy.
   C. wanted to make Rome the Italian capital city.
   D. crowned the king of Sardinia as king of Italy.

3. **Which phrase best describes Giuseppe Garibaldi?**
   A. a conservative minister of state
   B. a popular republican leader
   C. a liberal intellectual
   D. a moderate monarchist

4. **Bismarck provoked France into declaring war in 1870 with the goal of**
   A. creating an alliance with the southern German states.
   B. making Austria part of a new German confederation.
   C. forcing France to pay Germany a heavy war indemnity.
   D. forcing the king of France to abdicate.

5. **What was the main factor in the German victory over France in 1871?**
   A. factionalism within France
   B. German military superiority
   C. German diplomacy
   D. French diplomacy

6. **The German title kaiser, or emperor, suggested that Germany was symbolically connected to and descended from**
   A. the Austrian Empire.
   B. the Roman Empire.
   C. the Holy Roman Empire.
   D. the British Empire.

7. **_____ became the core of the new German Empire.**
   A. Austria
   B. Bavaria
   C. Alsace and Lorraine
   D. Prussia

8. **Which best describes the German legislative assembly?**
   A. a popularly elected house of representatives
   B. a largely symbolic house of hereditary nobles
   C. a parliament with one house of hereditary nobles and one elective house of representatives
   D. a parliament with one house of royally appointed ministers and one house of popularly elected representatives

9. **Which step toward German unification happened first?**
   A. Prussia defeated Austria and took sole control over Schleswig and Holstein.
   B. France declared war on Prussia.
   C. Prussia annexed Frankfurt.
   D. Prussia and Austria took over the duchies of Schleswig and Holstein.

10. **All these statements accurately describe both Cavour and Bismarck, except**
   A. they were both monarchists.
   B. they were both conservative.
   C. they were both adept at *Realpolitik.*
   D. they both wanted to become dictators.

chapter **14**

World Trade and Empires, 1839–1914

The nineteenth century was an age of imperialism—an age in which European nations expended a great deal of energy and money expanding their empires. Their motives were threefold. First, they expected economic profits from their colonies, many of which were rich in the natural resources and raw materials—including human beings—necessary to keep the European factories going. Second, no nation wanted to grant supremacy to the others; as long as one nation was establishing overseas colonies, other nations would follow suit simply to maintain a balance of power. Third, Christian churches that had steadily been losing power and influence in Europe saw colonization of Africa and Asia as a splendid opportunity for missionary work. Fourth, the sense of racial superiority that characterized Europeans made them feel it was their responsibility to impose their culture on peoples they regarded as uncivilized or inferior.

The opening of the Suez Canal connected the Mediterranean and Red Seas and thus provided a much shorter and more efficient shipping route between Europe and Asia. It also provided a means of communication and troop transport.

CHAPTER 14 OBJECTIVES

- Describe the motives that led various European nations to build foreign empires.
- Describe the period of British rule in India.
- Describe European colonization and conquest in Southeast Asia and Africa.

Chapter 14 Time Line

●	1840	First Opium War
●	1848	France annexes Algeria
●	1850	Britain gains control over India
●	1852	Boers (Dutch) establish South African Republic
●	1854	Boers establish Orange Free State
●	1856	Second Opium War
●	1857	Sepoy Mutiny in India
●	1880	France establishes protectorate in Congo
●	1882	Britain establishes protectorate in Egypt
●	1884	Nations meet at Berlin and agree on division of Africa
●	1886	British take Burma
●	1887	France conquers Indochina (Vietnam)
●	1898	Britain conquers the Sudan

India

England first established trade relations with India in 1608, with the arrival in India of the British East India Company. Its purpose was to make profits from trade between India and Europe. Such trade had been proved highly profitable by the experience of the Dutch and Portuguese in Southeast Asia. England was soon sailing west with shiploads of Indian cotton. As England's textile mills were the cornerstone of its economy, the trade with India assumed enormous importance. England could not grow its own cotton because it did not have the right climate.

Belatedly realizing that the British were establishing a trade monopoly with India, France formed the French East India Company in the 1700s. Hostility and resentment between the two companies broke out in 1744; during the Seven Years' War, the British drove France from India. As of 1765, Britain controlled one of the richest provinces in India—Bengal, on the east coast of India at the mouth of the Ganges River.

The collapse of India's Mughal Empire in the late 1700s allowed Britain to take over the entire nation from its power base in Bengal. This was a slow process, not completed until the annexation of Punjab in 1849. Many Indians resisted the British takeover, most famously during the Sepoy Mutiny of 1857. (*Sepoy* is an Indian term meaning "soldier.") In May 1857, Indian troops mutinied against British commanders at Meerut, near New Delhi. This touched off a wave of other mutinies and popular uprisings in central and northeastern India. The resistance was swiftly crushed, in part because different segments of Indian society were not united against the British; some even fought on the British side. In 1858, the East India Company was dissolved and Britain formally annexed India.

England maintained an exploitative and paternalistic relationship with India, which it valued not as an ancient civilization but as a source of manpower and a market for British manufactured goods. Since it was impossible to rule India effectively from faraway Britain, the British established both a bureaucratic and a military presence on the subcontinent. British military officers commanded both British and Indian troops, and British civil servants—along with Indians in subordinate positions—carried out the day-to-day business of governing. The British would occupy India until after World War II.

The British takeover and occupation had mixed effects on India. On the positive side, English became the one common language in a nation where hundreds of dialects were spoken; Britain also introduced Western ideas of education and women's rights to India. On the negative side, the British maintained an attitude of racial and cultural superiority throughout their stay in India, which the Indians naturally found both objectionable and unjustified, given that Indian culture, literature, and art long predated British. The spirit of nationalism was not confined to Europe; it arose in India too.

While Western European nations had a shared Classical heritage, a common way of life, a common cultural understanding, and a common religious history, Britain and India did not have these things in common. The Indian and European civilizations had created two cultures so different that there was almost no mutual understanding, and a great deal of suspicion and mistrust.

China and Southeast Asia

With the exception of Siam (present-day Thailand), nearly all the islands and kingdoms of Southeast Asia were under European sway by the outbreak of World War I in 1914. Most of the colonization took place after 1870. Thanks to the strength and military skill of Indian troops, Britain took over Burma and Singapore. Singapore was important for the protection of British shipping lanes, and Burma was ruled by an ambitious dynasty that threatened British supremacy in the region.

Britain's power base in India enabled it to open up trade with Manchu (Qing) China, which had maintained a highly favorable trade balance with Britain up to this time, for two reasons. First, the Chinese were not interested in acquiring Western goods, insisting instead on being paid in silver. Second, the Chinese did not desire any cultural exchange with the West; from the Chinese point of view, exposure to Western culture and ideas meant contamination. This attitude meant that only certain Chinese ports were open to Western traders, and the behavior of those who went ashore was strictly regulated.

Westerners traded with China despite the unfavorable financial balance, because China provided goods they could not purchase elsewhere. Tea was the favorite beverage in Britain, and China was also the source of porcelain, ceramics, silks, and other luxury goods. Britain and other Western nations pressured China to relax its restrictive policies, but to no avail—until the British hit on the effective but morally bankrupt notion of offering opium, cultivated in British India, as payment for Chinese goods.

The nineteenth century was an era of abysmal medical ignorance, and both Western and Eastern doctors prescribed opium as a painkiller. However, society was well aware that opium was a hallucinogenic, used illegitimately (not illegally in all countries) as what is today called a "recreational" drug. The Chinese had used opium for medicinal purposes for centuries, but placed a ban on its purchase or use without a doctor's prescription. However, China was not without its drug-dealers and opium addicts. The sudden rise in the availability of opium allowed the Chinese underworld excellent opportunities for profit, and the desirability of the opium caused a 180-degree shift in the trade balance between China and Britain.

The Manchus banned the importation of the drug. This provoked the British warships to fire on China, inaugurating the First Opium War in 1840. By 1842 the Chinese, unable to match the British military power, conceded defeat and accepted British demands to resume the importation of opium and to sign new treaties. Historians refer to these agreements as "unequal treaties" because they were all but signed at gunpoint, with one side dictating all the terms. The treaties specified that the Chinese would open several ports for trade; that China would provide equal access and privileges to all Western trading partners; and that foreigners, if accused of any crimes in China, would be tried by their own nations rather than in Chinese courts—a proceeding known as "extraterritoriality." The First Opium War effectively ended China's reign as a world power until after World War II.

Britain and France formed an alliance and won further concessions from the Manchus in the Second Opium War, fought from 1856 to 1860. At the same time, Russia took the opportunity to seize a large expanse of Siberian territory from China. After two more wars, one with France and one with Japan, China was cornered. The West forced the Qing government to adopt a free trade policy. Although the Qing emperor remained on the throne, he had little authority over events. Britain, France, Germany, Japan, and Russia established spheres of influence over most of China.

The Dutch won a power struggle on the island of Java in 1830 and gained huge profits by purchasing Javanese crops (sugar, coffee, and tea) very cheaply and selling them in Europe at much higher prices.

France was also active in Southeast Asia. In 1858–1859 the French invaded Vietnam and established a colony despite resistance from both Vietnam and China. By 1884, France had established protectorates in Annan and Tonkin; three years later they had taken over Cambodia. The French administered the area as the Union of Indochina. It was valuable for its natural resource of rubber, timber, and rice.

The Takeover of Africa

On the eve of World War I, in 1914, almost the entire continent of Africa was under European rule. The only exceptions were the independent nations of Ethiopia on the Red Sea and tiny Liberia on the Atlantic coast.

In the nineteenth century, Europeans regarded Africa as a literal and figurative economic gold mine. Literally, the southern half of the continent had fairly extensive resources of gold (and diamonds). Figuratively, Africa was a repository of natural resources that Europe could not provide for itself, such as rubber and a variety of minerals. Africa boasted a variety of climates, and many regions of the continent were ideal for the cultivation of cotton, coffee, and cocoa—all highly valued in Europe.

Europe had made enormous profits from the slave trade before the mid-1700s. Although European nations did not use African slave labor on the continent, they did carry shiploads of slaves to their colonies across the Atlantic. Millions of Africans—many sold to the traders by Africans from rival tribes—were kidnapped, transported, and sold into labor in the cotton or sugarcane fields of the Caribbean Islands, Latin America, and the southern United States. Britain alone shipped more than 3 million Africans across the ocean.

African tribal culture was centuries old by the time the first Europeans made contact with the continent. The continent was not culturally homogeneous; it was home to a large number of tribes who spoke different languages and had a great variety of customs. However, none of these was recognizable to a European as a civilized culture. European invaders of Africa behaved exactly as they had in the Americas in the 1500s: They conquered with their superior fire power, imposed their own culture and language on the native peoples, and exploited them.

In most cases, the Africans were simply not prepared for the European aggression. In some cases, Africans even welcomed Europeans as potential allies against their traditional local rivals. Africans were prone to accommodate the Europeans rather than risk armed confrontation, which they had no hope of winning due to their lack of sophisticated arms. Yet, they found many means of both passive and active resistance—everything from nonpayment of tributes and taxes to full-scale rebellion. European control was much more present in urban areas than in the countryside. Additionally, many areas of Africa were largely inaccessible without a modern transportation network, which took some time to build. European occupation therefore had relatively little effect on thousands of rural Africans.

Christian missionaries began playing an active role in Africa around the late 1700s, with the Baptist Missionary Society being founded in 1795. The men and women who traveled to Africa did not merely spread the gospel; they provided practical, down-to-earth help in a number of areas. First, they brought medicines and medical help. Malaria, which was spread by mosquitoes, was (and still is) epidemic throughout most of southern Africa. The missionaries brought and distributed quinine, which helped to combat it. Second, they were teachers. They held classes for children and adults, teaching them to read and write—not just in European languages, but in their own. Unlike the more secular colonizers, the missionaries lived among the people, ate the same food, and worked hard to learn the languages. It was the missionaries who were responsible, in many cases, for creating written forms of many of the African languages for the first time. This creation of a whole class of literate, educated Africans would prove crucial in the drive for African self-determination and independence that began after World War II. Third, the missionaries used what influence they had to try to persuade the Africans to discontinue some of their cruelest traditional practices, such as human sacrifice, slavery, and polygamy.

The European trade in African slaves was a source of vast profits for Britain, France, the Netherlands, and Portugal. Africans also profited; Europeans paid them large sums of money to round up victims from hostile tribes. From the mid-1700s until the slave trade died out, most African slaves were shipped across the ocean to work, usually in the worst and hardest jobs available, in the American colonies.

The vast majority of African slaves came from what Europeans had long called the "Gold Coast"—the coastal area of present-day Ghana, Ivory Coast, and Nigeria. The trade in slaves was so brisk for a time that the populations of these areas were decimated.

Olaudah Equiano (also known by the name of Gustavus Vasa), a slave who survived the notorious middle passage—the journey across the Atlantic—gained his freedom as an adult and wrote an important slave narrative. Equiano traveled to Britain in the early 1800s, becoming a well-known public speaker on the issue of abolition. He thus made an important contribution to the change of attitude in Britain that led to its 1807 ban on the slave trade.

Between 1858 and 1869, the French built the Suez Canal across a narrow neck of Egyptian land. This connection between the Mediterranean and Red Seas was to prove of major importance for communication, transport, and trade. The British seized the canal from the French in 1875, and soon after had established virtual control of the Egyptian government, largely for the sake of maintaining control of the canal. The British extended their authority in Egypt into neighboring Sudan. The Sudanese fought back under the leadership of Muhammad Ahmed ibn Ali, known as the Madhi. When the Madhi died, it became clear that effective Sudanese resistance depended on his leadership; without him, the Sudanese succumbed to the British in 1898. In 1899, Britain formally established Anglo-Egyptian rule in the Sudan. Britain also established itself in Nigeria and in the southern region in a colony it named Rhodesia (present-day Zambia and Zimbabwe).

Britain, France, Belgium, Germany, Italy, and Portugal all established a major presence on the African continent. Spain established one small colony on the

Atlantic coast. The Dutch settled in South Africa, where they established the Cape Colony, which the British took over during the Napoleonic Wars. The Boers, as the Dutch South Africans were known, established the South African Republic and the Orange Free State (named for the royal house of Orange) in the mid-nineteenth century. The British eventually drove them out in the Boer War, and South Africa was made a British dominion.

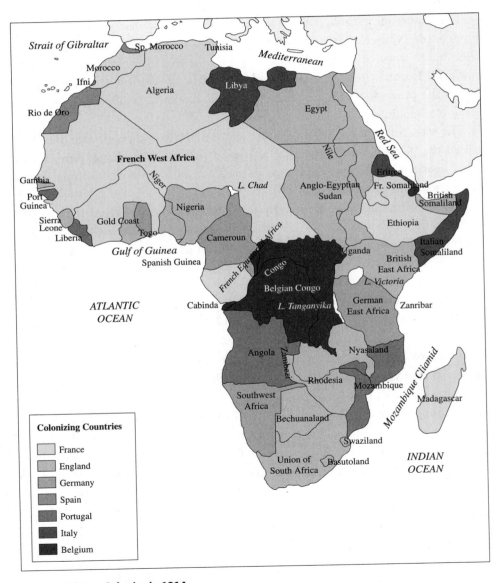

Europe's African Colonies in 1914

QUIZ

1. _____ was the Indian raw material most important to the British economy.
   A. Wool
   B. Rubber
   C. Cotton
   D. Diamonds

2. The British drove France out of India during _____
   A. the Sepoy Mutiny.
   B. the Seven Years' War.
   C. the Great War.
   D. World War II.

3. European religious organizations welcomed colonization primarily because
   A. they believed in European racial superiority.
   B. they wanted to make new converts.
   C. they no longer felt welcome in Europe.
   D. they hoped to make economic gains.

4. Why were rural Africans less affected than urban ones by the occupying Europeans?
   A. They were less accessible.
   B. They were less educated.
   C. They were less wealthy.
   D. They were less intimidated.

5. The Dutch were able to demand high prices in Europe for Javanese sugar, coffee, and tea because
   A. it cost them a lot of money to transport them to Europe.
   B. Europeans did not often travel to Java.
   C. the Suez Canal was not opened until 1869.
   D. these crops could not be cultivated in the European climate.

6. The Southeast Asian nation of _____ remained independent throughout the period of European colonization.
   A. Java
   B. Siam
   C. Vietnam
   D. Singapore

7. Britain established virtual rule over Egypt in order to maintain control over _____
   A. Nigeria.
   B. Rhodesia.
   C. the Suez Canal.
   D. the Bay of Bengal.

8. Europe made its greatest profits from the Atlantic slave trade between
   A. 1650 and 1750.
   B. 1750 and 1800.
   C. 1800 and 1850.
   D. 1850 and 1900.

9. After the British takeover, India was under the authority of the British monarch, but the day-to-day administration was carried out by
   A. the military.
   B. the civil service.
   C. the missionaries.
   D. the East India Company.

10. The Suez Canal connected the Red Sea with the
    A. Mediterranean Sea.
    B. Indian Ocean.
    C. Bay of Bengal.
    D. Arabian Sea.

PART II EXAM

1. _____ was the main factor in the economic crisis that led to the French Revolution.
   A. Reform of the French tax system
   B. Major public-works projects in the cities
   C. Excessive spending on the military
   D. The personal extravagance of the royal family

2. The Industrial Revolution began in Britain because of Britain's _____
   A. year-round temperate climate.
   B. northern European location.
   C. stable government and society.
   D. role in the Enlightenment.

3. Unlike the Enlightenment, the Renaissance was characterized by
   A. the admiration and imitation of the Classical past.
   B. the dedication of creative endeavors to the glory of God.
   C. an emphasis on the human being as a unique individual.
   D. an exchange of ideas among intellectuals of many nations.

4. Germany gained _____ from France as a result of the Franco-Prussian War of 1870.
   A. financial compensation
   B. Alsace and Lorraine
   C. Atlantic colonies
   D. favored trading status

5. _____ is the European minister whose name is most closely associated with the term *Realpolitik*.
   A. Otto von Bismarck
   B. Camilo di Cavour
   C. Charles Talleyrand
   D. Louis Philippe d'Orleans

6. **How did the Scientific Revolution affect the popular view of the Church in Europe?**
   A. It disproved the existence of God.
   B. It made people more skeptical of Church teachings.
   C. It inspired people to return to the Church in great numbers.
   D. It inspired people to abandon the Church in great numbers.

7. _____ **was the most cosmopolitan and artistically advanced city in Europe in the period just before the Napoleonic era.**
   A. London
   B. Florence
   C. Paris
   D. Vienna

8. **All the following nations remained absolute monarchies throughout the nineteenth century except**
   A. Austria.
   B. France.
   C. Prussia.
   D. Russia.

9. **The _____ provided an important shortcut for ships trading between Europe and Asia.**
   A. Mediterranean Sea
   B. Panama Canal
   C. Suez Canal
   D. Adriatic Sea

10. _____ **refers to the nineteenth-century movement in the arts that centered on the creative expression of the artist's individuality.**
    A. Renaissance
    B. Reformation
    C. *Reconquista*
    D. Romanticism

11. **The people of Paris rose up in arms against Charles X because**
    A. he revoked voting rights and freedom of the press.
    B. he dragged France into too many destructive wars.
    C. he refused to abdicate when the legislature ordered him to.
    D. his policies were too liberal to satisfy the aristocrats.

12. The _____ region of Africa was the major source of the European slave trade.
   A. Cape of Good Hope
   B. Mediterranean coast
   C. Nile River
   D. Gold Coast

13. The social reforms of Joseph II of Austria were unpopular with _____
   A. conservatives.
   B. liberals.
   C. intellectuals.
   D. artisans.

14. European governments passed laws encouraging industrialization because they expected to gain
   A. enormous profits for the treasury.
   B. up-to-date equipment for the military.
   C. universal employment for the people.
   D. major advantages in foreign relations.

15. Louis XVI agreed to all the following demands of the National Assembly except
   A. freedom of the press.
   B. reform of the tax code.
   C. individual liberty for the people.
   D. equal eligibility for high office.

16. Cavour and Garibaldi shared the common aim of
   A. marching on Rome.
   B. unifying Italy.
   C. establishing a monarchy.
   D. establishing a republic.

17. In 1870, the southern German states allied themselves with Prussia and the north German confederation against their common enemy _____
   A. Austria.
   B. Britain.
   C. France.
   D. Russia.

18. The main purpose of _____ was to defend the stability of European nation-states from any threat of popular rebellion.
   A. the Quadruple Alliance
   B. the Congress of Vienna
   C. the Holy Alliance
   D. the Romantic movement

19. Which of India's crops was of the greatest importance to the British economy?
   A. coffee
   B. tea
   C. pepper
   D. cotton

20. _____ was an important motivating force in the unification of Italy.
   A. Capitalism
   B. Nationalism
   C. Romanticism
   D. Catholicism

21. _____ is an important historical figure because he discovered that planets regularly orbit the sun in elliptical paths at varying speeds.
   A. Tycho Brahe
   B. Galileo Galilei
   C. Johannes Kepler
   D. Isaac Newton

22. Which of the following most accurately describes Joseph II of Austria?
   A. a constitutional monarch who ruled in concert with the legislative assembly
   B. an absolute monarch who did not believe in the rights of the people
   C. a benevolent autocrat who believed he was the best judge of how to rule his realm
   D. a warrior-king who was mainly interested in foreign affairs

23. _____ was the source of power that fueled the Industrial Revolution in Britain.
   A. Timber
   B. Steam
   C. Iron
   D. Steel

24. The support of _____ helped the people of Paris to achieve their goals during the French Revolution.
    A. the nobility
    B. the monarch
    C. the Church
    D. the military

25. Nationalism was dangerous to the stability of Austrian society because
    A. Austria was one of the Great Powers of Europe after 1815.
    B. Austria was ruled by a hereditary monarch.
    C. Austria was a large, contiguous landmass.
    D. Austria's population was ethnically and culturally diverse.

26. Which best describes the main reason for the Church's hostility toward the Scientific Revolution?
    A. Scientists suggested that their discoveries were compatible with biblical texts.
    B. Scientists flatly disagreed with biblical statements about how the universe functioned.
    C. Scientists wrote books and pamphlets suggesting that God did not exist.
    D. Scientists encouraged direct individual observation rather than blind acceptance of the assertions of those in authority.

27. The Kingdom of Sardinia joined in the Crimean War in order to
    A. establish an alliance with France.
    B. protect its trade interests in the Black Sea.
    C. help Russia drive the Ottoman Turks from Europe.
    D. prove that it had become one of the Great Powers of Europe.

28. Egypt was strategically important to the European economy because of the presence of
    A. the Suez Canal.
    B. the Orange Free State.
    C. diamonds and gold.
    D. mineral deposits.

29. Which event persuaded the National Convention of France to abolish the monarchy?
    A. the establishment of Napoleon Bonaparte as First Consul
    B. the king's attempt to escape to Austria
    C. the creation of the Committee of Public Safety
    D. the seventeenth-century takeover of the English throne by Oliver Cromwell

30. **James Hargreaves's most important contribution to the Industrial Revolution was**
    A. the flying shuttle.
    B. the steam engine.
    C. the electric motor.
    D. the spinning jenny.

31. **The Inquisition required Galileo to recant his published theories because**
    A. he had written about Copernican astronomy.
    B. his theories were inaccurate.
    C. his works were published in Italian, not Latin.
    D. he had disputed the existence of God in print.

32. **Which nineteenth-century political philosophy was most likely to appeal to the poorer classes of society?**
    A. conservatism
    B. liberalism
    C. Marxism
    D. nationalism

33. **On the eve of the First World War, in 1914, _____ was the nation with the greatest industrial output in Europe.**
    A. Britain
    B. France
    C. Germany
    D. Russia

34. **Czar Alexander II earned the enmity of the Russian nobility when he**
    A. built the Trans-Siberian Railroad.
    B. emancipated the serfs throughout the empire.
    C. concluded peace with the Turks in the Crimea.
    D. entered the Russo-Japanese War.

35. **_____ took over most of the Vietnamese peninsula, which became known as the Union of Indochina under its authority.**
    A. China
    B. France
    C. Britain
    D. The Netherlands

36. **What was the purpose of General Kutuzov's retreat toward Moscow in 1812?**
    A. to draw Napoleon's army far into Russia before winter came
    B. to acknowledge that Napoleon's army had defeated the Russians
    C. to prevent the French from invading and occupying Moscow
    D. to wait for help from Russia's Western allies

37. **French and Italian industry did not rely on coal power because**
    A. they relied on electrical power.
    B. they did not have large coal deposits.
    C. they did not know how to mine the ground for coal.
    D. they used timber instead of coal.

38. **_____ achieved unquestioned authority over India in 1815.**
    A. Russia
    B. China
    C. France
    D. Britain

39. **Business owners and managers opposed the unionization of workers during the Industrial Revolution primarily over the issue of**
    A. politics.
    B. wages and profits.
    C. child labor.
    D. benefits.

40. **Why was Jean-Jacques Rousseau considered the founding father of the Romantic movement in literature and the arts?**
    A. because he was a talented composer, painter, poet, and architect
    B. because he was an enthusiastic patron of the arts
    C. because he spent his career in Vienna
    D. because his philosophy focused on human emotions

41. **Which best describes the shift in thinking between the Scientific Revolution of the seventeenth century and the Enlightenment of the eighteenth century?**
    A. a rebirth of interest in Classical values and ideas
    B. a falling-off of the belief in the omnipotence of God
    C. a new interest in discovering how the universe functioned
    D. a reawakening of conservative ideas and ways of thinking

42. **Which best describes the relationship between France and Austria in the first decade of the nineteenth century?**
    A. Austria and France had no diplomatic relationship.
    B. France and Austria were allies.
    C. France dominated Austria.
    D. Austria dominated France.

43. **Why did the Congress of Vienna recommend German unification?**
    A. because the small German states were fighting too many wars with one another
    B. because a unified Germany would be a check on France's strength
    C. because the Germans had defeated the French in the Napoleonic Wars
    D. because Napoleon had already created the Confederation of the Rhine

44. **Which best describes the trade relationship between Britain and China before the First Opium War of 1840?**
    A. China profited more than Britain from the trade relationship.
    B. Britain profited more than China from the trade relationship.
    C. Both nations profited equally from the trade relationship.
    D. The two nations did not trade with one another.

45. **A nineteenth-century European who supported absolute monarchy would be described as _____**
    A. a conservative.
    B. an anarchist.
    C. a liberal.
    D. a socialist.

46. **Which best describes the administrative structure of the Austro-Hungarian Empire?**
    A. The two kingdoms were entirely independent from one another administratively.
    B. The two kingdoms were a joint monarchy with no written constitution or legislative assembly.
    C. Each kingdom had its own monarch, but they shared the same constitution and legislature.
    D. Each kingdom had its own constitution and legislature, but they shared a monarch.

47. **What effect did the European rail system have on the Industrial Revolution?**
    A. It brought industrialization to areas that had not yet begun to build factories.
    B. It provided efficient overland connections among industrial areas.
    C. It gave rise to a new industry known today as tourism.
    D. It made it possible to move armies around Europe more efficiently.

48. _____ conceived, edited, and contributed articles to the French Enlightenment's great achievement, the *Encyclopédie*.
    A. Diderot
    B. Montesquieu
    C. Rousseau
    D. Voltaire

49. **All of the following were important figures in the Romantic movement in music except**
    A. Hector Berlioz.
    B. Wolfgang Amadeus Mozart.
    C. Pyotr Ilyich Tchaikovsky.
    D. Giuseppe Verdi.

50. **The deputies at the Congress of Vienna established the Quadruple Alliance with what purpose?**
    A. to create a lasting peace in Europe by maintaining a balance of power
    B. to establish parliamentary democracies in all European nations
    C. to set up an international court of justice to try war criminals
    D. to work out a plan for a common European currency

Part III

Twentieth-Century European History

chapter 15

The Great War (World War I) and Its Aftermath, 1914–1919

Historians generally agree that the nineteenth century did not begin and end with the calendar, but that it began and ended with two major historical milestones. It began with the Congress of Vienna in 1815 and ended abruptly with the outbreak of the Great War in 1914. (The name "World War I" did not come into use until much later, since of course no one knew at the time that there would be a World War II.)

The war happened primarily for two reasons. The first was nationalism: Serbian nationalism was the motive for an assassination in the Austrian royal family, and German nationalism was the motive for the major buildup of the German military in the years before the war. The second reason for going to war was maintaining the balance of power. The unification of Germany had changed things by creating a large, strong, powerful entity in central Europe— a nation-state whose ambitions caused grave concern to Britain, Russia, and especially France.

The war would be fought between the Allied or Entente powers (Britain, France, and Russia) and the Central powers (Germany, Austria, Bulgaria, and the Ottomans). The United States and Italy would later enter the war on the side of the Allies.

Europe had never seen violence on the scale of the Great War. The Industrial Revolution made it possible to transport more troops longer distances more quickly, and had enabled the invention of a variety of mechanized weapons. The clumsy muskets of earlier wars were replaced with much more efficient guns. Cavalry regiments were replaced with tanks. Hand-to-hand combat was replaced by long-distance sniper fire.

At the end of the war, the three most powerful European nations—Britain, France, and Germany—were severely weakened. Millions of their young men had been slaughtered, their military forces were destroyed, their economies were devastated, and vast swaths of northeastern France, site of four years of trench warfare, lay in ruins. The United States came out of the war as the world's strongest nation.

CHAPTER 15 OBJECTIVES

- Identify the causes of the Great War.
- Identify the Allied or Entente powers and the Central powers, and explain how each nation chose which side to fight on.
- Describe the course of the fighting.
- List and explain the major provisions of the Peace of Versailles.

Chapter 15 Time Line

- 1908   Austria-Hungary annexes Bosnia-Herzegovina
- 1914   **June 28** Gavrilo Princip assassinates Franz Ferdinand and Sophie of Austria-Hungary

  July 28 Austria-Hungary declares war on Serbia

  July 30 Russian troops mobilize against Austria-Hungary

  August 1 Germany declares war on Russia

  August 3 Germany declares war on France; German troops invade Belgium

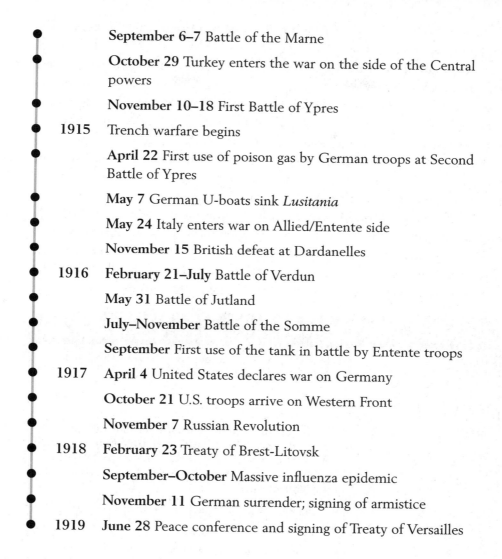

September 6–7 Battle of the Marne

October 29 Turkey enters the war on the side of the Central powers

November 10–18 First Battle of Ypres

1915 Trench warfare begins

April 22 First use of poison gas by German troops at Second Battle of Ypres

May 7 German U-boats sink *Lusitania*

May 24 Italy enters war on Allied/Entente side

November 15 British defeat at Dardanelles

1916 **February 21–July** Battle of Verdun

May 31 Battle of Jutland

July–November Battle of the Somme

September First use of the tank in battle by Entente troops

1917 **April 4** United States declares war on Germany

October 21 U.S. troops arrive on Western Front

November 7 Russian Revolution

1918 **February 23** Treaty of Brest-Litovsk

September–October Massive influenza epidemic

November 11 German surrender; signing of armistice

1919 **June 28** Peace conference and signing of Treaty of Versailles

Buildup to the War

World War I was largely a struggle among the Great Powers of Europe—Germany, France, Britain, Russia, and Austria. No one nation had dominated Europe since the defeat of Napoleon; an entire century had gone by in relative peace among the Great Powers.

All this began to change with the unification of Germany in 1871. Previously, it had been a collection of small states. Now it was a large and powerful state. Germany's new position of power came from two major sources: geography and economy.

Geographically, Germany's central position on the continent made it a dangerous neighbor. It was in a position to attack several nations simply by marching over the border. Because this central position made it equally vulnerable to attack in its turn, Germany invested heavily in its army and navy, continuing the aggressive policy inaugurated under Frederick the Great see Chapter 6.

Economically, Germany had become Europe's strongest nation. Germany had been quick to industrialize after unification, and the country soon surpassed even Britain in this regard. National prosperity gave rise to an excess of boastful national pride—particularly as embodied in Kaiser Wilhelm II, crowned in 1888—that made Germany unpopular among its neighbors.

Between German unification and 1910, the European powers formed a series of alliances. These agreements established relationships that would pit the nations of central Europe against the nations on either side.

EUROPEAN ALLIANCES, 1881–1907

1881 "Three Emperors' Alliance" Germany, Russia, Austria	This alliance crumbled because Germany quickly came to view Russia as a threat rather than an ally.
1882 "Triple Alliance" Germany, Austria, Italy	This alliance brought all of central Europe together. It divided the eastern and western nations, making it difficult for them to help one another; on the other hand, it meant that the Central powers would have to defend themselves on two fronts if war broke out. The alliance with Italy did not last; Italy joined the Entente powers in 1915.
1894 France and Russia	These nations were natural allies against the threat of the nations that lay geographically between them. Neither had enough natural resources or manpower to defeat the Central powers on its own.
1904 France and Britain	France and Britain had been enemies ever since the Norman conquest of England in 1066. However, German industrialization and the massive buildup of the German navy alarmed Britain and contributed to British desire for a strong ally on the continent.
1907 Britain and Russia	This agreement cemented the "Triple Entente" among Britain, France, and Russia.

The alliances showed another new factor that had emerged in European politics—the direct involvement of Britain. Britain had largely remained aloof from continental border wars and power struggles. British troops had occasionally participated, especially in the Napoleonic Wars, but Britain's geographical detachment from the continent had generally reflected its lack of central involvement in major power struggles among the other nations. This changed with the series of alliances made in the years before the Great War.

Ironically, three of the European monarchs were closely related family members: George V of Britain and Kaiser Wilhelm II of Germany were first cousins, and Czar Nicholas II of Russia was their first cousin by marriage. However, the family relationships among the monarchs did not prevent them from going to war against one another.

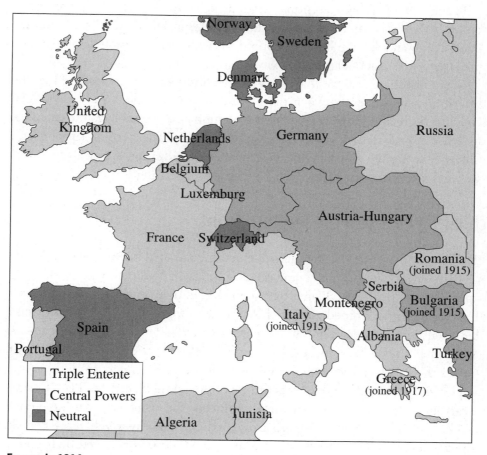

Europe in 1914

The Outbreak of War

In the last decades before the outbreak of war, almost all the Balkan states won their independence from the Ottoman Empire: Romania and Serbia in 1878, Thessaly in 1881, Bulgaria in 1908, and Albania and Macedonia in 1913. The only exception was Bosnia-Herzegovina, which remained under Austrian control (see Chapter 12).

Serbia resented Austria's takeover of Bosnia for two reasons. First, Bosnia was a Slav nation, populated by a mix of ethnic Croats, Serbs, and Turks—people who had little in common with their Austrian rulers. Second, Serbia had hoped for a political union with Bosnia, so that the two states together could form one larger and stronger one.

In June 1914, Serbian resentment found expression by means of an assassin's bullet. A Serbian named Gavrilo Princip shot and killed Austrian Archduke Franz Ferdinand and Archduchess Sophie as they rode in an open car through the streets of Bosnia's capital, Sarajevo.

Many historians believe that if Austria had immediately invaded Serbia, the war would have been between these two nations only and would have been concluded quickly. However, while Austria hesitated, Russia began to mobilize its army in preparation for the defense of Serbia, which it would support as a fellow Slav nation. Germany considered this mobilization a serious threat of war and promptly came to Austria's defense by declaring war on Serbia.

The Schlieffen Plan and the Western Front

The German military had long since assumed that it would one day have to fight a war against France and Russia, and it had worked out a war plan, known as the Schlieffen Plan after the officer who designed it. The Schlieffen Plan called for an immediate march on France through Belgium, which stood between their borders. The German army would then march south, capture the capital city of Paris, and thus sew up a quick victory on the Western Front before the Russians had time to muster an attack on Germany from the east.

However, the army did not proceed according to the Schlieffen Plan. Due to disagreements among the commanding officers, the army turned aside before reaching Paris, and met the French army on the Marne River. When the French unexpectedly won the Battle of the Marne, the Germans changed their plans;

the Western Front would now become a setting for trench warfare. By this time, Britain had declared war on Germany as well.

Both sides dug hundreds of miles of trenches stretching roughly along the north-south axis of Europe, from the North Sea to the border of Switzerland. The trenches served the infantry on both sides as both home and fort throughout four years of fighting. The trenches were dreadful places, especially on the British-French side. The Allies had assumed the war would be over quickly and had dug the trenches hastily. They were always muddy, often knee-deep in rain water, crawling with lice and rats, sweltering in summer and freezing in winter. Soldiers had no way to keep themselves, their sleeping places, their rations, or their precious personal possessions clean or dry. The German trenches were somewhat more bearable; the German army had taken a much more methodical approach to trench-building, laying down board floors and installing electricity.

German and French trenches were only a few miles apart, with the zone between them labeled "no-man's-land." When the order came for attack, soldiers would leap out of the trenches and rush at the enemy trenches with their guns firing.

No-man's-land had no cover; it was open and barren ground. For centuries, European soldiers had been fighting battles in which the armies clashed on open ground, with the stronger side usually winning a decisive victory in short order. The types of weapons used meant that most combat was up close and hand-to-hand; eighteenth- and nineteenth-century muskets and rifles had little accuracy over a long distance, and of course swords and sabers were only meant for hand-to-hand combat.

Modern weapons were entirely different. Machine guns, grenades, and other new weapons developed during the Industrial Revolution were most effective from a distance. They were best suited to an ambush-style combat, with soldiers firing on the enemy from the protection of trees, buildings, or, in this case, trenches. Since the attacking soldiers were charging forward across open ground, the defenders in the trenches could fire on them from a position of relative safety. Through four years of trench warfare, neither the Germans nor the French seemed to grasp this lesson; the generals continued to send their men forth from the trenches to be slaughtered by enemy fire. Millions of soldiers died on both sides, and neither side ever advanced its lines more than a few miles into enemy territory. The Western Front was a stalemate throughout most of the war.

The War at Sea

Thousands of British troops joined the French in the trenches, but Britain also used its powerful navy against the Germans. The British navy blockaded Germany and set mines in the North Sea. The British searched all ships entering the North Sea and intercepted any goods that appeared bound for Germany. On its side, Germany had always planned to use its U-boats (*unterseeboots*, literally "undersea boats," or submarines) to cripple the British navy. The U-boat was a highly effective weapon because it could sail silently under water, unheard and unseen, and then suddenly blow up a ship on the surface that had had no warning of its approach. The Germans published advertisements warning the public that they intended to attack passenger ships as well as cargo steamers; of course, many people still took the risk of sailing. On May 7, 1915, when the Germans sank the British passenger liner HMS *Lusitania*, more than a hundred American passengers died. This event proved a major catalyst in the United States' decision to join the war in 1917.

The Eastern Front

The sheer size of the Russian population and the enormous dimensions of the country made it a formidable opponent. However, the Germans won a major early victory against the Russians at Tannenberg on the Russian border. The Russians fought back decisively during 1915, but over the next two years the German army advanced some distance into Russia. By 1918, the Germans were halfway to Moscow.

Events took an unexpected turn when Russia abruptly withdrew from the war. The Russian Revolution (see Chapter 16) brought a new government to power in Russia, whose only desire was to get out of the war as quickly as possible so it could settle its own domestic affairs. Russian leader Vladimir Ilyich Lenin signed a peace treaty with Germany in the city of Brest-Litovsk in 1918, surrendering a good deal of territory in exchange for the German withdrawal from Russia. This freed the German army to turn all its attention to the Western Front.

The End of the War

In the fall of 1917, French troops began to mutiny. They had been fighting in the trenches for what seemed to them like a lifetime, making no advance against the enemy, watching their comrades get blown to pieces, and knowing that all the time the generals and commanders were safe behind the lines of fire. They put down their guns and refused to fight. The arrival of American troops in 1917 put new heart into the French troops: in addition to manpower, the Americans provided fresh supplies and weapons.

The Germans now launched a massive attack on the Western Front, which would prove to be their final attempt at victory. With the added strength of the American troops, the French and British were able to beat back the German offensive. Fighting raged on into the autumn of 1918. Finally, in the Battle of the Argonne Forest, it became clear that Germany would have to surrender. On November 9, the Germans formally announced the abdication of Kaiser Wilhelm. Early in the morning of November 11, the leaders on both sides signed the armistice. At 11 A.M., the guns stopped firing for the last time.

The Terms of the Peace

The peace conference that would settle the issues of the war convened at Versailles. A powerful symbol of French authority and supremacy, it had been deliberately chosen to intimidate the German delegation. The Germans were humiliated still more by being brought to France by train, along a route that took them through many of the battlefields and forced them to view the devastation for which the world would demand they take sole blame.

For the first time in history, a non-European nation would play a major role in the peace settlements. U.S. troops had been a decisive factor in the last year of fighting and had a level of industrial and economic might that dwarfed all the European nations; additionally, the United States had lost comparatively few troops during the war.

The leaders of the Great Powers were divided in their goals. U.S. President Woodrow Wilson wanted to establish a lasting peace in Europe. Premier Georges Clemenceau of France wanted to humiliate Germany. Prime Minister David Lloyd George of Britain wanted to achieve a new balance of power, rather than weakening Germany so much that France would take its place as the sole great power on the European continent. Italian Prime Minister Vittorio Orlando wanted to recover certain Italian territory from Austria.

Despite having fought on the winning side, Russia—soon to become the Soviet Union—took no part in the negotiations at Versailles. Far too much mutual distrust existed between Russia and Western Europe on both political and economic grounds. The Russians resented the lack of European support for their new government, while the Europeans considered that the Russians had sold them out by withdrawing from the war and making a separate peace with Germany. Economically, the forces of communism and capitalism were inherent enemies.

Provisions of the Treaty of Versailles

- Created new nations (Czechoslovakia and Yugoslavia)
- Restored the independence of Poland, Finland, Latvia, Lithuania, and Estonia
- Restored Alsace and Lorraine to France
- Gave France control of Saarland region until 1934
- Designated the Rhineland a demilitarized zone between Germany and France
- Created the League of Nations, an international peacekeeping force
- Drastically and permanently reduced the German military
- Forced Germans to admit full responsibility for the war
- Charged Germany billions of dollars in reparations

Restoring the balance of power and achieving peace involved three measures. The first was to redraw European borders along ethnic lines to achieve self-government by nationality. This had been tried in 1815 with mixed success, since the lines had been rather arbitrary. This time the leaders took more care to accommodate the forces of nationalism; they created several new states, expanded others, and broke up the Austro-Hungarian Empire. Once again, their aims were not entirely successful.

The second measure was to reduce Germany's strength and increase France's. Alsace and Lorraine changed hands once again, this time returning to French control. The Rhineland on Germany's western border would be maintained as a demilitarized zone. Additionally, the Germans were to admit full responsibility for the war, to pay enormous reparations, and to reduce their army and navy to small forces. Although the United States argued against these punitive measures, France insisted on them. The United States argued that they would ruin the German economy for decades to come and that it was not reasonable to reduce the German military to the point where the country could not defend itself. The French argued that Germany was the aggressor nation and thus fully responsible for the war—which had devastated France and murdered an entire generation of its young men. Since Clemenceau refused to compromise on this issue, Wilson reluctantly consented. A storm of protest from the German delegates had no effect. The "war guilt clause," as it came to be known, would largely contribute to the German aggression of the 1930s and 1940s.

The third measure toward maintaining a balance was President Wilson's suggestion for an international peacekeeping force. Wilson had recently given a speech in which he laid out "Fourteen Points"—a list of measures that he believed would lead to a lasting peace throughout Europe and the world. The last point on his list proposed an international peacekeeping organization that would protect large and small nations on an equal basis. Members of this League of Nations could discuss conflicts over a conference table and resolve them peacefully, with war becoming a last resort. If one nation behaved aggressively, all other nations would unite against it, effectively putting a stop to attacks.

The League of Nations eventually came about in 1920. Ironically, the United States did not become a member of the League. The American system of government required that Congress approve international treaties; the opposition party refused to approve the League of Nations clause in the Treaty of Versailles on the grounds that it committed the United States to defend any European nation attacked by an outsider.

The War's Impact on Europe

Casualties of the Great War totaled more than 37 million people—an entire generation of Europeans of all nations, either dead or severely wounded. Millions more died of a severe flu epidemic that struck not only Europe but the rest of the world as well. Many soldiers would never recover from the horrors of combat; they were left in a condition of mental illness called shellshock. Chronic nightmares, hallucinations, severe depression, lethargy, and outbreaks of violent behavior were common symptoms of shellshock. Today doctors refer to this result of combat experience as post-traumatic stress disorder.

Moreover, "an age was dead and gone," as Woodrow Wilson commented in a 1918 speech. The tank had replaced the cavalry regiment. The machine gun had replaced the bayonet. Elected ministers of state had replaced almost all the hereditary monarchs. Mechanized warfare was a horror that no one had anticipated.

The United States, geographically far removed from the combat, emerged from the war far stronger than the European powers. The war effort had bolstered the American economy; in addition, fighting side by side with the British and French cemented good relations between the nations and gave the United States a level of power and influence over Europe that would persist for the rest of the twentieth century. This influence showed at Versailles, where the United States was an equal participant in the peace process despite not having participated equally in the fighting. The balance of international power had shifted from the Old World to the New. The United States was on its way to becoming a superpower.

QUIZ

1. _____ was forced to assume total responsibility for World War I.
   A. Austria-Hungary
   B. France
   C. Germany
   D. Russia

2. Britain's main source of anxiety during the years before 1914 was
   A. the buildup of the German navy.
   B. the success of Russian industrialization.
   C. the status of its colonies in the Middle East.
   D. the Austrian annexation of Bosnia.

3. _____ was the main motive for the assassination of Franz Ferdinand and Sophie in Sarajevo in 1914.
   A. Anarchism
   B. Nationalism
   C. Economics
   D. Religion

4. **Why did other nations consider the unified Germany a threat to the balance of power?**
   A. because it created a new hereditary monarchy
   B. because it annexed a number of small neighboring states
   C. because it combined size and power with a central continental location
   D. because it was a long-standing enemy of France

5. **Trench warfare resulted in a stalemate primarily because**
   A. weather conditions made it too problematic.
   B. modern weapons were not suited to that style of combat.
   C. the German army had to divide its forces on two fronts.
   D. the French trenches were badly and hastily dug.

6. **The Schlieffen Plan failed because**
   A. the German army did not march all the way to Paris.
   B. the Russians won a major victory in their first clash with the Central powers.
   C. the Italians deserted the Central powers and fought on the Entente side.
   D. Britain used its navy to blockade Germany in the North Sea.

7. **Which of the following nation-states was newly-created by the leaders at Versailles?**
   A. Austria
   B. Greece
   C. Poland
   D. Yugoslavia

8. **Which of the great powers did not take part in the negotiations at Versailles?**
   A. Britain
   B. Germany
   C. Russia
   D. United States

9. **France's main goal at Versailles can best be described as**
   A. the achievement of a lasting peace in Europe.
   B. the reestablishment of a balance of power.
   C. the humiliation and ruin of Germany.
   D. the redrawing of national borders along ethnic lines.

10. **A major "first" in the Great War was**
    A. the outbreak of battles in the empires outside of Europe.
    B. the impressive military force demonstrated by Germany.
    C. the alliance between France and Russia.
    D. the decisive participation of a non-European nation.

chapter 16

Revolution in Russia: 1917 to the Eve of World War II

The Russian Revolution, also called the Bolshevik Revolution after the victorious political party, is unique in history. Unlike earlier revolutions in France, England, and other European nations, it was not a simple desire to overthrow and replace the government then in power. Instead, it was an attempt to overthrow the social and political order of all Europe.

The Russian Revolution brought about the prediction Marx and Engels had made in *The Communist Manifesto*: the violent overturning of the social order by the workers. This had not happened elsewhere in Europe because conditions in Russia were more extreme. During the nineteenth century, most European nations had acquired some form of representative government. Liberal political parties had acquired some measure of power and influence, and even Socialists were a recognized force in the political order. In Russia, no such tradition of representative government existed. Although there was a parliament of sorts, the Russian czar was an autocrat who still believed in bygone traditions of the divine right of kings.

The new order that arose in Russia after the revolution had a great deal in common with the old order. In both cases, the head of state was an autocrat, the army and the police were loyal to the state and were regularly used to put down opposition among the people, and there was no tolerance of dissent.

One major difference between the old regime and the new was that the new regime was determined that the state should be the only influence on the lives of the people. The Bolsheviks disbanded practically every independent organization in Russia, including the Orthodox Church. Since the Church might conceivably disagree with many of the harsh measures undertaken by the state, the Church could no longer be allowed to exist.

CHAPTER 16 OBJECTIVES

- Explain the causes of the Russian Revolution.
- Describe the course of the Russian civil war.
- Compare and contrast the policies and leadership of Lenin and Stalin.

Chapter 16 Time Line

- **1917**   **March** Czar Nicholas II abdicates

    November Bolshevik Revolution; Lenin takes power

- **1918**   Treaty of Brest-Litovsk; outbreak of civil war; assassination of royal family

- **1920–1921**   War with Poland

- **1921**   Peasant uprising: New Economic Policy established

- **1922**   Soviet Union is formally founded

- **1924**   Lenin dies; Stalin takes power

- **1928**   First Five-Year Plan

- **1936–1938**   Great Purges

The Russian Revolution

World War I played a major role in bringing about the Russian Revolution. The advance of the German army into Russia brought food shortages, famine, and starvation; it smashed the Russian railway system in the west; it diverted thousands of able-bodied men from their jobs to serve in the army. As it had elsewhere in Europe, war brought industrialization to a halt and wrecked the economy. It was easy for ordinary Russians to see that the czar was helpless to take control and improve matters.

Czar Nicholas II had succeeded to the Russian throne in 1894. Like most of his predecessors, Nicholas believed that he ruled by divine right and that no one should question him. The revolution of 1905 forced him to acknowledge that times had changed—that the people demanded some say in how they were governed. Although Nicholas made some concessions toward the demands of liberalism and republicanism, his reforms were too timid and slight to satisfy any but the most conservative. Resentment against the czar led to a popular uprising in 1917, as a result of which Nicholas abdicated.

There was no orderly transfer of power. In the wake of the czar's abdication, the Socialists and moderates set up a Provisional Government, which shared its power with the Petrograd (formerly St. Petersburg) Soviet of Workers' and Soldiers' Deputies. The aims of these two bodies were not the same. The Provisional Government concentrated all its planning on defeating the Germans in the Great War. The Soviet, on the other hand, made the domestic economy its priority. Its goal was to set up a legislative assembly that could address pressing concerns about land ownership, grain prices, and food shortages.

Vladimir Ilyich Lenin, born in 1870 in Simbirsk on the Volga River, quickly rose to prominence as the leader of the Bolshevik (Russian for "majority") Party. Lenin made a great impression on the people by continually repeating the slogan "Peace, Land, and Bread"—the three issues of greatest concern to the ordinary people.

By November, the government had become so unpopular that the Bolsheviks were able to grab power in a successful *coup d'etat*, orchestrated by Lenin's close associate Leon Trotsky. Lenin lost no time in setting up one-party rule, with himself as the party dictator. Lenin's most pressing concern was to end the war with Germany. He cared nothing for victory over Germany, nor did he respect alliances made by the former Russian regime with the Western capitalist nations he despised and hoped one day to overthrow. Therefore, the quickest way to achieve peace was through diplomacy. In December of 1917, Russia and Germany agreed on peace terms; German forces would withdraw in exchange for a vast swath of Russian territory (Latvia, Lithuania, Russian territory in Poland and Finland, and the Ukraine). The terms were made official in the Treaty of Brest-Litovsk, signed in March 1918.

By signing this treaty with Germany, the Bolsheviks aroused strong opposition in two groups of people. The first was Russia's former allies, still fighting the First World War. Britain and France felt that Russia had betrayed and abandoned them. The second group was the many Russians who were alarmed at the terms of the treaty. The loss of the western territory was significant because this was the most "modern" part of the country. Western Russia was better developed, more densely populated, and more industrialized than the central and eastern portions of the country. However, Lenin believed that the first thing he must do in power was to seize control and hold it. This did not allow for the niceties of pleasing his future constituents or kowtowing to his power base. He needed to demonstrate that he was in charge and that he knew what he was doing. Therefore, he ignored all opposition to the treaty.

The Russian Civil War

By 1918, an all-out civil war was raging in Russia between the Whites and the Reds. The Whites were royalists, moderates, anti-Communists, and non-Russian Europeans who wanted to overpower the Bolsheviks and restore some semblance of reasonable government to Russia. The Reds supported the Bolsheviks, who renamed themselves "Communists" during this period. (The terms *Bolshevik* and *Communist* can be used interchangeably to refer to the ruling political party when discussing Russia under Lenin's rule.) The Red Army's loyalty to the Communist Party and the state would make it one of the Party's most effective tools in the following years.

The civil war lasted for about three years, during which there were mass desertions on both sides; in the end, the Reds prevailed. There were several reasons for their victory. First, they outnumbered the Whites. Second, their commanders were much better organized than those on the White side. Third, they had in Lenin an identifiable strong leader with clear goals. The Whites consisted of too many groups whose interests were not necessarily identical. Fourth, the Reds controlled Moscow, which meant they controlled the railroads. Finally, the Reds enjoyed tremendous popular support within Russia. Workers naturally rallied behind the Bolsheviks because they were the self-proclaimed Workers' Party. Peasants distrusted the Whites because the Whites did not immediately promise them ownership of the land. Russian leaders also supported the Reds; they considered the Whites to be foreign interlopers and they resented Europe's hostility toward the new Russian government. On their side, the Europeans bitterly resented the timing of the revolution because it had meant Russia's withdrawal from World War I. This era created distrust between Russia and the rest of Europe that lasted the rest of the century and lingers even to the present day.

Russia and the Soviet Union Under Lenin

The Communist regime that emerged from the civil war was characterized by chaos. Lenin and his associates had no experience of governing and had to create a system by trial and error. Lenin knew that he wanted an autocratic regime in which he would be sole dictator. He never considered establishing a parliamentary system; he believed this to be simply a rubber stamp for the capitalist forces of society.

A major goal of the Russian revolutionaries was to incite similar revolutions throughout all of Europe; to destroy not just a type of government but an entire existing social and political order. To help bring this about, Lenin and his associates formed the International Communist Party, known as the Comintern, in 1919. The Comintern was characterized by rigid, uncompromising rules. Although the Socialist movement was strong throughout Europe, European Socialists were more moderate than Communists; they were on the whole satisfied with the greater degree of representation that ordinary citizens acquired during the nineteenth century. For example, by 1914 universal or near-universal adult male suffrage was the law in Britain, France, Germany, Italy, and elsewhere. Additionally, women acquired unprecedented freedom and political power during and immediately after World War I. In this acceptance of the system, Lenin saw the defeat of everything he wanted to accomplish; the Socialists of Europe simply were not prepared to go to the same extremes as the Communists. Through the Comintern, Lenin hoped to change this. Moscow controlled the Comintern from the early 1920s.

In 1919, after World War I was over, the Great Powers met at Versailles to negotiate the peace. Russia took no part in the negotiations, but the country was nonetheless affected. The Russian territory that Germany had taken at Brest-Litovsk was made into independent nations; had Russia sent a delegation to Versailles, this might have been arranged differently. As matters stood, the Communist government refused to acknowledge the loss of the western territory until some time after Versailles. In the end, of course, Russia lost the fight to keep its land.

War between Russia and Poland broke out in 1920. It did not last long. In March 1921 the peace treaty established the Russian-Polish border that would remain in place until 1939. Poland had become an enemy for Lenin to reckon with, for several reasons. First, it had a long-standing history of resentment toward Russian oppression. Second, it was a large nation with a large population, capable of holding its own in a struggle with Russia. Third, the Poles were fiercely anti-Bolshevik, in part because Poland was largely a Catholic nation and the Bolsheviks were atheists.

The early 1920s in Russia can accurately be called "a Second Time of Troubles." As a true Marxist, Lenin believed above all in policies that favored the workers. He also believed that industrialization was the key to Russia's economic recovery. Therefore he instituted the New Economic Policy in 1921. It called for peasants to sell their surplus grain to the state at a fixed price in either money or kind (such as clothing or tools); the grain would be used to feed the urban industrial workers.

The peasants reacted to the government orders in a way the Communists had not foreseen. Industry was crippled from the war and was not producing anything for the peasants to buy, so money was not useful to them; and the state rarely remembered to pay them in kind. Therefore, instead of working hard to provide the necessary surplus, they hoarded their grain, fearful of not having enough to feed their families. With no grain coming in from the country, the urban workers were going hungry; soon many of them were fleeing to the country in search of food. Severe droughts at this time led to widespread famine. Historians estimate that perhaps 6 million Russians died of starvation and disease during this period.

In 1922, Russia was renamed to reflect the new government's philosophy: it became the Union of Soviet Socialist Republics, called the Soviet Union or USSR for short. The twelve individual republics—including Georgia, Kazakhstan, and Russia—were equals, each with its own soviet, and all firmly under control of the dictator.

The Communists made it clear to the old guard that there was no place for them in the new workers' state. In the Soviet Union, the concept of private property disappeared. The wealthy were stripped of their homes, which were turned into apartment houses for workers, with the original owners perhaps being allowed to rent one room as their own family apartment. At least 2 million aristocrats packed what they could carry and fled to Western Europe. Those who stayed had to learn hard manual labor like all other Soviets.

Stalin

After suffering a series of strokes, Lenin died in 1924 without naming a successor. Two men, both of whom had been close to Lenin but neither of whom he believed should rule, emerged as the most likely candidates for dictator: Leon Trotsky and Joseph Stalin.

Trotsky was born Leon Bronstein in 1879 in the Black Sea province of Kherson. A political protestor in his youth, he had been imprisoned and exiled to Siberia. On his successful escape, he took the name Trotsky. He had been Lenin's closest associate, despite violent disagreements between them, and had played a major role in the coup of 1917. Joseph Stalin was born Joseph Dzhugashvili in 1878 in Georgia. An early follower of Lenin, he led an outlaw existence throughout much of his youth and was imprisoned on a number of occasions. He founded the workers' newspaper *Pravda* (*Truth*). Stalin, based on the Russian word for "steel," was a pen name he used throughout his career. Like Trotsky, Stalin rose to a prominent position of leadership among the Communists, although he had serious and frequent disagreements with Lenin. In the power struggle following Lenin's death, Stalin triumphed over Trotsky and became dictator; it was not long before he forced Trotsky to leave the country for good.

Stalin has earned the reputation of being history's most ruthless dictator, with the possible exception of Adolf Hitler. Under his rule, the Soviet Union could accurately be described as a police state. Stalin enforced his policies with no evidence of a conscience and no regard whatsoever for human life. Historians have estimated that about 30 million Russians died during his regime—some of starvation or disease, but most either in the brutal conditions of the labor camps or because their executions were ordered by the state. The government was careful to conceal evidence of Stalin's brutality from the outside world; even many Russians were not aware of its full extent.

The Communists all believed that industrialization was of paramount importance in making the Soviet Union a major European power once again. However, they differed over the means toward achieving this end. Some believed that since the grain harvests were needed to feed the industrial workers, the state should try to gain the peasants' support. Others believed that it was not necessary to conciliate the peasants, since the state could force them into obedience. Stalin was one of the latter group.

Stalin's policy, called the Five-Year Plan, was implemented in 1929. It involved two goals. The first was collectivization, in which small independent farmers (known in Russian as *kulaks*) and subsistence farmers were forced to pool their land and work the new, giant farms together, with the state dictating prices. Since the *kulaks* were accustomed to independence, owning their own land and farming it as they saw fit, they naturally had no desire to join state-run collectives. Their lack of cooperation made Stalin decide to get rid of them; he was genuinely at odds with the peasants, considering them nothing more than a means for providing the urban workers with food. Between 1930 and 1933, more than 2 million *kulaks* and "sympathizers" were deported, either to collective farms far from their own districts or to prison camps.

The second goal of the Five-Year Plan was to develop heavy industry. Russia had been slow to industrialize but had begun to catch up to the rest of Europe by 1913. Although the war and revolution put a stop to this process, production had risen nearly to its 1913 levels by 1927. As part of the Five-Year Plan, the state called for major public-works projects, including the Moscow Metro, railways, canals, and power plants. Many were built with prison-camp labor. As a result of the Five-Year Plan, employment doubled and industrial output more than doubled by 1932—but not without taking a toll on the workers. Other Five-Year Plans would follow.

Artists and intellectuals had a particularly bad time of it under the new regime. Under the New Economic Policy, some bold experimentation had occurred in the arts, but Stalin immediately put a stop to it. He believed that the purpose of all art was to serve the state, not to express what an individual artist wished to communicate. Books, films, popular songs, symphonies, paintings, plays—works of art in all genres were banned if they hinted at any criticism of the regime or suggested that social conditions in Russia were anything short of ideal. Some emigrated to Europe or the United States; others stayed and did their best to come to terms with the policies.

Although Stalin achieved an impressive degree of control over the state and the people, there were some things he could not control, even with his willingness to use any means necessary. During his first few years in power, the Soviet Union experienced severe food shortages, widespread lack of cooperation from the peasants, mass migrations to the cities that left fewer people to farm the land, a typhus epidemic, and in 1933, a famine that probably killed more than 4 million people. The nation's economic gains during this period are especially impressive considering the harsh conditions in which the people were living.

During the mid-1930s, a wave of executions and banishments known as the Great Purges did much to establish Stalin's historical reputation. Historians' interpretations of the Great Purges vary, but most agree that Stalin set about them as a means of preserving his autocratic powers. Between 1936 and 1939, at least 750,000 people were executed or banished to the labor camps. Anyone who opposed Stalin publicly, or was unfortunate enough to be caught denouncing him privately, was purged—military officers, high-ranking politicians or economists, artists and intellectuals, and political dissenters.

Communism Elsewhere in Europe

Lenin had originally expected that the Communist Revolution would sweep through Europe. His expectations were only partially fulfilled. Socialist and Communist uprisings took place throughout Germany and Eastern Europe, but none lasted more than five months. Outside Russia, Socialists could generally find their place in a parliamentary system of government.

Germany underwent a chaotic period of popular uprisings during the fall of 1918. In January 1919, the monarchy was replaced by the Weimar Republic, named for the city in which the legislative assembly met and wrote the new German constitution. The Weimar Republic lasted only until the rise of Adolf Hitler in 1933. (See Chapter 17.)

The Communists were closest to achieving success in Hungary, where a workers' republic was established in 1919 under Bela Kun. This Communist state lasted five months—a period of brutal oppression known in Hungary as the Red Terror—before it was replaced by something resembling a constitutional monarchy under former diplomat and naval commander Miklos Horthy. Communists in Bavaria and Slovakia also established workers' states, but each lasted for a few weeks only.

QUIZ

1. **What was the immediate result of the abdication of Czar Nicholas II?**
   A. The Provisional Government assumed power.
   B. Lenin founded the International Communist Party.
   C. The state introduced enforced collectivization.
   D. Russia signed a peace treaty with Germany.

2. **The primary goal of the Five-Year Plan was**
   A. to pass major social legislation.
   B. to recover territory lost during World War I.
   C. to write a new constitution.
   D. to improve industrialization.

3. **The Russian Revolution was unique among all European revolutions because**
   A. a dictator rose to power after the abolition of a monarchy.
   B. it was intended to overturn the social order throughout Europe.
   C. the new government was established only after a civil war was fought.
   D. it replaced one form of government with an entirely different form.

4. **In what way was the new order in Russia exactly like the old order?**
   A. The head of state and the head of the Orthodox Church were allies.
   B. The head of state was an autocrat whose dictates could not be questioned.
   C. The government relied on and courted the support of the people.
   D. The government supported revolutionary activity in other European nations.

5. **Why did European nations oppose the Bolshevik government when it was first established?**
   A. They were afraid of the Bolsheviks' influence in Eastern Europe.
   B. They did not want an alliance to form between Russia and Germany.
   C. They resented Russia's withdrawal from the First World War.
   D. They did not believe in government by the people.

6. **Which of the following choices best describes the White forces during the Russian civil war?**
   A. workers and peasants
   B. international Communists
   C. royalists and anti-Communists
   D. liberals and Socialists

7. **In the Treaty of Brest-Litovsk, Russia agreed to give up western territory to Germany in exchange for** _____
   A. German surrender to Russia.
   B. German withdrawal from Russia.
   C. a German-Russian defensive alliance.
   D. German reparations.

8. **Why did Communism not take a stronger hold in Europe after World War I?**
   A. Socialists were contented with representative European governments.
   B. There was no international Communist party.
   C. Europeans were shocked by stories of Stalin's brutal policies.
   D. Nations were too busy rebuilding their economies.

9. **Russian peasants supported the Reds during the civil war because the Reds promised them** _____
   A. land.
   B. money.
   C. the vote.
   D. freedom.

10. **Stalin is considered an especially brutal dictator because**
   A. he led the nation into wars it could not win.
   B. he was an absolute ruler who did not accept advice or counsel.
   C. he ordered the exile, imprisonment, and/or execution of millions.
   D. he used the army and police as tools of oppression.

17

The Rise of Totalitarianism, 1919–1939

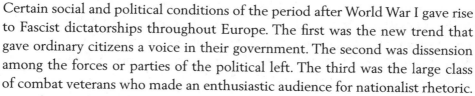

Certain social and political conditions of the period after World War I gave rise to Fascist dictatorships throughout Europe. The first was the new trend that gave ordinary citizens a voice in their government. The second was dissension among the forces or parties of the political left. The third was the large class of combat veterans who made an enthusiastic audience for nationalist rhetoric.

Widespread participation in government by the citizens was something new in the twentieth century. For the first time, each man had one vote, regardless of his birth or education. Fascist leaders found that propaganda techniques were enormously effective with uneducated voters; simple images and slogans were often repeated, easily remembered, and immediately appealing to a class of people who were accustomed to obeying and accepting authority. Since the uneducated vastly outnumbered the rest of the population, Fascists always made sure to commandeer their support.

Political theorists speak of "the left" when they refer to liberal politicians who look to the future, and of "the right" when they refer to conservatives who look to the past. In the years after the Great War, the forces of the political left found themselves in disagreement. The radicals had become so radical that they alienated the Socialists and liberals, whose political aims were more moderate. Many Socialists reasoned that a conservative government would be more moderate than a radical one; in other words, they believed that fascism (a conservative government) was a better alternative to communism (a radical government).

A high degree of nationalism always exists among the military; this is natural and inevitable among a profession of people who risk their lives in combat for their nation, while regarding other nations as the enemy. Many veterans of World War I, especially the Germans, believed that their sacrifices had been in vain and their nation had been damaged and humiliated. Dictators could give extreme, angry, high-flown patriotic speeches that sounded excessive to any reasonable person, but that veterans could be counted on to applaud enthusiastically. Dictators actively courted the support of veterans because they wanted the personal loyalty of the military. Control of the military made any leader practically invulnerable to opposition because the military had control of the guns.

In practice, as it turned out, fascism and communism amounted to the same thing—totalitarianism. Each dictatorship of the period between the world wars was fiercely nationalist, espousing an extreme form of patriotism that, at least in Germany's case, developed into active, malevolent racism. Each established government controls over what had been a market economy. Each used the army as an instrument to control the people. Each employed a police force that reported only to the dictator and that was hated and feared by the citizens. None tolerated dissent in any form; none tolerated free speech, free expression in the arts, or a free press.

CHAPTER 17 OBJECTIVES

- Compare and contrast fascism and communism.
- Identify the facts that gave rise to totalitarian governments after World War I.
- Identify the dictators of the era and discuss how each one rose to power.
- Describe, compare, and contrast the dictatorships in Italy, Germany, and Spain.

Chapter 17 Time Line

- **1921** Mussolini founds Fascist Party in Italy
- **1922** Mussolini becomes prime minister of Italy
- **1929** U.S. stock market crashes; beginning of Great Depression
- **1933** Adolf Hitler becomes chancellor of Germany
- **1936–1939** Spanish Civil War
- **1939** Francisco Franco establishes dictatorship in Spain

Italy—The Rise of Fascism

In 1919, the Italian economy was suffering from massive unemployment and high inflation. In areas where fighting had occurred, cities and land would have to be rebuilt and recultivated. Politically, the country became divided between the Socialist and nationalist parties. The situation was ripe for the rise to power of Benito Mussolini.

Born in 1883 in the ancient town of Forlì in northern Italy, Mussolini was a very well-read intellectual, a combat veteran, and a former journalist. He had once been a committed Socialist, but his ideas changed during the war. In 1919, Mussolini held the first meeting of the group that would become the Fascist Party of Italy. (The Italian word *fascio* means "union" and comes from the Latin *fasces*, a sheaf of grain that had been a symbol of the authority of the Roman state in ancient times.)

As the leader of the Fascist movement, Mussolini explicitly encouraged violence against the Socialists, thereby attracting new members who were little better than thugs. Their extreme nationalism found expression in gang-style violence. In April 1919, Mussolini's supporters stormed into the offices of the Milan newspaper *Avanti* (*Forward*) and destroyed the printing presses. This act of violence was typical of the terrorist tactics that would become the signature of the totalitarian regimes of the next two decades.

Mussolini had one serious rival in the person of Gabriele d'Annunzio, already famous as a playwright, poet, and hero of World War I. In September 1919, D'Annunzio led his followers in an invasion and occupation of the Yugoslavian city of Fiume, on the nationalist grounds that nearly 90 percent of its citizens were ethnic Italians. Once in power in Fiume, D'Annunzio behaved like the

Caesars of ancient Rome, staging military parades and bombastic daily speeches to impress and intimidate the people.

Italian Prime Minister Giovanni Giolitti eventually negotiated a settlement with Yugoslavia. In exchange for Yugoslavia's making Fiume independent, Giolitti forced D'Annunzio to step down. D'Annunzio's supporters, balked of their prize, turned to Mussolini.

Mussolini was nothing if not pragmatic; he was guided much more by practicality than by principle. He was quite willing to negotiate with anyone or any group if he saw a chance of strengthening his own base of power. In the days after Fiume, Mussolini negotiated with leading moderate political leaders, treated the chastened D'Annunzio generously, and encouraged his own supporters to take action against Socialists.

In northern Italy, major landowners had lost a great deal of their negotiating power to the forces of socialism. Therefore, the landowners decided that the Fascists, as anti-Socialists, were their natural allies. Between November 1920 and April 1921, the Fascists gave free rein to their aggressiveness. They destroyed the offices of Labor Exchanges throughout the region, dragged labor organizers into the street and beat them up, and smashed printing presses of any newspapers whose editors favored socialist politics. At the same time, the Fascists won support among the peasants by giving some of them land outright. This convinced many farmers to desert the Socialists, since the goal of socialism was state-owned land. Farmers preferred the possibility of private ownership of their own farms.

The Fascists stepped up their campaign of terror and intimidation, taking over entire towns and cities in the region. With the help of local police, nationalist veterans, and their own organized military squads, called "Blackshirts" because of the uniforms they wore, the Fascists occupied public buildings and forced local governments to do what they wanted, including instituting public-works programs that gave jobs to the unemployed. Naturally, this won them a great deal of support among the people.

By May of 1921, the Fascists had become so strong that Giolitti felt it was better to assimilate them than fight them. He formed a coalition government that included seats in Parliament for Mussolini and thirty-four other Fascists.

In October 1922, Mussolini staged what became known as the March on Rome. The Blackshirts commandeered and boarded trains to Rome from three different starting points, taking over towns along the three routes. The new prime minister, Luigi Facta, resolutely prepared to stop them, assembling troops and asking the king to declare martial law in Rome. However, the king refused, fearing that a confrontation between the Fascists and the Italian army would lead immediately to civil war. Unwilling to risk this, he offered the office of prime minister to Mussolini. Four years later, Mussolini had become Il Duce—the absolute dictator of Italy. (*Duce* is Italian for "leader.")

Like all dictators, Mussolini was quick to establish one-party rule. During the 1920s, his policies brought economic recovery to the nation. Additionally, he struck a bargain with the Catholic Church. In the Lateran Treaty of 1929, the Church officially and formally recognized the nation of Italy for the first time in exchange for broad authority over the everyday lives of Italian citizens.

European economies collapsed in the crash of 1929 and the Great Depression (see later in this chapter), and Italy's was no exception. In 1935, Mussolini ordered the invasion of Ethiopia, for both political and economic reasons. Politically, the invasion was a sign of the desire to subdue and control other lands that was typical of a fascist state. Economically, Mussolini hoped to counter the effects of the Depression by subduing a nation that was rich in natural resources. He intended Ethiopia to provide Italy with both natural resources and a market for Italian manufactured goods.

Germany—Hitler and the Nazis Seize Power

The rise of an extreme nationalist party in Germany was all but inevitable after the Treaty of Versailles. Germany's industry was destroyed, its military greatly reduced, some of its territory gone, and its economy devastated. Workers' revolutions broke out in several German cities, but all were eventually put down. With the proclamation of the Weimar Republic in 1919, Germany could begin to pick up the pieces and move forward.

The Treaty of Versailles required Germany to reduce the size of the army to a very small force. Already bitter because they had lost the war, thousands of veterans now found themselves out of a job. Blaming the new German government for abandoning them, they took revenge at the polling place. Robbed of their parliamentary majority, the Social Democrats—those committed to a democratic constitutional government—had no choice but to form a coalition with representatives of the other parties. These coalition governments, of which there were more than a dozen between 1919 and 1933, were unable to accomplish much because their members had too many different goals. Conservatives, monarchists, and Democrats could not work together effectively even in the area of foreign policy, which traditionally united political opponents against the common enemy. Unable to negotiate effectively, Germany lost a series of arguments over Versailles Treaty provisions during the 1920s. As a result, Germans grew more nationalist and at the same time more contemptuous of their own government.

By 1922 France had determined the amount of the reparations Germany owed: more than 130 billion marks. The German people reacted furiously to the news that their government had agreed to this demand. As far as the people were concerned, the demand was unjustified; it was simply revenge on a defenseless nation. Moreover, the money simply was not there.

The French, deciding to take in fuel what Germany would not hand over in money, marched into the Ruhr—the coal-producing region of western Germany that had been made a demilitarized zone by the Treaty of Versailles. Although this was not cost-effective for the French, it brought economic ruin to Germany. Inflation soared to unimaginable levels. In December 1921, a loaf of bread cost 4 marks; in December 1922 it cost 163 marks; by December 1923 the price had risen to a staggering 400 *billion* marks!

This was the low point of German fortunes after World War I. Beginning in 1923, France and Britain showed a willingness to compromise over the payment of reparations, and France began to withdraw troops from the Ruhr. The United States also loaned money to Germany, and the ensuing years saw a steady recovery of the German economy as prices dropped back to normal levels. In another sign that the rifts of the war were beginning to heal, the Western nations welcomed Germany into the League of Nations in 1926. In addition, the Weimar Republic became famous for bold, experimental works by such artists as composer Kurt Weill, writers Bertolt Brecht and Thomas Mann, painters George Grosz and Wassily Kandinsky, and film director Joseph von Sternberg.

The U.S. stock market crashed in the fall of 1929. It had been soaring on an insubstantial foundation of margin buying and unpaid debts. When people began selling stocks to pay debts, others lost confidence in the market and it collapsed with stunning speed. When the market collapsed, the banks failed; when the banks failed, the businesses closed; when the businesses closed, the workers lost their jobs and could find no others. This economic failure is known as the Great Depression.

The Depression was not confined to the United States; the fact of international banking and trade made it a universal economic crash. Banks closed throughout Europe and prices dropped. No one could find a market for goods because no one had cash with which to buy them. The Great Depression was the deathblow to the recovery that Germany and other European nations had been making since the end of the Great War. The German government, faced with strikes, violent protests in the streets, and rising unemployment, collapsed. The Nazi Party (the name is an abbreviation of "National Socialist German Workers' Party") now rose to power under its founder and leader, an obscure Austrian named Adolf Hitler.

Born in 1889 in Branau on the Austrian-German border, Hitler had been a failure all his life, often living on charity, unable to settle down to any profession until he joined the German army during World War I. Hitler served with some distinction in a low rank and felt great personal bitterness over Germany's defeat. He used his extraordinary ability to stir the emotions of crowds to gain power; his rhetoric about the greatness of the German Empire hit a nerve with people who desperately needed decisive leadership. Hitler believed that the way to win the support of the voters was to use simple slogans and propaganda to appeal to their national pride, their emotions, and their prejudices. He had no experience of government or politics, nor the skill or the desire to present logically thought-out social programs. Because of this, the established German political parties made the great mistake of underestimating him and his mass appeal.

In 1930, the Nazis won a large number of seats in the Reichstag (the German parliament). Hitler never looked back from this success. He and his closest followers now carried out a campaign of intimidation that brought him quickly to the top position in the German government. By 1932, the Nazis had become the most powerful party in Germany. In 1933, Hitler was appointed chancellor of Germany. It was not long before he exchanged this democratic title for the imperial title "Führer (Leader) of the Third Reich." With the eager collaboration of the majority of Germans, this foreign nobody had made himself an absolute dictator whose orders could not be questioned by anyone.

One of Hitler's first acts was to establish one-party rule by the Nazis. His close associate Heinrich Himmler soon created the Gestapo, a secret state police force responsible only to the führer. Hitler also had the SS (*Schutzstaffel*, or "Protection Squadron"), a rogue militia like Mussolini's Blackshirts, at his command. These two organizations promptly and efficiently carried out many of the orders—executions and other acts of brutal violence against German citizens—that have cemented Hitler's reputation as the greatest villain in modern European history.

Hitler soon made it evident that he espoused two of the most common aspects of fascism: expansionism and racism. In Hitler's case, the two impulses were linked. He considered that Germans and other northern European nationalities, such as Scandinavians and British, were racially superior, while Slavs and southern Europeans were inferior. Territorial expansion would provide living space for the Aryans (his term for the racially superior) while at the same time subduing the *Untermenschen* (literally "subhumans," or inferior races). His persecution of the Jews was the most obvious manifestation of his prejudices. Under Hitler's rule, German Jews were soon stripped of all civil rights, deprived of their professions, and forced into menial jobs. Later, conditions would become much worse for them (see Chapter 18). Historians estimate that perhaps one-fourth of all German Jews fled the country in the early 1930s.

Although the mass of the population had confidence in Hitler's leadership, thousands of Germans considered him a demagogue and a madman and were dismayed and appalled by his lightning rise to absolute power. Tight censorship of the press and the arts made it clear that Germany simply was not a safe place to live for those who were not committed to the Nazi ideology. Many German intellectuals, artists, journalists, and teachers packed up and left the country, hoping that Hitler would soon fall.

In order to expand, Germany needed to rearm. In 1933, Hitler withdrew Germany from the League of Nations, and the country began to rearm despite the ban contained in the Versailles Treaty. Rearming increased considerably in 1936, as Hitler made it clear that he expected Germany to be ready to launch a war of aggression by 1940.

Spain and the Spanish Civil War

Spain spent the first half of the 1930s trying to settle what type of government it wanted: republican or nationalist. The dictatorship of Miguel Primo de Rivera ended in 1930. It was replaced by the republican administration of Prime Minister Azaña. For three years Azaña carried out a program of egalitarian reforms. In 1933, Azaña was forced out of office due to the bitter opposition of the anti-reform establishment.

Over the next three years, two opposing political philosophies struggled for power. The Popular Front was the left-wing side, composed of Communists, anarchists, and Socialists. The National Front was the right-wing side, composed of conservatives, monarchists, and Catholics in positions of power and influence. In 1936, the Popular Front carried the elections, executing Primo de Rivera by firing squad and restoring Azaña to power.

General Francisco Franco had been waiting with the army in Morocco for news of the elections. When he learned that the National Front had been defeated, he led an invasion into Spain, where he laid siege to Madrid. The fascist Falange party supported Franco, as did Italy and Germany. The Germans were able to supply Franco through Portugal, which was then ruled by a regime that sympathized with fascism. The Soviet Union supported the Popular Front for a time but eventually withdrew its support; this enabled the National Front to win the civil war, and as of 1939 Spain was a military dictatorship under Franco.

The Rise of Totalitarianism in Other European Nations

The small states of Eastern Europe, several of them newly created by the Treaty of Versailles, were the perfect breeding ground for totalitarianism for three reasons. First, nationalism was a divisive factor in these ethnically diverse countries. Second, this area suffered economically as much as any other during World War I. Third, several of these nations were newly created, and none had more than a few decades' experience in self-government. All these factors combined to create unstable societies that were ripe for a seizure of power. Except for Czechoslovakia, which established and managed to maintain a democratic government, all the nations of Eastern Europe succumbed to dictatorship between 1919 and 1936.

QUIZ

1. **Why was Europe affected by the crash of the U.S. stock market in 1929?**
    A. European economies depended on American loans.
    B. European nations had loaned money to the United States.
    C. The European branches of American banks failed.
    D. International banking and trading connected the two economies.

2. **The personal loyalty of _____ was crucial to the success of all European dictators in the 1920s and 1930s.**
    A. the army or militia
    B. the intellectuals and artists
    C. the press
    D. the civil servants

3. **Which European nation supported the Popular Front in Spain?**
    A. Britain
    B. France
    C. Germany
    D. the Soviet Union

4. **In 1930s Spain, high-ranking Catholics usually supported _____**
    A. Prime Minister Azaña.
    B. the Communist Party.
    C. the National Front.
    D. the Popular Front.

5. **Which best describes the Spanish government in 1939?**
    A. an absolute monarchy
    B. a constitutional monarchy
    C. a parliamentary republic
    D. a military dictatorship

6. **Large landowners in Italy supported the Fascists because both were _____**
    A. liberal.
    B. royalist.
    C. anti-Catholic.
    D. anti-Socialist.

7. **The king of Italy refused to put down the Blackshirts because**
   A. he was personally afraid for his own life.
   B. he did not command the loyalty of the Italian army.
   C. he wanted to avoid a full-scale civil war.
   D. he had made a secret bargain with Mussolini.

8. **Why was Germany unable to negotiate effectively with other nations in the early 1920s?**
   A. because of the Great Depression
   B. because of high unemployment
   C. because of dissension within the coalition government
   D. because of the invasion of the Ruhr

9. **Adolf Hitler rose to power primarily by**
   A. commanding the loyalty of the German army.
   B. demonstrating his intention to repair the economy.
   C. expressing support for social programs.
   D. appealing to the force of German nationalism.

10. **Why did France invade the Ruhr in 1922?**
    A. to commandeer the coal
    B. to annex the region
    C. to aid the striking workers
    D. to protect itself from German invasion

chapter 18

World War II, 1939–1945

Historians agree that the peace treaty signed in 1919 at the Congress of Versailles was one of the major causes of World War II. The second war arose as a natural consequence of the first, and both can fairly be described as wars of German aggression. Many historians consider the two world wars (and the smaller-scale wars that occurred in between) as one war. Some historians refer to the period 1914–1945 as "the Second Thirty Years' War."

The Axis powers (Germany and Italy) had the upper hand on the battlefield until late 1942, for several reasons. First, they were the aggressors and were therefore able to control the course of events. Second, their leaders had been planning for the war for years, while the Allied nations (Britain, France, and the USSR—the U.S. would join the Allies later) were taken more or less by surprise. Third, the German troops were extremely well-disciplined. Fourth, Germany and Italy between them controlled almost all of Europe and a sizable chunk of North Africa.

The Allied powers were eventually able to seize the upper hand for two reasons, both very important. First, numerical strength was on their side. The United States and the USSR could provide fresh troops in almost unlimited numbers, and the Italians changed sides in 1943, which left Germany alone. Second, American factories were far from the fighting, out of danger of Axis bombing or capture, and were a source of virtually unlimited supplies: weapons, ammunition, ships, tanks, and so on.

Perhaps the major reason for the German defeat in the war lies in the personality of Hitler. As sole dictator of Germany, Hitler made all the crucial decisions in the early days of the war; many of these turned out to be serious strategic errors. As the war dragged on, Hitler seemed less and less aware of events. Historians are generally agreed that he was not entirely sane.

In terms of lost lives and ruined cities, World War II was by far the costliest war in history. It ended a long historical era of European domination. As it ended, the Allies began to realize they would have to take extraordinary steps to prevent such wholesale violence and slaughter from occurring in the future.

CHAPTER 18 OBJECTIVES

- Identify the major causes of World War II.
- List the Allied and Axis nations and identify their leaders.
- Describe the major battles of the war and locate them on the map.
- Explain what happened at the Yalta and Potsdam conferences.

Chapter 18 Time Line

- **1933**   Adolf Hitler becomes chancellor of Germany
- **1935**   Nuremberg Laws deprive Jews of German citizenship
- **1936**   Germany annexes Rhineland; Germany and Italy unite as Axis powers
- **1938**   Germany annexes Austria
- **1939**   **August 23** Germany and Soviet Union sign nonaggression pact

  September Germany and Soviet Union annex Poland from opposite sides; Britain and France declare war on Germany
- **1940**   **May 10** Germany invades Belgium and marches into France; Winston Churchill becomes prime minister of Britain

  May 20 Allies retreat at Dunkirk

  June 10 Italy declares war on Britain and France

  July 10 Germany sets up Vichy regime in southern France

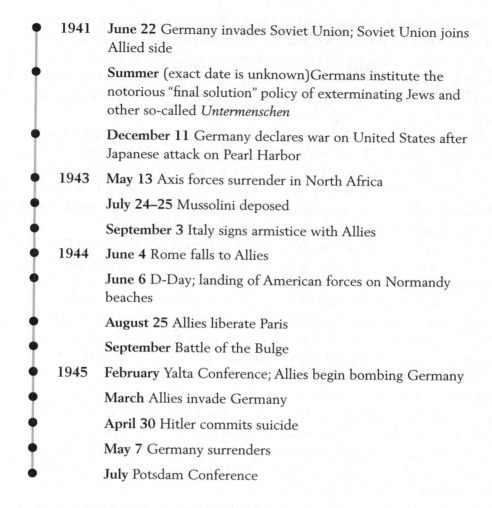

1941   **June 22** Germany invades Soviet Union; Soviet Union joins Allied side

Summer (exact date is unknown)Germans institute the notorious "final solution" policy of exterminating Jews and other so-called *Untermenschen*

December 11 Germany declares war on United States after Japanese attack on Pearl Harbor

1943   **May 13** Axis forces surrender in North Africa

July 24–25 Mussolini deposed

September 3 Italy signs armistice with Allies

1944   **June 4** Rome falls to Allies

June 6 D-Day; landing of American forces on Normandy beaches

August 25 Allies liberate Paris

September Battle of the Bulge

1945   **February** Yalta Conference; Allies begin bombing Germany

March Allies invade Germany

April 30 Hitler commits suicide

May 7 Germany surrenders

July Potsdam Conference

1933: The Beginning of German Aggression

In flat defiance of the Versailles Treaty, Hitler ordered Germany to begin rebuilding its military shortly after he became chancellor. Rearming began in 1933 and escalated in 1936 as part of Hitler's plan to begin a war of aggression in which he would restore Germany to its mythical imperial glory. In concrete terms, his plan in the late 1930s was to create a culturally and ethnically German empire in central Europe, and to annex an undetermined number of the smaller Eastern European states.

Germany moved into the Rhineland and occupied it in 1936. In 1938, the German army invaded and annexed Austria (the Germans referred to this event as the *Anschluss,* or "union"), and in 1939, Czechoslovakia. Other European nations watched with concern, but there was no popular support anywhere for another war with Germany. Hitler was therefore allowed to proceed almost unchecked, and he proved he was entirely capable of effective intimidation tactics against anyone who did object. The next step required forming an alliance with the Soviet Union.

Secretly, Hitler and Stalin signed a nonaggression pact with two major provisions. First, neither nation would attack the other. Second, both nations would invade Poland from opposite sides and divide it between them. Stalin's motive was to recover Polish territory that had been under Russian control before World War I. Hitler's motive was to recover a stretch of formerly German territory known as the Danzig Corridor.

Danzig was an important port city on the Baltic; the fifty-mile-wide Danzig Corridor provided overland access to it. The Versailles Treaty had declared Danzig a free city and had given the corridor to Poland, thus separating East Prussia geographically from the rest of Germany. Hitler intended to take over the corridor and the port, thus reuniting the German state into one landmass. Of course, the invasion of Poland would also allow the German army direct overland access to the Soviet Union—something the usually distrustful Stalin apparently had not considered.

Britain and France were agreed that Germany could not be permitted to upset the balance of power by taking over all of Eastern Europe and had formally guaranteed Poland's sovereignty. Hitler's closest associates, knowing of the agreement, had tried to dissuade him from provoking a war against the Allies by invading Poland, but Hitler refused to listen to them, considering the agreement a bluff. He promptly realized his mistake: Britain and France declared war on Germany immediately after the German invasion of Poland.

1940: The Fall of France and the Battle of Britain

In April 1940, the German army invaded Denmark and Norway. In May the army staged a successful two-pronged attack on France, with one division invading through Belgium and the other through the Ardennes, south of Paris. The advancing German divisions cut off the British troops, who were forced to retreat across the English Channel. On June 21, Marshal Pétain of France asked for an armistice. Thus Hitler won an easy victory over Germany's historical enemy. The Germans would occupy Paris until late 1944. Hitler maintained control over southern France, Morocco, and Algeria throughout the Vichy regime.

Now that the Germans were firmly installed only a few miles away across the Channel, the British knew that a change in their leadership was overdue. Winston Churchill had warned Parliament for years about German rearmament and its probable consequences. He had vigorously opposed his predecessor Neville Chamberlain's policy of appeasement. The people turned to Churchill in their fear, and he became prime minister on May 10.

No wartime leader in history ever played a more important role than Churchill in maintaining the morale of his people. Churchill may have been the only man in Europe whom Hitler could not intimidate. His refusal to even consider the possibility of a British defeat was communicated to his people in his radio addresses. Churchill and the Royal Family set an example of courage by refusing to leave London, despite the nightly bombing of the capital by the German air force.

This attack from the air is known as the Battle of Britain, fought entirely between the two air forces. The bombardment began as a prelude to a planned German invasion that never took place. The German Luftwaffe bombed Royal Air Force bases and airfields throughout southern England into the late summer of 1940. The result was costly for the Germans; they lost more than half their fighter planes and took revenge by bombing London and other heavily populated civilian areas. The purpose of the Blitz, as the attack on the civilians is called, was to intimidate the British into surrender or withdrawal from the war. In 1941, the Germans realized this purpose had failed. They would return to bomb London again in 1943, but for now the Battle of Britain was won.

The Eastern Front

In perhaps his most serious error of judgment, Hitler abandoned the nonaggression pact he had signed with Stalin and invaded the Soviet Union in 1941. The Soviets were taken completely unawares, but they soon rallied against the enemy and proved fierce and stubborn in opposition. The German attack immediately brought the Soviet Union into the war on the Allied side. With its enormous army, the USSR would be a crucial factor in the ultimate Allied victory.

In their attack on the eastern front, the Germans made two crucial mistakes. First, they seriously underestimated the vast size of the Soviet army and the production capacity of the Soviet munitions factories. Second, Hitler genuinely believed that Russians, like all Slavs, were an inferior people who would not be capable of defeating the German army. Of course, this was a delusion with no basis in reality. In fact, the Soviets were highly disciplined, having learned obedience under the harsh rule of Stalin; in that way at least, he proved an important unifying force for his people during wartime. Both these mistakes led the Germans to believe they could achieve an easy victory; hence they did not send a large enough army to the eastern front.

In September 1941, the Germans laid siege to Leningrad. Penned inside their city with an ever-dwindling supply of food, all the Russians could do was tighten their belts and wait and hope for rescue. By the time the siege was lifted in 1944, more than one million Russian civilians had died of starvation and related illnesses. The Soviets would retaliate for this when they marched into Berlin in 1945.

In the summer of 1942, the industrial city of Stalingrad on the Volga River became a major battleground. The Germans nearly secured a victory, but the Soviets refused to give up, eventually winning the battle in January 1943.

North Africa and the Italian Front

In 1941, Japan took a hand in the game by bombing the U.S. naval base at Pearl Harbor in a surprise, unannounced attack. The United States immediately declared war on Japan. Honoring an agreement signed with Japan in 1940, Hitler then declared war on the United States. He seriously underestimated the efficiency of the American response and the speed with which the Americans would come to the rescue of their European allies.

When the Americans arrived in Europe, they planned with Allied leaders to begin their attack in the Mediterranean. Under the overall command of U.S. General Dwight D. Eisenhower, the Allies invaded North Africa in November 1942. British forces under General Montgomery pursued German forces lead by General Erwin Johannes Rommel. Despite Rommel's great skill and tactical ability, his forces were outnumbered and he lost ground at the Battle of El Alamein. The Allies soon controlled North Africa and blocked supply lines between Italy and Germany. In May 1943, the Allies forced the surrender of Axis troops in Tunisia, their last African stronghold. The combinations of the Soviet and North African victories turned the tide of war in the Allies' favor.

With North Africa under their control, the Allies invaded Sicily in July 1943, using it as a base from which to plan their attack on the Italian mainland. Italy gave way promptly. Many Italians had come to despise the Fascists, and the nation as a whole felt little loyalty to Mussolini by this time.

The king of Italy had Mussolini arrested and replaced him with a new prime minister. In September, the Germans rescued Mussolini and helped him establish a new Fascist power base in northern Italy. Meanwhile, the new Italian government signed an armistice with the Allies. Allied forces, including Italian troops, liberated Naples in October 1943 and Rome in June 1944. By then, Italian rebels had located Mussolini and executed him.

The Western Front

The Allies bombed Germany throughout 1943. The goal of the bombing was twofold: first, to destroy strategic locations such as railroad lines and factories, and second, to break the spirit of the German people by destroying their civilization, just as the Germans had tried to do against Britain. Allied bombs killed tens of thousands of German civilians and reduced virtually every large German city to rubble. The Allied bombing of the ancient and beautiful city of Dresden later became a byword for senseless, vicious destruction far beyond what was necessary in strategic terms.

The navies carried on the Battle of the Atlantic. Until 1943, German U-boats held the upper hand, attacking Allied ships with great success. The tide turned when the Allies developed sonar technology that helped them pinpoint the U-boats' locations, invisible far below the surface. By 1944 the Allies had regained control over the oceans.

The Allies agreed that the war would be won or lost on the western front. The United States and Britain combined forces to launch a surprise offensive in Normandy, on the French side of the English Channel. Working with Allied military staff, Eisenhower laid a trail of misinformation and false clues that led the Germans to expect an invasion at Calais, some distance away.

On D-Day, June 6, 1944, 150,000 Allied troops crossed the English Channel, landed on the beaches of France, and began marching toward Paris. No German troops were there to stop them; Eisenhower's deception had fooled Hitler. On August 25, 1944, the Allies liberated Paris.

After the shock of losing the French capital, the Germans launched a fierce assault on the Allied troops in the Ardennes region. They pushed Allied troops so far back at one location that they nearly broke through the line of defense, forming a "bulge" in the front line and thus giving the Battle of the Bulge its name. The Allies, outnumbered by nearly two to one, held out until reinforcements arrived and helped them push the Germans back. By January, it was clear that the Germans had lost any chance at victory.

In February 1945, Churchill, Roosevelt, and Stalin met at Yalta to plan for the peace they knew lay in the near future. Stalin promised that after Germany surrendered, Soviet troops would help the United States defeat Japan. (The Soviets made good on this promise; Japan surrendered in September 1945.) The three leaders then agreed to occupy Germany after the war, and discussed plans for a new League of Nations.

The End of the War

In 1945, Soviet troops were marching westward toward Berlin, while Allied troops approached it from the southeast. In April, the Soviets were the first to march into Hitler's capital city, where they took brutal revenge on the people. Unable to face the loss of his power, or to contemplate the punishment and public humiliation he would undergo as the loser of the war, Hitler committed suicide on April 30. Germany surrendered a week later, ending the war in Europe.

As the British and American troops marched eastward, liberating Austria and Poland, they discovered the concentration camps where millions of Jews and other "non-Aryans" of central and eastern Europe, notably the migratory Sinti and Romany peoples, had been rounded up for slaughter in a deliberate massacre of innocents known to history as the Holocaust.

Since the camps were in their own backyards, and since their own friends and neighbors had been dragged away and imprisoned in them, a fair number of Europeans, especially Germans and Poles who lived nearby, were more or less aware of the camps and their significance. Across Europe, many courageous individuals helped to hide their Jewish friends or aid them in other ways. However, no nation made any official attempt to put a stop to what was happening. Historians continue to debate the leaders' reasons, with explanations ranging from deep-seated racism to the belief that the survival of Europe as a whole was a more urgent priority than protecting the inmates of the camps.

The Allied troops, particularly the Americans, were unprepared for what they found when they liberated the camps. The prisoners had been shorn of their hair and starved to two-thirds or one-half their normal body weight; registration numbers were tattooed on their arms; exhaustion and disease had robbed them of all their vitality. There was large-scale cremation equipment at some camps, and massive common graves at all of them. There were huge, neatly sorted piles of human hair, gold dental fillings, eyeglasses, clothing, and shoes. Almost all the camp guards had committed suicide or fled in terror of the approaching Allied armies.

World War II 1939-1945

Results of the War

The Allied forces had crushed the German attempt to conquer Europe. The Nazi Party was disbanded and discredited; many of its key figures killed themselves or fled to South America. A number of the rest were tried as war criminals. Germany lost all the territory it had conquered during the war.

Europe's population was devastated by the war. The Soviet Union was the hardest hit of all, with 9 million soldiers and 19 million civilians dead. The total deaths for all other European nations combined were about 5 million soldiers and about 7 million civilians, including the refugees of all nations who died of starvation, disease, or stray bullets. Approximately 6 million Jews, Sinti, and Romany were massacred in the Nazi concentration camps. Thousands more Europeans were lucky enough to emigrate overseas before or during the war; most would never return.

Not only people but whole cities were casualties of the war. Much of central Europe lay in ruins. Germany was utterly destroyed by Allied bombs. The beautiful cities of Berlin and Vienna were unrecognizable, nothing but smoking heaps of loose bricks, chunks of concrete, and wrecked hulks of buildings. Cities and villages across Italy and Poland had been reduced to piles of stones. Transportation systems across the continent were wrecked. Everyday necessities such as fresh water, fuel, electricity, and food were unavailable. Sanitation was impossible in bombed-out cities. Governments were in disarray or had been removed from power.

The war ended a long era of European domination of the globe. For the next fifty years, only two nations dominated world affairs: the United States and the Soviet Union. The tremendous power the Soviet Union would soon wield was not immediately apparent at the end of World War II; the case was quite otherwise with the United States. The United States emerged strong from the war for three reasons. First, the munitions industry had completely reinvigorated the American economy. Second, American casualties had been very low compared to European losses. Third, the war had had only a minimal impact on American civilians, since apart from the one bombing attack on Pearl Harbor, they were far removed from the combat zones.

The leaders meeting in Potsdam for the peace conference had an enormous rebuilding task before them.

Provisions of the Potsdam Conference

- Austria and Germany would each be divided into four zones of occupation: Soviet, British, U.S., and French.
- The capital cities of Vienna and Berlin would be divided into four zones of occupation, as above.
- The Allies would help to rebuild German industry and reestablish local German governments.

- German refugees would be helped to return to their homes.
- Poland would retain German territory it had taken during the war.
- Germany would pay reparations to all Allied nations, with the Soviet Union taking the largest share as the greatest sufferer.

The leaders at Potsdam were outwardly civil but inwardly distrustful of one another. Stalin did not want the United States imposing a capitalist economy on Germany. In addition, he deeply resented the fact that the Allies had waited until 1944 to invade Normandy, while Soviet soldiers were fighting desperately in the east. On his side, U.S. President Harry Truman did not want the Soviets to gain too much control over Poland and Eastern Europe. These mutual suspicions grew as time went on. Before long, they led the world into the Cold War.

The United Nations

The League of Nations had failed to prevent World War II. National leaders agreed that they needed to design a new, stronger peacekeeping organization. Delegates from the United States, China, the Soviet Union, and Britain wrote a proposal for an organization to be called the United Nations. Delegates from fifty nations then met to discuss the proposal and write a UN charter. It established a General Assembly in which all member nations would have an equal voice, and a fifteen-member Security Council. Ten of the fifteen seats on the Security Council would rotate among nations; the other five would be permanently held by Britain, China, France, the Soviet Union, and the United States.

QUIZ

1. **Stalin joined the Allied nations in 1941 because**
   A. Germany invaded Poland.
   B. Germany reneged on the nonaggression pact.
   C. the United States entered the war.
   D. Italy entered the war.

2. **Why did the Germans fail to prevent the Allied invasion at Normandy in 1944?**
   A. They did not believe the Allies intended to invade France.
   B. They were concentrating on winning the war at sea.
   C. They already knew that they would lose the war.
   D. They expected the Allies to invade at a different location.

3. **Which European nation suffered by far the heaviest losses in the war?**
   A. Austria
   B. Germany
   C. Poland
   D. Soviet Union

4. **Which nation changed sides in the war once it was liberated?**
   A. Austria
   B. Britain
   C. France
   D. Italy

5. **Which best sums up Germany's main foreign-policy goal at the beginning of the war?**
   A. to annex other central European nations
   B. to conquer Britain and France
   C. to subjugate all of Europe
   D. to divide Poland with the USSR

6. **When the Americans arrived in Europe, they began a concerted war effort**
   A. on the eastern front.
   B. on the western front.
   C. in North Africa.
   D. in the Balkans.

7. **What eventually became of Benito Mussolini?**
   A. He surrendered to the Allies.
   B. He escaped to South America.
   C. He was executed by Italian rebels.
   D. He committed suicide when Italy was liberated.

8. **The Danzig Corridor was strategically important because**
   A. it provided an overland route from central Europe to a major Baltic port.
   B. it had once been controlled by the Russian Empire.
   C. it was a demilitarized buffer zone between Austria and Poland.
   D. it was the heart of the Polish coal reserves.

9. **When Germany invaded France, the British army _____**
   A. asked for an armistice.
   B. began bombing Germany.
   C. attacked the German troops.
   D. retreated to Britain.

10. **What was the immediate effect of Germany's invasion of Poland?**
    A. The United States declared war on Germany.
    B. Britain and France declared war on Germany.
    C. The Soviet Union abandoned the nonaggression pact.
    D. The Soviet Union joined the Allies against Germany.

chapter 19

The Cold War, 1945–1968

World War II was over, but it did not bring peace to the world. It ushered in a new era of conflict, known as the Cold War, that would last for forty-five years. The conflict was called a "cold" war because the opponents—the United States and the Soviet Union—did not actually fire shots at one another. Instead, they maintained a hostile standoff.

The Soviet Union was the only European nation to emerge from the destruction of World War II as a superpower. By 1949, it had begun to manufacture and stockpile nuclear weapons in order to keep pace with the world's only other superpower, the United States. With their antithetical political systems and economic policies, the United States and the Soviet Union were natural enemies; throughout the Cold War, each tried to contain the other's sphere of influence. However, the development of nuclear weapons in the 1940s meant that both sides had to move very carefully; neither was willing to risk a nuclear holocaust that would literally destroy the world.

The former Great Powers of Europe played only secondary roles during the Cold War. The two devastating world wars had ended their era of supremacy. While the Western nations concentrated on restabilizing their societies and economies, the Eastern nations—those behind what Winston Churchill described as the "Iron Curtain" of communism—learned to survive under regulated economies and governments that were imposed on them from above.

From the Asian point of view, the term *cold war* is a misnomer. When civil wars erupted in Korea and Vietnam, the Soviets backed one side and the United States the other. Hundreds of thousands of civilians and soldiers died during the Korean and Vietnam wars, and neither outcome made much difference to the overall Cold War.

CHAPTER 19 OBJECTIVES

- Define the term *Cold War* and identify the nations on each side of the conflict.
- Identify the international treaties of the era and the member nations.
- Compare and contrast Eastern and Western Europe after World War II.
- Discuss the international conflicts that arose during the Cold War.

Chapter 19 Time Line

- **1945**   United Nations founded
- **1946**   Winston Churchill gives "Iron Curtain" speech; Allies divide Korea into two zones
- **1948**   Marshall Plan goes into effect
- **1949**   North Atlantic Treaty Organization (NATO) founded
- **1950**   Korean War begins
- **1955**   Warsaw Pact signed
- **1956**   Hungarian uprising
- **1960**   Vietnam War begins
- **1961**   East Germans put up Berlin Wall
- **1962**   Cuban Missile Crisis
- **1968**   Prague Spring

The Cold War in Eastern Europe

In 1946, Winston Churchill made an important speech on the current state of world affairs. He spoke the following memorable sentences:

> From Stettin in the Baltic to Trieste in the Adriatic, an iron curtain has descended across the Continent. Behind that line lie all the capitals of the ancient states of Central and Eastern Europe. Warsaw, Berlin, Prague, Vienna, Budapest, Belgrade, Bucharest and Sofia, all these famous cities and the populations around them lie in what I must call the Soviet sphere, and all are subject in one form or another not only to Soviet influence but to a very high and, in many cases, increasing measure of control from Moscow.

Between about 1944 and 1947, Churchill's analysis was proved correct. Every Eastern European nation except Greece either established a Communist state (usually called a "people's republic") or was absorbed into the Soviet Union. Being a member of the Comintern meant answering to the absolute authority of the Soviet dictator; therefore all the Eastern European nations were now Soviet satellites, just as Churchill had described. One-party rule under an absolute dictator was the most common form of government behind the Iron Curtain.

Stalin claimed that the USSR needed these allies as a safety zone between itself and the West for its own security. Germany had twice invaded Russia and inflicted tremendous damage and loss of life; Stalin was determined to prevent any further overland attacks. Additionally, from the Communist point of view, capitalist nations were inherently enemies.

Czechoslovakia

After World War I, Eduard Beneš and Thomas Masaryk had made Czechoslovakia a democratic republic—a multinational state dominated by the Czechs. Subdued by the Nazi regime during World War II, the nation was reestablished in 1945 as an independent socialist state under President Beneš. In 1948, the Communist Party managed to shoulder Beneš aside, replacing him with Communist Klement Gottwald. Czechoslovakia struggled under an oppressive dictatorship until 1968, when Alexander Dubcek took power. Although a

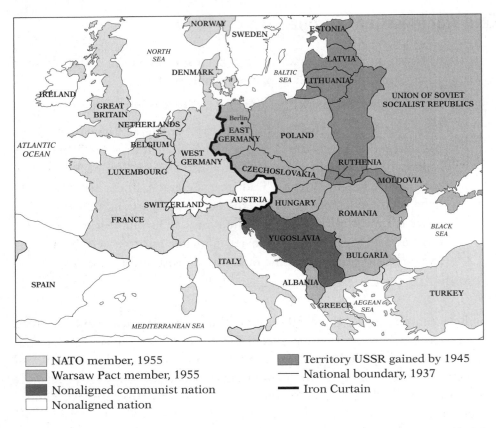

NATO member, 1955
Warsaw Pact member, 1955
Nonaligned communist nation
Nonaligned nation

Territory USSR gained by 1945
— National boundary, 1937
— Iron Curtain

Party member, he was a moderate who immediately brought about meaningful reform, such as the abolition of censorship and the granting of real legislative powers to the National Assembly. This brief period of reform is known as the Prague Spring. The Soviets, furious at this apparent defection from the Communist bloc, sent troops into the country to replace Dubcek and restore the status quo.

Hungary

The Soviets drove the Nazis out of Hungary in 1944. In 1947, Stalinist dictator Matias Rakosi took power. Moderate Imre Nagy replaced Rakosi in 1953, but was forced out of office when he tried to introduce economic reform. Nagy headed a successful popular uprising in 1956, formed a new government, and instituted widespread reform. A brief era of freedom was put down by a Soviet military invasion in November; the Soviets executed Nagy and replaced him with their own candidate, János Kádár.

Poland

After the 1939 German-Soviet invasion, the Polish government fled the country, eventually making its way to London. The Soviets installed a puppet regime of their own in Lublin in 1944. At Yalta, Stalin made two demands concerning Poland. First, the Soviet Union should receive a large swath of territory in eastern Poland. Second, the Allies should recognize the Lublin regime as the official Polish government. In return for losing territory on the eastern border, Poland gained German-controlled territory in the west.

The first postwar Polish elections were held in 1947, bringing one-party Communist rule to the nation. This marked the beginning of a long period of political and social unrest in Poland.

Yugoslavia

The state of Yugoslavia was highly unstable even before World War II broke out; like the former Austro-Hungarian Empire, it contained too many ethnic groups who would only be satisfied by self-determination. The Croats hated and resented the ruling Serbs so much that they actually regarded the invading German army as liberators. Yugoslavs soon found themselves divided into two warring factions. The Chetniks were Serbian and royalist; the Partisans included Communists, anti-Nazis, and a variety of Yugoslavs who wanted self-rule. In 1945, the Allies agreed to support the leader of the Partisans, the Communist Josip Broz, who had called himself Tito since his release from prison for political protest in 1933.

Although Tito ruled as a Communist dictator, he refused to recognize Soviet authority over Yugoslavia. When he expelled the occupying Russian military forces in 1948, the Comintern revoked his Party membership.

Germany

At Potsdam, the Allies agreed to occupy Germany. There were several reasons for the occupation. First, they wanted to purge Germany of Nazism and punish any surviving Nazis. Second, they intended to help the Germans set up a new, democratic government. Third, they would work with the Germans to install a new bureaucracy, including a police force. Fourth, they would work to reestablish society and the German economy, including everything from the school systems to the postal service to the transportation network.

The Soviets occupied the eastern half of Berlin; the western half was divided among American-, British-, and French-occupied zones. Before long, the three

Western powers united their zones into one for economic purposes; Stalin's refusal to go along with their plan effectively made Berlin into two cities.

Since Berlin was many miles behind the Iron Curtain, West Berlin was entirely isolated and geographically very vulnerable to threats from the Soviets. In 1948, the Soviets blocked all ground access to West Berlin, claiming they had the right to do as they saw fit with East German roads, bridges, and railways. This was in effect an attempt at a siege; if supplies could not be delivered, the city would be forced to capitulate to Soviet control. The United States immediately organized the Berlin Airlift, which brought in food, fuel, and other supplies by plane. It took a good many flights to supply an entire city; on some days American planes landed in West Berlin every few minutes. In 1949, the Soviets accepted defeat and ended the blockade. Soon after this, West Germany officially parted from East Germany. At that point the two nations became known as the Federal Republic of Germany (West), a parliamentary democracy headed by Chancellor Konrad Adenauer, and the German Democratic Republic (East), a one-party Communist state headed by Chancellor Walter Ulbricht.

During the 1950s, hundreds of thousands of East Germans sought economic opportunity, intellectual and artistic freedom, and political asylum by the simple means of walking across the border into West Berlin, then relocating to West Germany or another western nation. By 1961, nearly 20 percent of the East German population had defected. The East Germans and the Soviets were well aware of this and knew that it was the worst possible publicity for their system. They were especially concerned because the people most likely to escape to the West were intellectuals, artists, professors, scientists, and other valuable and highly trained professionals. They took drastic measures to stop the flow of emigration. One August morning in 1961, Berliners woke up to discover that during the night, the army had secretly begun construction of a physical barrier that entirely encircled West Berlin—a barbed-wire fence that would soon be replaced by a massive concrete wall, complete with armed guards and dogs.

The Berlin Wall stopped the free westward migration. From that time on, East Germans had to have special permits to cross the wall and could only stay in the West for very limited periods of time. Travel from West to East was still unrestricted, but West Berliners had to be sure to carry identification so the guards would allow them to return home. In the Berlin metro system, the border between the two halves of the city became the last stop on all westbound trains. Many people still found ways to escape. Some hid in the trunks of cars; some clung to the undercarriage of trains; some openly made a run for it. Some escapes were successful; others ended in death. The Berlin Wall soon became the most recognizable symbol of the Cold War era. In June 1963, U.S. President John F. Kennedy gave a memorable speech on the western side of the wall, in which he summed up the basic flaw in the Communist system thus: "Freedom has many difficulties and democracy is not perfect, but we have never had to put a wall up to keep our people in—to prevent them from leaving us."

International Organizations

Since the Communist and non-Communist members of the United Nations were mutually hostile and distrustful, many heads of state felt that they would do well to form smaller international unions for their mutual protection. Two such organizations were formed; members agreed that if any nation were attacked, all the others would come to its defense.

Organization	Date Formed	Members
North Atlantic Treaty Organization (NATO)	1947	Canada
		Belgium
		Britain
		Denmark
		France
		*Greece
		Iceland
		Luxembourg
		Netherlands
		Norway
		Portugal
		*Turkey
		United States
		*West Germany
Warsaw Pact	1955	Albania
		Bulgaria
		Czechoslovakia
		East Germany
		Hungary
		Poland
		Romania
		Soviet Union
* nation that joined NATO after 1947		

Rebuilding Europe

When Communist forces took over Czechoslovakia in 1948, the U.S. Congress realized the seriousness of the Soviet threat to European democracy. They voted for full funding of the European Recovery Program, universally known as the Marshall Plan.

General George C. Marshall, the American secretary of state and former army chief of staff, created a foreign-aid plan by which the United States would provide almost unlimited funding for the necessary repairs to Europe's cities, highways, and railways. Any European nation that requested such aid would receive it. In the end, the Marshall Plan provided $13 billion to war-torn Europe as an outright gift, not a loan. Although the economies of Europe were already achieving near-miracles of recovery by their own efforts, Marshall Plan funds played a crucial role in rebuilding—but only in the West. Stalin, who regarded the Marshall Plan as a blatant American attempt to subjugate Western Europe, would not allow any nation behind the Iron Curtain to accept American aid.

Thanks to their people's superhuman efforts plus the boost provided by the Marshall Plan, Western European nations returned to normal much faster than anyone would have expected on seeing the destruction wrought by the war. Infrastructure was rebuilt, theaters reopened, people went back to work. Many difficulties, including food shortages and rationing, still existed for some time after the war, but governments took what steps they could to bring their nations back to prosperity.

Behind the Iron Curtain, conditions were quite different. Although one benefit of Communist rule was full employment, jobs were assigned without regard to individual preference and wages were low. Housing was overcrowded—an entire family sharing a one-room apartment without a private kitchen or bathroom was typical in any Russian city. In addition, there were constant shortages of necessities, and luxury goods were a thing of the past. Behind the Iron Curtain, there was never any guarantee that shops would have anything to sell. When people heard that a market had just received a truckload of, say, fresh eggs, a long line of customers would appear as if by magic at that market, because it might be the last chance for eggs for a month or more. People carried shopping bags called "perhaps-bags" everywhere they went, just in case—perhaps—there might be something to buy and carry home. Barter, rather than cash purchases, became common. Luxuries were completely out of reach. The state owned and ran all businesses and industries, so no one had any personal pride or vested interest in doing a good job or seeing his or her business succeed.

Cold War Conflicts

Until 1949, the United States was the only nation that had the technology to make nuclear weapons. However, Soviet scientists, following the same research path as the Western scientists, had their own bomb by 1949. A nuclear arms race ensued. By 1960 the United States had about five times as many nuclear weapons as the Soviets. Nuclear weapons were enormously expensive, and during the 1950s the U.S. economy was thriving.

The possession of nuclear weapons made both superpowers very cautious. The United States had dropped nuclear bombs on Japan in 1945, so the world knew exactly how destructive such weapons were. Neither side in the Cold War wanted to cause a nuclear holocaust. However, they played key roles in two conventional wars and arrived at one dangerous standoff.

Korean War

Japan occupied Korea during World War II. During the war, the Soviet Union had fostered a Korean Communist Party within the USSR. In 1945, the victorious Allied leaders agreed to divide Korea geographically. The Soviets occupied industrial North Korea, which was proclaimed the Korean Democratic People's Republic under chairman Kim Il Sung in 1948. The Americans occupied agricultural South Korea, withdrawing in 1949 after the election of Syngman Rhee as president of the Republic of Korea. North Korea invaded South Korea in 1950 with the goal of uniting the nation under Communist rule. U.S. troops fought on the side of South Korea, while Communist China sent troops to aid the North Koreans. Fighting ended with a 1953 truce that left matters where they were in 1950—with two independent Koreas, one Communist, one democratic.

Cuban Missile Crisis

The closest the world came to nuclear war was an event known as the Cuban Missile Crisis. In 1959, rebel leader Fidel Castro seized power in Cuba, turning the country into a Communist dictatorship. The presence of a Communist nation—a Soviet ally—only ninety miles from the Florida coast was a grave concern to the Americans. A botched American attempt to remove Castro from power increased Cold War hostility between the superpowers.

Soviet premier Nikita Khrushchev, meeting U.S. President John F. Kennedy face to face at a European summit, came away mistaking Kennedy's youth and inexperience for weakness. Believing the United States would be easy to intimidate, Khrushchev began building up nuclear arms in Cuba. As soon as the United States learned of the presence of the missiles, it established a naval blockade of the island. Both sides prepared for battle, but at the last moment the Soviet ships turned back. Khrushchev offered Kennedy an exchange: if the United States would withdraw its nuclear missiles from its European bases, the USSR would do the same with the Cuban missiles. Nuclear war had been avoided and from that time forward, both sides worked slowly and cautiously toward achieving what later became know as *détente*, loosely translated as "peaceful coexistence."

Vietnam War

France controlled what it called Indochina—Vietnam, Laos, and Cambodia— from 1883 to 1945. (See Chapter 14.) Japan occupied Indochina during World War II. When the Japanese withdrew, rebel leader Ho Chi Minh declared Vietnamese independence. The United States backed France's refusal to grant independence for two reasons: first, Ho was a Communist; second, the United States felt obliged to support France because they were longtime allies.

The United States poured money into the French effort to regain control over Indochina, while Communist China aided the Vietminh. The guerilla tactics of the Vietminh were very effective against a French fighting force that was unfamiliar with the Vietnamese jungles. At Dien Bien Phu in northern Vietnam, the Vietminh outnumbered and trapped the French. President Eisenhower was unwilling to send American troops to Vietnam. Unable to win without reinforcements, the French surrendered to Ho's troops on May 7, 1954.

France, Britain, the United States, the USSR, China, Vietnam, Cambodia, and Laos all met for a peace conference in Geneva. The conference ended in a stalemate, dividing Vietnam into a northern half ruled by Ho and the Vietminh and a southern half ruled by France. The representatives agreed that in 1956, the two Vietnams would hold general elections and reunite under one government.

With American backing, government official Ngo Dinh Diem became president of South Vietnam. Widely and deservedly unpopular, Diem refused to hold the agreed-on elections for fear of losing. Meanwhile, the Vietminh began sending weapons to their fellows in the South, who would become known as the Vietcong.

Fighting between the Vietcong and North Vietnamese troops on one side and American and South Vietnamese troops on the other side dragged on from the early 1960s through 1975. French troops had abandoned the area in 1956, as agreed at the peace conference. The Americans held out until the end, finally acknowledging in 1975 that they had reached an impasse. The war ended in a victory for the Communist North, who were quick to unite the two halves of the country under one rule.

QUIZ

1. **The Marshall Plan offered aid to**
   A. all the nations of Europe.
   B. all nations behind the Iron Curtain.
   C. all nations that had fought for the Allies during the war.
   D. all nations west of the Iron Curtain.

2. **What was the purpose of the Berlin Airlift?**
   A. to get supplies to West Berlin in spite of the blockade
   B. to help people escape from East Berlin or East Germany
   C. to return German refugees to their homes after the war
   D. to provide aid to any Iron Curtain nation

3. **One important reason for the Allied occupation of Germany was**
   A. to help Germany rearm.
   B. to discuss plans for the United Nations.
   C. to obliterate all surviving elements of Nazism.
   D. to divide the country into two independent nations.

4. **The Berlin Wall was built in order to**
   A. prevent Westerners from entering East Berlin.
   B. prevent East Germans from entering West Berlin.
   C. block Allied or Western access to West Berlin.
   D. prevent violence from breaking out in Berlin.

5. At the end of the civil war in Vietnam, the North and South were united under _____
   A. a constitutional monarchy.
   B. a democratic republic.
   C. a Communist dictatorship.
   D. a hereditary monarchy.

6. _____ was one advantage of life under Communist rule.
   A. Freedom of expression
   B. Comfortable housing
   C. High wages
   D. Full employment

7. Which of the following best describes the result of the Korean War?
   A. a victory for Communist North Korea
   B. a victory for democratic South Korea
   C. a stalemate
   D. anarchy

8. Recent memories of _____ persuaded Stalin to maintain a safety zone of friendly states on the western border of the USSR.
   A. czarist rule
   B. international peace treaties
   C. nuclear bombings
   D. German invasions

9. _____ was the only Eastern European Communist nation to avoid Soviet domination.
   A. Czechoslovakia
   B. East Germany
   C. Poland
   D. Yugoslavia

10. _____ rebelled against the forces of communism by emigrating westward.
    A. Czechoslovakians
    B. East Germans
    C. Soviets
    D. Yugoslavians

chapter 20

The Fall of Communism, 1945–1989

Between 1989 and 1991, several key events signaled the end of the Cold War. First, Communist dictatorships collapsed throughout Eastern Europe. Second, the Berlin Wall fell and East and West Germany were reunited. Third, the Soviet Union broke up.

To many people, it had appeared as though the Cold War would drag on permanently. When it ended, it did so abruptly and rapidly and with almost no bloodshed (the disastrous civil war in Yugoslavia was not the result of Cold War issues). The swiftness of the change happened for a variety of reasons: peace and prosperity in the West, the unifying factor of the destruction of World War II, and the persistent underground resistance to communism behind the Iron Curtain throughout the Cold War.

Economically, the West had prospered during the Cold War years. Those in the East were well aware that their own governments prevented them from enjoying much of a share in the postwar boom. The Communists always insisted that workers in the capitalist nations were oppressed and unhappy, but Eastern Europeans knew that Westerners enjoyed higher wages and a higher standard of living than they did.

World War II had been enormously destructive, but Europeans managed to create positive effects from the destruction. It created a genuine spirit of cooperation among Western nations, including the United States. With all nations working busily to rebuild and repair, employment was high and the atmosphere was one of courage and hope. Eastern nations also had to repair and rebuild, but without the freedom to choose their own employment, to form trade unions, or to install the latest technology, they felt less of a personal stake in the outcome. The atmosphere was one of stagnation and resignation.

The basic philosophy behind communism is that each person should contribute what he or she can to society and the economy and take as much as he or she needs. Most would agree that such an idea is compassionate, generous, and fair. Unfortunately, communism in practice did not reflect its philosophy. It meant censorship and oppression. When people are not permitted to say what they think, to write what they please, to travel where they wish, or to describe accurately the conditions they live in, they are not free. The history of modern Europe shows a constant progress toward freedom—the human freedom to live as a reasonable being with the right to make one's own basic choices. Communism was intolerable to many precisely because it refused to allow such freedom. Throughout the Cold War, many Eastern Europeans resisted it—some vocally, some silently, but all consistently. Individuals—sometimes prominent ones—defected to other nations. Writers smuggled their works out of the country for publication. Leaders led actual armed revolutions. Workers fought for their rights to bargain for higher wages and safer conditions. Without courageous resistance from within, the Communist governments of the East would never have fallen so rapidly.

CHAPTER 20 OBJECTIVES

- Describe the important events that marked the end of the Cold War.
- Describe the course of events in the Soviet Union after the death of Stalin.
- Explain the purpose of the European Union.

Chapter 20 Time Line

- **1953** Death of Stalin
- **1957** Treaty of Rome establishes EEC (later European Union)
- **1968** Prague Spring
- **1980** Formation of Solidarity in Poland
- **1985** Mikhail Gorbachev becomes head of Soviet Union
- **1989** Velvet Revolution in Czechoslovakia; Grosz lifts Iron Curtain in Hungary; Berlin Wall falls; Communist governments throughout Eastern Europe fall
- **1990** East and West Germany are reunited; civil war begins in Yugoslavia
- **1991** Soviet Union is dissolved; Commonwealth of Independent States is established

Soviet Leadership After Stalin

The major turning point in the rise and fall of the Soviet Union took place in 1953, with the death of seventy-four-year-old Joseph Stalin. His successors would never impress their personalities on the nation as he had done. They lacked both his personal brutality and his insistence on personal control over every aspect of Soviet life as well as Soviet government.

In terms of the rivalry with the United States, Stalin had followed a policy of bluffing. He deceived the United States and the world into believing the USSR was much stronger militarily than was in fact the case. In truth, so many millions of Soviets had been killed during the wars, and the western region of the country had been so badly damaged by the German invasions, that the USSR would take a long time to recover. Stalin created an atmosphere of secrecy and mystery that was highly successful in maintaining the illusion of the Soviet state as a mighty superpower. The purpose of his bluff was mainly defensive; he wanted at all costs to prevent any American attack on the USSR. In fact, there was never any real danger of such an attack. The United States had no desire to engage in all-out war with the Soviet Union unless such a situation absolutely could not be avoided. Stalin, however, always believed that capitalist nations were his natural enemies and that they would crush the Soviet Union if they could.

A gradual thaw in Soviet foreign and domestic policy followed Stalin's death. Nikita Khrushchev, his successor, clearly showed the course of the future when he gave a 1956 speech denouncing Stalin's crimes against humanity. From this time on, the cult of personality that Stalin had cultivated began to fade; he was no longer officially venerated in the USSR. This "de-Stalinization" process helped lead to the Hungarian revolution of 1956 (see Chapter 19).

Khrushchev also oversaw substantial domestic reforms. Although he could not have predicted the breakup of the Soviet Union that would come later, he helped lay the groundwork for it by decentralizing the bureaucracy of the state, shifting authority from Moscow to the fifteen individual republics. He also relaxed censorship in the arts, although he did not by any means eliminate it. New agricultural policies led to a short-term economic surge. In addition, Khrushchev presided over the space race, in which Soviet astronaut Yuri Gagarin became the first person to orbit the Earth.

In 1964, Party leaders forced Khrushchev to resign from his post. A downturn in the economy, plus long-standing discontent with some of his policies, had made him unpopular among the leadership. His successor, Leonid Brezhnev, is most notable for signing the Strategic Arms Limitation Talks (SALT) Treaty with U.S. President Richard Nixon. This treaty limited the number of intercontinental nuclear missiles for both nations. In addition, the two leaders discussed relaxing trade restrictions between their countries.

The milder political climate under Stalin's successors gave rise to some degree of political protest within the Soviet Union. Soviet workers were well aware that while they were badly housed, poorly paid, and had little access to consumer goods or even much choice in basic items like groceries, the Party elite lived in comparative luxury. Since everyone in a Communist state is supposed to be treated equally, this had long caused resentment. That resentment began to find public expression under Khrushchev and those who succeeded him. Soviets were no longer content to accept the high degree of inequality, nor the censorship that was an international embarrassment to a nation that had always prided itself on its great artists. For example, Boris Pasternak, an acclaimed poet and the author of the novel *Dr. Zhivago*, was ordered to refuse the 1958 Nobel Prize for literature, and Alexander Solzhenitsyn was deprived of his Soviet citizenship because he wrote honestly about the gulags (the notorious Soviet prison camps).

The Gorbachev Era

In 1985, Mikhail Gorbachev became the head of the Soviet Union. Born in 1931 to a peasant family in the North Caucasus region, Gorbachev was well aware that major political changes were necessary. Beginning around 1980, the United States had enormously increased military spending; the Soviet Union simply could not afford to keep up without ruining its own economy. To remedy the economic and social problems in the USSR, Gorbachev instituted *glasnost* (openness) and *perestroika* (a restructuring of the economy and society). *Glasnost* was intended to encourage open debate within the Soviet Union. Gorbachev believed that the economic and social problems the country faced demanded input from all segments of society, not just Party members. He relaxed censorship and instituted policies that encouraged writers and intellectuals to speak out about society's problems and suggest their own solutions.

Perestroika called for increases in foreign trade and reductions on military spending. During a 1987 meeting with U.S. President Ronald Reagan, Gorbachev signed the Intermediate-Range Nuclear Forces Treaty, eliminating all medium-range nuclear missiles from Europe. This made Gorbachev very unpopular with the Soviet military, who were convinced it made the USSR vulnerable to attack.

In 1988, Gorbachev thoroughly reorganized the Soviet government. He called for a Congress of People's Deputies, whose members would then elect the Supreme Soviet (the federal legislative assembly). Under Gorbachev's predecessors the Supreme Soviet had simply served as a rubber stamp for the Party; from now on it would function as a powerful lawmaking body. Deputies for the Congress represented all segments of society and government: one-third represented the interests of the many nationalities within the USSR, one-third were freely elected on a geographical basis, and one-third were directly nominated by major institutions such as the Orthodox Church, the trade unions, and the Communist Party. The new Supreme Soviet was bicameral and would meet twice a year for three- or four-month sessions. The era of one-party rule in the Soviet Union was over. Non-Communists were allowed to run for office at the national, republic, and local levels in 1989.

In July 1988, due to a severe economic slump and his own awareness of the changed atmosphere in Eastern Europe, Gorbachev announced that the Soviet Union would withdraw from any interference in the self-government of other nations. Eastern Europe would have to take care of itself from now on; the

Soviet Union could no longer afford to control and monitor nations outside its own borders.

The Cold War Ends in Europe

To the Western world, communism appeared to collapse almost all at once. In fact, there were different degrees of communism in the Eastern European nations. In some nations the level of authority was much harsher than others, and some began an active fight against communism sooner than others. By 1990, all the Communist governments of Eastern Europe had fallen.

Poland

In 1978, Karol Cardinal Wojtyla of Poland became Pope John Paul II—the first non-Italian to hold the Church's highest office since the early 1500s. In the wake of his election, Poland became the focus of a great deal of international attention. This played a significant role in bringing about political reform.

Beginning in 1980, soaring prices led Polish laborers to stage a series of strikes and to demand the right to form trade unions. The Polish government gave in to the workers' demands in September, and the workers formed Solidarity, a national council to coordinate independent trade unions. Solidarity members created a list of demands that made it clear they wanted real reform, not just higher wages: a union's right to strike, freedom for dissenters being held in prison, and the lifting of censorship. Dock worker Lech Walesa, who headed Solidarity, would later become the president of a democratic Poland.

The Polish government was naturally hostile to Solidarity, which had made itself a national political party rather than just a labor organization. Despite an outright 1981 ban on Solidarity, the political tide had turned in Poland. By 1989 the government was forced to legalize Solidarity once again, and the party swept the elections held that year. Combined with Gorbachev's public withdrawal of Soviet influence in Iron Curtain nations, the Communist Party in Poland was thrust aside for good.

Hungary

Although several years of Stalinist repression had followed the 1956 rebellion, Hungary had been gradually flexing its political muscles since the Soviet thaw of the early 1960s. In 1968, Hungary announced the New Economic

Mechanism, which moved state controls on the market and allowed for free enterprise. Karol Grosz, who took office in 1987, supported Gorbachev's policies of openness and greater political freedom. With the 1989 withdrawal of Soviet interference in Hungarian affairs, Grosz ordered the opening of the border between Hungary and Austria. This was the first official lifting of any part of the Iron Curtain, and it caused an immediate flood of Eastern European immigrants into Hungary and across the border.

Czechoslovakia

In the wake of Communist crackdowns meant to prevent the workers from uniting in imitation of Solidarity, popular demonstrations occurred in the streets of Prague and other cities in the fall of 1989. In a series of events known as the Velvet Revolution, the Communist premier Gustav Husak resigned and was replaced within the month by the democratically elected Vaclav Havel. Alexander Dubcek, the hero of the 1968 Prague Spring, became the head of the Czechoslovak Parliament. Longstanding ethnic hostility between Czechs and Slovaks caused the 1993 separation of Czechoslovakia into Slovakia (also called the Slovak Republic) and the Czech Republic.

East Germany

Perhaps the most emotional and dramatic moment of the entire Cold War came on November 9, 1989, when the Berlin Wall came tumbling down.

Gorbachev had visited East Berlin in October. As he watched the East German crowds during an outdoor ceremony, he was amazed to hear them calling to him by name, appealing for help against their leaders. This was all the more astounding as the crowd was made of handpicked Communist Party activists. Clearly, the days of Communist rule in East Germany were numbered. A police crackdown took place a few days after the demonstration, but the government realized it could not stem the tide of popular resistance any longer.

Travel restrictions were relaxed in early November, and on the evening of the ninth, one ill-prepared official, flustered by a reporter's question, announced that the new rules would "immediately" take effect at the border. East Berliners flooded to the wall checkpoints in such huge crowds that the guards could not hold them back. By midnight, young Germans were attacking the wall on both sides with sledgehammers and pickaxes, clambering to the top and pulling up their friends to dance and cheer alongside them. Berliners poured freely through the Brandenburg Gate in both directions for the first time since 1961. During the following weeks, border restrictions throughout Eastern Europe were removed, and easterners could freely travel to the West once again. In 1990, East and West Germany were officially and formally reunited under one government. After nearly fifty years, the Iron Curtain had come down.

Yugoslavia

Marshall Tito was a Communist, but he had such independent ideas that the Comintern actually expelled him from the Party. Tito governed Yugoslavia from 1945 until his death in 1980, managing to keep the mutually hostile forces of ethnic nationalism under control. In the great revolutionary year of 1989, however, civil war broke out, with Serbians wanting to dominate the power structure of the nation and Croatia, Macedonia, Slovenia, and Bosnia agitating for independence and self-determination. Fierce fighting among the various ethnic groups—Serbs against Croats, Bosnians against Serbs, Albanians against Serbs—continued through 1995. By 2008, Yugoslavia had broken into independent states—Slovenia, Croatia, Bosnia-Herzegovina, Serbia, Montenegro, and Macedonia.

The Breakup of the Soviet Union

The USSR had instigated the Cold War; fittingly, it was the last European nation to let go of Communist rule. In 1991, Party leaders attempted a coup against Gorbachev, who had been losing popularity due to a severe economic crisis and the Communist Party's dismay at the loss of influence in Europe. Additionally, the Baltic republics had been agitating for self-determination.

The actual coup attempt was inept and an embarrassing failure; however, it gave the western republics the opportunity to seize their independence. Gorbachev realized that he could no longer hold the Soviet Union together. In late 1991, all the Soviet republics became independent nation-states; all except Latvia, Lithuania, and Estonia formed an association known as the Commonwealth of Independent States (CIS). This association was intended as a successor to the USSR, which was officially dissolved on December 31. Members of the CIS are entirely independent, self-governing nations. The CIS unites them for purposes of security, economics, internal and external trade, and justice.

The European Union

The foundation of the European Union goes back to the 1957 Treaty of Rome. Astonishingly, this agreement was first set in motion by the two nations that had perhaps the deepest and longest-standing traditional enmity in Europe: France and (West) Germany. For the first time in centuries, the two largest and strongest nations of central Europe realized that they could accomplish much more as allies than they ever had as enemies.

The richest coal-producing region in central Europe lay on the Franco-German border. In 1950, France proposed to West Germany that an international organization be created to administer the region so that all of Europe could benefit from the coal. An immediate and enthusiastic agreement led eventually to the creation of what was then called the European Economic Community (EEC) and the European Atomic Energy Commission. In 1957, the EEC had six members: France, West Germany, Belgium, the Netherlands, Luxembourg, and Italy. In addition to overseeing coal production, the nations lifted tariffs among themselves, thus encouraging internal trade, and agreed to establish common tariffs for imports from non-EEC nations.

Soon other nations became eager to join the EEC and share its benefits. French concerns about possible American influence, and objections to certain British demands for special treatment, held up any expansion of membership until 1973. In 1991, the present-day European Union was founded, with fifteen member nations; between 2004 and 2007, membership was extended to almost all the nations of Eastern Europe.

Member nations of the EU are entirely separate and self-governing, but they share a common foreign and security policy and cooperate on domestic affairs and affairs of international justice. Since 1999, the EU nations also have had a shared currency, the euro. Member states are required to have stable, freely elected governments; to guarantee basic rights and protections to their citizens; to manage their economies; and to abide by EU laws and treaties.

QUIZ

1. _____ issues were the primary motivation for the creation of the EEC and later the European Union.
   A. Cultural
   B. Philosophical
   C. Economic
   D. Political

2. What was the major cause of the civil war that broke out in Yugoslavia in 1989–1990?
   A. ethnic nationalism
   B. resistance to Communist rule
   C. economic concerns
   D. censorship

3. The Polish Solidarity is best described as
   A. a trade union of skilled workers.
   B. a major political party.
   C. an underground resistance movement.
   D. a one-party system of government.

4. The political concept of *glasnost* welcomes
   A. free expression of political opinions.
   B. universal suffrage for adults.
   C. the lifting of restrictions on travel.
   D. the establishment of a strong legislature.

5. Which best describes the change in the Soviet government after the death of Stalin?
   A. It became substantially harsher and more repressive.
   B. It became somewhat less repressive.
   C. It became more centralized.
   D. It became radically more democratic.

6. The people of Eastern Europe caused the downfall of communism by means of
   A. changes in domestic policy.
   B. ethnic civil wars.
   C. passive and active resistance.
   D. establishing a free press.

7. **Why do people consider the fall of the Berlin Wall to be the symbolic end of the Cold War?**
   A. because East Germany was the last European nation to abandon communism
   B. because it happened as the result of a fluke
   C. because it signaled the reunification of East and West Germany
   D. because the wall was the most visible symbol of the Iron Curtain

8. **Which best describes the members of the Soviet Congress of People's Deputies?**
   A. They all belonged to the Communist Party.
   B. They represented all aspects of Soviet society.
   C. They all served by appointment from above.
   D. They were elected on a strictly geographical basis.

9. **Which best describes the Commonwealth of Independent States?**
   A. It is a parliamentary democracy.
   B. It is a federal republic.
   C. It is an economic union of self-governing nations.
   D. It is an international peacekeeping force.

10. **The USSR was bound to lose the arms race with the United States because the USSR was**
   A. a smaller nation.
   B. a poorer nation.
   C. a wealthier nation.
   D. a more democratic nation.

PART III EXAM

1. Which nation did not fight on the side of the Allied/Entente powers during
    World War I?
    A. Austria
    B. Britain
    C. France
    D. Italy

2. Which Soviet leader announced that the USSR would take no further part in
    the self-government of other nations?
    A. Leonid Brezhnev
    B. Mikhail Gorbachev
    C. Nikita Khrushchev
    D. Joseph Stalin

3. During the revolutionary period and the civil war in Russia, members of the
    old guard _____ by the thousands.
    A. joined the Red Army
    B. emigrated to Europe
    C. committed suicide
    D. ran for political office

4. In what respect was World War I different from any European war that pre-
    ceded it?
    A. It was fought among the traditional Great Powers of Europe.
    B. It was largely motivated by nationalism.
    C. It caused major changes to the map of Europe.
    D. It involved the major participation of a non-European nation.

5. What effect did the first Five-Year Plan have on the Russian peasants?
    A. They gained the right to own their own land.
    B. They were forced to work on collective farms.
    C. They gained the right to vote.
    D. They lost the right to vote.

6. _____ was established after World War II as an international peacekeeping organization.
   A. The Quadruple Alliance
   B. The League of Nations
   C. The United Nations
   D. The Warsaw Pact

7. In 1917, Germany agreed to withdraw troops from Russia if the Russians would agree to
   A. sign a nonaggression pact.
   B. cooperate with them in a double invasion of Poland.
   C. cede a large swath of territory to Germany.
   D. pay an annual tribute to the German government.

8. _____ succumbed to a period of nationalist civil war after the end of the Cold War.
   A. Germany
   B. The former Soviet republics
   C. Poland
   D. Yugoslavia

9. The most successful of the short-lived Communist regimes that arose after the First World War was in
   A. Bavaria.
   B. Czechoslovakia.
   C. Germany.
   D. Hungary.

10. _____ suffered by far the largest number of casualties in World War II.
    A. France
    B. Germany
    C. Italy
    D. Soviet Union

11. _____ disappeared from the map at the end of the Cold War.
    A. Austria
    B. Czechoslovakia
    C. Poland
    D. Romania

12. _____ is one major reason the Soviet Union withdrew from the affairs of state of the Iron Curtain nations in the 1980s.
    A. The high expense of the arms race
    B. The prospect of an all-out war with the United States
    C. The threat of revolution within the USSR
    D. The establishment of the Commonwealth of Independent States

13. Lenin opposed a parliamentary form of government because he believed that it was only a mouthpiece for
    A. artists and intellectuals.
    B. large and small farmers.
    C. business owners and managers.
    D. workers.

14. After World War I, northern Italian landowners were anti-Socialist primarily because the Socialists
    A. supported the overthrow of the monarchy.
    B. had unionized and thus acquired negotiating power.
    C. were agitating for ownership of their own land.
    D. had new demands after their return from military service.

15. Which non-European nation would play a major role in European history from World War I to the end of the Cold War?
    A. China
    B. India
    C. Soviet Union
    D. United States

16. _____ was divided by the Iron Curtain and broke into two nations in 1949.
    A. Austria
    B. Germany
    C. Hungary
    D. Poland

17. **The USSR installed nuclear missiles in Cuba in order to**
    A. expand its power base.
    B. make an ally of Cuba.
    C. intimidate the United States.
    D. fulfill a UN requirement.

18. **As a result of an agreement with Mussolini, the Catholic Church _____ in 1929.**
    A. ceded control of the public school system
    B. officially recognized the state of Italy
    C. supported the underground anti-Fascist movement
    D. shut down its seminaries throughout Italy

19. **At Yalta in 1945, the Soviet Union promised the United States that it would _____ after victory was declared in Europe.**
    A. be the first to march into Berlin
    B. join U.S. troops in the war with Japan
    C. hold free elections in Moscow
    D. establish communism throughout Eastern Europe

20. **All these means of popular resistance contributed to the end of the Cold War except**
    A. demonstrations in the streets.
    B. assassinations of Communist leaders.
    C. publication of writings that criticized the Communist regimes.
    D. support for non-Communist leaders.

21. **The king of Italy refused to put down the Blackshirts in 1922 because**
    A. he hoped that they would form part of the new coalition government.
    B. he had made a secret agreement with Mussolini.
    C. he believed the army and the Blackshirts would both turn on him.
    D. he was afraid a confrontation would lead to civil war.

22. **_____ was the primary reason for Serbia's resentment of the Austrian takeover of Bosnia in 1908.**
    A. Anarchism
    B. Communism
    C. Nationalism
    D. Imperialism

23. What was the main reason for Stalin's distrust of the other Allied leaders during the peace process in 1945?
   A. He felt that they had allowed the Soviets to do most of the fighting.
   B. He resented their sharing of the credit for taking Berlin.
   C. He had to rely on interpreters to tell him what they said.
   D. He believed they intended to impose a capitalist economy on Germany.

24. What effect did World War II have on the international status of the Great Powers of Western Europe?
   A. They became superpowers.
   B. They became secondary or minor powers.
   C. They fell under Communist control.
   D. They became American satellite states.

25. _____ was the German equivalent of Mussolini's Blackshirts.
   A. The Nazi Party
   B. The Gestapo
   C. The SS
   D. The Luftwaffe

26. _____ is notable for being the only Communist head of state in Eastern Europe to successfully defy the authority of the Soviet Union.
   A. Vaclav Havel
   B. Josip Broz (Tito)
   C. Walter Ulbricht
   D. Konrad Adenauer

27. All these statements are true of both Hitler and Napoleon except
   A. he was not born in the country in which he seized power.
   B. he awarded himself an imperial title once he was in power.
   C. he attempted to take over most of Europe.
   D. he was an extreme nationalist.

28. In what way was Yugoslavia in the 1920s similar to the Austro-Hungarian Empire in the late 1800s?
   A. Both were Communist states.
   B. Both were constitutional monarchies.
   C. Both had conservative leaders.
   D. Both had diverse ethnic populations.

29. **Before the outbreak of World War II, which two nations signed a nonaggression pact?**
    A. Britain and France
    B. France and Germany
    C. Germany and the Soviet Union
    D. the Soviet Union and Britain

30. **Which two forms of government amount to exactly the same thing?**
    A. communism and fascism
    B. communism and anarchism
    C. fascism and republicanism
    D. democracy and fascism

31. **The term *Velvet Revolution* refers to a 1989 regime change in**
    A. Czechoslovakia.
    B. East Germany.
    C. Poland.
    D. Yugoslavia.

32. **_____ defeated Russia in a short-lived war between 1920 and 1921.**
    A. Austria
    B. Germany
    C. Poland
    D. Hungary

33. **The chief Soviet goal during the Cold War was**
    A. to annex new territory into the USSR.
    B. to set up Communist governments throughout the world.
    C. to rebuild the Soviet economy and infrastructure.
    D. to take over West Berlin.

34. **Politically, the National Front in 1930s Spain is best described as**
    A. Communist.
    B. Socialist.
    C. conservative.
    D. democratic.

35. **Which best describes the purpose of the North Atlantic Treaty Organization?**
    A. to eliminate nuclear missiles from the world
    B. to make communism illegal throughout the West
    C. to provide for the defense of any member nation that was attacked
    D. to maintain international peace

36. **Which best describes a major weakness in the German strategy for World War II?**
    A. dividing the armed forces to fight on multiple fronts
    B. forming an alliance with the Soviet Union
    C. attacking the western front before the east was secured
    D. relying on insufficient industrial output

37. **Historians agree that _____ was a main contributing cause to World War II.**
    A. the Great Depression
    B. the Treaty of Versailles
    C. the Spanish Civil War
    D. the Lateran Treaty

38. **Among the Communist states that briefly arose in Europe after the First World War, which lasted the longest?**
    A. Bulgarian
    B. German
    C. Hungarian
    D. Slovakian

39. **_____ led most combat veterans to support Fascist leaders.**
    A. Extreme nationalism
    B. Economic concerns
    C. Income-tax issues
    D. The desire for peace

40. **After 1945, which best describes the nations of Western Europe (i.e., those not behind the Iron Curtain)?**
    A. puppet governments subordinate to the United States
    B. Communist states subordinate to the USSR
    C. major world powers with international empires
    D. minor or secondary world powers

41. **Trench warfare during World War I resulted in a stalemate primarily because of**
    A. the technological changes in weapons.
    B. the imbalance in numbers of troops on the two sides.
    C. the location of the trenches in central Europe.
    D. the lack of sufficient weapons, rations, and other supplies.

42. **Prime Minister Azaña of Spain was forced out of office due to the opposition of the _____**
    A. reformers.
    B. liberals.
    C. workers.
    D. establishment.

43. **All of these nations were members of the Warsaw Pact of 1955 except _____**
    A. Austria.
    B. Hungary.
    C. Poland.
    D. Romania.

44. **The European Union became possible when the traditional enemies _____ became allies.**
    A. Britain and France
    B. France and Germany
    C. Germany and Russia
    D. Russia and Britain

45. **The 1919 Treaty of Versailles imposed all the following conditions on Germany except**
    A. the drastic reduction of its army.
    B. the payment of billions of marks in reparations.
    C. the admission of full responsibility for the war.
    D. the replacement of its monarch with a freely elected government.

46. **The siege of _____ caused the Soviets to take a brutal revenge when they marched into Berlin in 1945.**
    A. Moscow
    B. Leningrad
    C. Kiev
    D. Warsaw

47. **Which best explains why West Berlin became the symbolic heart of the Cold War struggle?**
    A. It was the largest city in Europe.
    B. It was the only free city behind the Iron Curtain.
    C. It demonstrated the failure of capitalism.
    D. It refused to accept Marshall Plan aid.

48. **Why did the Russian peasants hoard grain under the New Economic Policy?**
    A. because they hoped to overthrow the new regime
    B. because the state usually failed to pay them for the grain
    C. because they planned to migrate to the cities to find work
    D. because they needed grain to bribe the state police

49. **Which national leader did not take part in the Potsdam Conference of 1945?**
    A. Joseph Stalin of the Soviet Union
    B. Harry Truman of the United States
    C. Winston Churchill of Britain
    D. Charles de Gaulle of France

50. **The Great Powers redrew the European map at Versailles in order to**
    A. create new states on the basis of a population's ethnic identity.
    B. take Russian territory away from the new Communist government.
    C. create an alliance between Germany and France.
    D. eliminate the need for European nations to maintain standing armies.

Final Exam

1. **Which nation changed sides during the Second World War?**
   A. Austria
   B. Italy
   C. Poland
   D. Soviet Union

2. **Which was the first nation to establish settled colonies in North America?**
   A. England
   B. France
   C. Germany
   D. Spain

3. **Iron Curtain nations refused to accept Marshall Plan aid because**
   A. they blamed Germany for destroying the European economy.
   B. there was too much distrust between the former Allied and Axis nations.
   C. they knew they would never be able to repay the United States.
   D. Stalin refused to allow any ties between his satellites and his only strong national rival.

4. **Constantinople was named "the New (Second) Rome";** _____ **later became known as "the Third Rome."**
   A. Madrid
   B. Moscow
   C. Paris
   D. Vienna

5. **At the end of the Thirty Years' War,** _____ **emerged as the dominant European power.**
   A. England
   B. France
   C. the Holy Roman Empire
   D. Sweden

6. **The Holy Roman Empire was officially and permanently dissolved during**
   A. the Reformation.
   B. the Thirty Years' War.
   C. the Napoleonic Wars.
   D. the Great War.

7. **The Peace of Augsburg of 1555 declared that each German Prince**
   A. could choose the religion of his state.
   B. could cast one vote for Holy Roman emperor.
   C. must vote for a Protestant for the post of Holy Roman emperor.
   D. must vote for a Catholic for the post of Holy Roman emperor.

8. **In Italy, the Fascists and the major landowners united forces against** _____
   A. the conservatives.
   B. the Socialists.
   C. the monarchy.
   D. the Church.

9. In nineteenth-century Europe, both conservatives and liberals believed that

   A. there should be separation among the branches of the central government.

   B. a written constitution was necessary for political stability.

   C. a nation should be ruled by a benevolent, but absolute, hereditary monarch.

   D. the working class should not have any voice in the government.

10. The term *Renaissance* refers to a reawakening of interest in art and ideas from which period?

    A. the Middle Ages

    B. the Classical age

    C. the Romantic era

    D. the prehistoric era

11. What was the purpose of the Great Purges of the 1930s?

    A. to eliminate political opposition in the Soviet Union

    B. to massacre specific ethnic groups within Europe

    C. to provide necessary labor for major construction projects

    D. to draft men into the armed forces in the Axis nations

12. The development of _____ gave the working class some leverage over business and factory owners for the first time in history.

    A. communism

    B. steam power

    C. the railway

    D. trade unions

13. Control of _____ constituted a major bone of contention between France and Germany for nearly four hundred years.

    A. the Rhine River

    B. the Danube River

    C. Alsace and Lorraine

    D. Belgium and Flanders

14. **Britain and France went to war in North America over conflicting claims to**

    A. the Ohio River valley area.

    B. the city of New Orleans, Louisiana.

    C. territory west of the Mississippi River.

    D. the colonies along the Atlantic coast.

15. **Which major figure of the Enlightenment first suggested a government of multiple branches with checks and balances?**

    A. René Descartes

    B. the Baron de Montesquieu

    C. Jean-Jacques Rousseau

    D. Voltaire

16. **The Austrian Empire created in 1815 included all these states except _____**

    A. Bavaria.

    B. Bohemia.

    C. Hungary.

    D. Transylvania.

17. **During the _____, Vasili II established a hereditary monarchy in Russia.**

    A. 1300s

    B. 1400s

    C. 1500s

    D. 1600s

18. **A major goal of the Congress of Vienna was to ensure that _____ would no longer be a major European power.**

    A. Britain

    B. France

    C. Germany

    D. Russia

19. **Michelangelo's frescoes on the ceiling of the Sistine Chapel are an important reflection of their historical period because**

    A. they are almost entirely the work of a single painter.

    B. they cover an enormous surface.

    C. they treat Christian and pagan elements equally.

    D. they were commissioned by the pope.

20. **The Weimar Republic provided ineffective leadership primarily because**

    A. the leaders in the Reichstag could not agree on policy.

    B. most German voters did not want a democratic government.

    C. France had sent an occupying force into the Ruhr.

    D. the leaders suppressed free speech and a free press.

21. **One reason the Industrial Revolution was slower to come about on the continent was the lack of political influence among the _____**

    A. aristocracy and nobility.

    B. mercantile middle class.

    C. working class and farmers.

    D. students and intellectuals.

22. **The Japanese victory over Russia in 1905 stopped Russia's expansion into _____**

    A. Africa.

    B. China.

    C. Poland.

    D. Germany.

23. **What was the most important purpose of the Berlin Wall?**

    A. to prevent any possibility of a Berlin airlift during the blockade

    B. to prevent Iron Curtain nations from accepting Marshall Plan aid

    C. to prevent West Germans and other Western Europeans from defecting to East Germany

    D. to prevent citizens of East Germany and other Iron Curtain nations from defecting to the West

24. **Which accurately describes the main difference between Lutheranism and Calvinism?**

    A. Calvinists believe in predestination; Lutherans believe in salvation by faith.

    B. Calvinists believe in salvation by faith; Lutherans believe in predestination.

    C. Calvinists believe in salvation by good works; Lutherans believe in salvation by faith.

    D. Calvinists believe in salvation by faith; Lutherans believe in salvation by good works.

25. **The British enclosure movement of the late eighteenth and early nineteenth centuries caused**

    A. a drop in production in British textile mills.

    B. a mass migration from the villages to the large cities.

    C. a rise in subsistence farming.

    D. hostile relations between Britain and France.

26. **The Romantic movement in the arts stressed the importance of**

    A. the great value of the worker to society.

    B. the individual personality of the artist.

    C. the glorification of religion.

    D. the random chances that make up human life.

27. **Machiavelli's *The Prince* was revolutionary because it asserted**

    A. that a ruler should do whatever was necessary to maintain power, including acting unethically or dishonestly.

    B. that women were just as competent and qualified to rule kingdoms as men.

    C. that rule over a nation-state should be decided by merit, not by birth.

    D. that all human beings had certain natural rights.

28. **Britain defeated France in a power struggle over India during** _____

    A. the Seven Years' War.

    B. the Napoleonic Wars.

    C. the Sepoy Mutiny.

    D. World War I.

29. **One important reason Elizabeth I supported the Anglican Church was that**

    A. the Catholic Church considered her parents' marriage invalid.

    B. she welcomed the chance to share her royal authority with the pope.

    C. the majority of ordinary English people preferred the Catholic faith.

    D. she was a devout Protestant who hoped to spread the Anglican faith throughout Europe.

30. **What was the key factor in Britain's being the first European nation to industrialize?**

    A. the supremacy of its navy

    B. its leading role in the Scientific Revolution

    C. its political, social, and financial stability

    D. the extent of its colonial empire

31. **During the Reformation, _____ became the state religion of Scotland.**

    A. Anglicanism

    B. Calvinism

    C. Lutheranism

    D. Presbyterianism

32. **_____ brought an abrupt end to the European economic recovery of the late 1920s.**

    A. Hitler's rise to power

    B. Stalin's rise to power

    C. The Great Depression

    D. The Spanish Civil War

33. **Which European nation emerged from World War II as a great world power?**

    A. Britain

    B. France

    C. Poland

    D. Soviet Union

34. The term *Indochina* refers to a group of Southeast Asian states collectively ruled by
    _____ at the end of the nineteenth century.

    A. Britain

    B. France

    C. Germany

    D. the Netherlands

35. The invention and development of the _____ allowed Galileo to make
    crucial observations about the planets and other heavenly bodies.

    A. pendulum clock

    B. printing press

    C. telescope

    D. microscope

36. Minister of state _____ deliberately used the press to provoke France to
    attack Prussia in 1870.

    A. Napoleon III

    B. Otto von Bismarck

    C. William Gladstone

    D. Klaus von Metternich

37. Jean-Jacques Rousseau's belief in _____ aroused the contempt of most
    other *philosophes*.

    A. the nobility of primitive man

    B. the importance of the hereditary class system

    C. the influence of education

    D. the importance of religious beliefs

38. Which nation did not participate in the peace conference held at Versailles in 1919?

    A. France

    B. Germany

    C. Italy

    D. Russia

39. _____ was the main cause of both world wars.

    A. Anti-communism

    B. Extreme nationalism

    C. Defense against aggression

    D. Religious conflict

40. During the Reformation, which nation adopted a Protestant religion by legislative act rather than popular rebellion?

    A. Germany

    B. France

    C. England

    D. Sweden

41. Britain imposed its authority on Egypt in the late nineteenth century in order to maintain

    A. a trade monopoly on Egyptian cotton.

    B. a friendly alliance with a large Arab nation.

    C. control over the Suez Canal.

    D. control of Egypt's foreign relations within Africa.

42. The loyalty of _____ may have been Hitler's most important asset in his rise to the office of chancellor of Germany.

    A. the wealthy

    B. the middle class

    C. the intellectuals and artists

    D. the World War I veterans

43. Which nation was the aggressor in the Crimean War of the 1850s?

    A. Britain

    B. France

    C. Russia

    D. Italy

44. **Count Camillo di Cavour is historically significant for his central role in**

    A. the unification of Italy.

    B. the Russian defeat of Napoleon.

    C. the restoration of Charles II of England to the throne.

    D. the Congress of Vienna.

45. **Why did the Catholic nation of France not support the Catholic side in the Thirty Years' War?**

    A. because the king of France was married to an Austrian princess

    B. because the pope was a traditional enemy of the French kings

    C. because a Catholic defeat in the war would strengthen France's position

    D. because France's ministers were sympathetic to the Protestant side

46. **Britain drove _____ out of power in South Africa and the Orange Free State.**

    A. the Dutch

    B. the French

    C. the Portuguese

    D. the Germans

47. **The USSR and the United States nearly reached the point of nuclear war during _____**

    A. the Cuban Missile Crisis.

    B. the Strategic Arms Limitation Talks.

    C. the partition of Germany into four zones of occupation.

    D. the signing of the Warsaw Pact.

48. **As a result of the 1438 Council of Florence,**

    A. Martin Luther published his Ninety-Five Theses in Wittenberg.

    B. a major cultural and intellectual exchange took place among scholars.

    C. Pope Leo X commissioned Michelangelo to paint the Sistine Chapel ceiling.

    D. the Italian city-states became a unified nation under one monarch.

49. **Which nation began World War I by declaring war on Serbia?**

    A. Britain

    B. France

    C. Germany

    D. Russia

50. **All of these were important causes of Napoleon's downfall, except**

    A. France had become the common enemy of all other European nations.

    B. the mainly non-French army felt no loyalty to either Napoleon or France.

    C. the anger of the legislature over being ruled by a non-French emperor.

    D. the development of nationalism in other European nations.

51. **Which best describes the overarching goal that united all the eighteenth-century *philosophes*?**

    A. education

    B. freedom

    C. anarchy

    D. political unification

52. **In *The Communist Manifesto*, Marx and Engels stated that _____ was the most valuable member of society.**

    A. the constitutional monarch

    B. the soldier

    C. the worker

    D. the artist or intellectual

53. **The Catholic Church helped to bring about its own loss of power and influence by**

    A. failing to reunite the Orthodox and Roman Catholic denominations.

    B. establishing seminaries for the education and training of priests throughout Europe.

    C. sponsoring Johannes Gutenberg's work on movable type and the printing press.

    D. encouraging and fostering the revival of interest in the arts and ideas of Greece and Rome.

54. **All these nations fought on the same side during World War I except** _____.

    A. Britain

    B. France

    C. Germany

    D. Russia

55. **One factor that enabled Napoleon to become first consul of France, then emperor, was**

    A. his long absences from France while leading the troops in battle.

    B. a long period of economic prosperity that followed the execution of the king.

    C. the restoration to authority and dignity of the Catholic Church in France.

    D. the lack of a coherent legislative assembly despite several attempts to create one.

56. **Which best explains why communism, as it was practiced, was not satisfactory to the peoples of Eastern Europe?**

    A. It left them feeling constantly vulnerable to foreign invasion.

    B. It refused them basic freedoms they demanded as a human right.

    C. It was a corrupt system of government.

    D. It was a barrier to economic progress.

57. **Why did Louis XIV require that the hereditary nobles spend part of each year at Versailles?**

    A. to curtail their freedom and thus prevent possible conspiracies or attacks on the throne

    B. to drive a wedge between them and the peasants on their estates

    C. to have them on hand to counsel and advise him in foreign and domestic policy

    D. to protect him in case of a popular uprising or revolution

58. **What is the main reason the Anglican religion, as established in 1534, was so similar in practice to Catholicism?**

    A. because the Anglican church hierarchy did not want to give up any of their authority

    B. because Anglicanism was established for political, not spiritual, reasons

    C. because the people of England did not want major changes in the way they worshiped

    D. because the pope pressured the archbishop of Canterbury not to make major changes to the worship service

59. _____ declared war on Germany when Germany invaded Poland in 1939.

    A. Britain and France

    B. France and Italy

    C. Italy and Austria

    D. Austria and Britain

60. Sweden briefly achieved the status of a major European power during

    A. the Renaissance.

    B. the Industrial Revolution.

    C. the Thirty Years' War.

    D. the Napoleonic era.

61. Which best describes Stalin's attitude toward Soviet peasants?

    A. They were an inferior race of people.

    B. They were a means of providing grain for the industrial workers.

    C. They were the Communist Party's natural base of support.

    D. They should overthrow the social order and take control.

62. _____ was the first modern European nation to establish a constitutional monarchy.

    A. Belgium

    B. England

    C. France

    D. Italy

63. Which nation appeared to be upsetting or disturbing the peaceful balance of power in Europe in the years leading up to World War I?

    A. Austria-Hungary

    B. Germany

    C. Italy

    D. Russia

64. The *philosophes* of the Enlightenment admired Britain because
    A. it had a stable government and a prosperous economy.
    B. it was a great world power despite its relatively small size.
    C. it had a relatively free press and relative religious tolerance.
    D. it was the birthplace of some of the greatest *philosophes*.

65. Which of the following is an important scholar and writer associated with the Humanist movement of the sixteenth century?
    A. Niccolò Machiavelli
    B. Desiderus Erasmus
    C. Johannes Kepler
    D. Denis Diderot

66. The history of Russia as a nation-state began during the era when the Russians managed to expel _____ from their lands.
    A. the Chinese
    B. the Indians
    C. the Tatars
    D. the Arabs

67. _____ is an important figure in history because he defied Soviet authority in post–World War II Czechoslovakia during the Prague Spring.
    A. Alexander Dubcek
    B. Mikhail Gorbachev
    C. Imre Nagy
    D. Lech Walesa

68. _____ was the major battleground during the Thirty Years' War.
    A. Austria
    B. France
    C. The Holy Roman Empire
    D. Poland

69. **Why was Newton's discovery and explanation of the principle of gravity important?**

    A. It proved that travel in space would be possible one day.

    B. It disputed the findings of previous scientists and astronomers.

    C. It showed that the workings of the universe were intelligible to ordinary people.

    D. It demonstrated that the Earth and other planets moved around the sun.

70. **What was the Polish government's initial response to the rise of Solidarity?**

    A. to ban it legally

    B. to ignore it

    C. to start a civil war

    D. to resign in the face of its widespread support

71. **In the Sepoy Mutiny of 1857, _____ troops rose up against the British.**

    A. South African

    B. Chinese

    C. Indian

    D. Korean

72. **The Declaration of the Rights of Man and of the Citizen contains important ideas from _____**

    A. the Glorious Revolution.

    B. the Renaissance.

    C. the Enlightenment.

    D. the Scientific Revolution.

73. **One very basic reason Germany was bound to lose World War II was that**

    A. the German troops were greatly outnumbered.

    B. the Germans were not loyal to their government.

    C. the German generals were poor strategists.

    D. the Germans had violated the Versailles Treaty.

74. **The Iron Curtain was first lifted on the border between**

    A. Austria and Hungary.

    B. East and West Germany.

    C. East and West Berlin.

    D. Germany and Austria.

75. **One major factor that caused Europeans to question the omnipotence of the Catholic Church in the 1300s was**

    A. new developments in medical science.

    B. the Church's inability to combat the Black Plague.

    C. the pope's refusal to grant Henry VIII a divorce.

    D. the publication of *The Prince*.

76. **Lenin founded the Comintern with the goal of**

    A. forming alliances with European leaders.

    B. spying on foreign governments.

    C. achieving international peace.

    D. spreading communism throughout Europe.

77. **The attempted coup against Mikhail Gorbachev in 1991 was motivated by**

    A. economic and political concerns.

    B. lack of popular support for his policies.

    C. chaos in Eastern Europe.

    D. the civil war in Yugoslavia.

78. **The absolute monarchs of the seventeenth and eighteenth centuries consistently granted major privileges to _____ as a means of defusing possible disloyalty or opposition.**

    A. the military

    B. the pope

    C. the hereditary nobility

    D. the wealthy merchant class

79. **The original motive for sponsoring European voyages to other continents was** _____

    A. to establish foreign military bases.

    B. to expand the empire by setting up permanent European colonies.

    C. to convert native populations to Christianity.

    D. to establish profitable trade relations.

80. **Which new thought process arose during the Scientific Revolution?**

    A. interpreting one's own direct observations and data

    B. studying and interpreting the great writings of the past

    C. asking questions of educated philosophers and teachers

    D. accepting what one was told by leaders of the Church

81. **Between the reign of Edward VI and the Glorious Revolution, the position of the Anglican Church varied according to**

    A. the state of the English economy.

    B. the religious preferences of the English monarch.

    C. whether England was at peace or at war.

    D. the political relations among England, Scotland, and Ireland.

82. **The political concept of *perestroika* is best described as**

    A. an openness to political discourse from all social ranks.

    B. a restructuring of government and society.

    C. the universal right of an adult to vote.

    D. the right of a head of state to choose the national religion.

83. **One important reason the French Revolution succeeded in abolishing the monarchy was that**

    A. France had no formal political parties and no legislative assembly.

    B. the king was unable to escape from Versailles.

    C. the hereditary aristocracy did not want to give up any of its privileges.

    D. the armed National Guard sided with the common people.

84. **Conflict between King Charles I and the British Parliament erupted into open warfare over the issue of**

    A. the balance of power between the legislature and the throne.

    B. religious disagreements between England and Ireland.

    C. Parliament's dislike of being ruled by a Protestant monarch.

    D. Charles's prospective marriage to a French Catholic princess.

85. **Why did Peter the Great establish St. Petersburg as the new Russian capital city?**

    A. to establish and maintain new trade routes with Europe

    B. to indicate that he saw Russia as a nation belonging to Western Europe

    C. to command the attendance and service of the hereditary nobles

    D. to protect the nation from invasion from the west

86. **Russian peasants generally supported the Bolsheviks because the Bolsheviks promised them _____**

    A. land.

    B. education.

    C. the right to vote.

    D. employment.

87. **_____ became the core of a unified Italy in 1861.**

    A. Rome

    B. The Papal States

    C. Piedmont

    D. The former Duchy of Florence

88. **During the Reformation, Protestantism failed to establish itself firmly and securely in France because**

    A. the French were involved in a series of civil wars.

    B. the granting of indulgences had not spread to France.

    C. the monarchs were Catholics and supported the Catholic cause.

    D. the French people were not interested in the teachings of Calvin or Luther.

89. **The first soviets—workers' councils—in Russia were established in the wake of**

    A. the Revolution of 1905.

    B. the Bolshevik Revolution of 1917.

    C. the Great War.

    D. World War II.

90. **One reason non-Russians joined the White forces during the Russian civil war of 1918 was**

    A. to reestablish a legitimate Russian government.

    B. to recover territory Russia had ceded to Germany.

    C. to take revenge on the Russians for abandoning World War I.

    D. to establish cordial relations with the Russian leaders.

91. **In the years leading to the First World War, Britain's primary concern was _____**

    A. the buildup of the German navy.

    B. the alliance between France and Russia.

    C. the ascension to the German throne of Wilhelm II.

    D. the establishment of independent states in the Balkans.

92. **The British Parliament deposed King James II because he was _____**

    A. Anglican.

    B. Calvinist.

    C. Catholic.

    D. Presbyterian.

93. **What false assumption led Hitler to underestimate the Soviets as opponents?**

    A. that the country was not that large

    B. that they had a powerful navy

    C. that they were not really loyal to Stalin

    D. that they were racially inferior to the Germans

94. **Which nineteenth-century political philosophy is furthest to the political left?**

    A. conservatism

    B. communism

    C. liberalism

    D. socialism

95. **What was the most important reason for the Europeans' success in establishing dominance over the native populations in the Americas?**

    A. They had deadlier weapons.

    B. There were more of them.

    C. They were physically healthier and stronger.

    D. They were more familiar with the local geography.

96. **The kingdom of _____ eventually became the core of a united German nation.**

    A. Austria

    B. Bohemia

    C. Poland

    D. Prussia

97. **_____ was created at the end of the Napoleonic Wars to maintain a peaceful balance of power in Europe.**

    A. The League of Nations

    B. The European Union

    C. The Quadruple Alliance

    D. The United Nations

98. **Which influential group, class, or institution fiercely opposed Italian unification in the nineteenth century?**

    A. the Italian monarch and the royalists

    B. the pope and the Catholic Church

    C. the political conservatives and the wealthy

    D. the republicans and intellectuals

99. **King James I of England is a notable figure in history because he**

   A. closed all the theaters in London due to his strict religious beliefs.

   B. was the last English monarch to reign before the monarchy was abolished.

   C. passed a law requiring all gentlemen to shave their beards.

   D. commissioned a brilliant new English translation of the Bible.

100. **What was Frederick the Great's main reason for making the Prussian army the strongest and most impressive fighting force in Europe?**

   A. to gain the approval of his father, King Frederick William I

   B. to take military revenge on the nations that had defeated the Holy Roman Empire during the Thirty Years' War

   C. to discourage other nations from invading Prussia despite its geographically vulnerable position

   D. to invade and conquer Austria and make it part of a united German state

Afterword

Europe Since the Cold War

A typical European history survey course will end with the fall of communism, or perhaps go as far as the formation of the current European Union. The course is called *history*, not *current events*, because it deals with the past. However, it is a good idea to arm yourself with knowledge of developments that have taken place in Europe, and are currently taking place, since the early 1990s. This Afterword describes some of the trends and issues that European nations are trying to come to terms with for the future.

Immigration

Since about 1990, Europe has had to absorb an enormous influx of immigrants, almost all from Africa and the Middle East. Immigration has had a tremendous impact on the economy, as many of these immigrants have entered Europe illegally and are working without proper documentation.

Immigration has also had a significant cultural impact. Many Europeans feel grave concern that their own cultures are disappearing as African and Arab populations rise and the native population falls. Unlike the United States, a nation populated entirely by immigrants and their descendants (even the "native" peoples of the Americas originally came from Asia), European countries have been, for the most part, culturally homogeneous for centuries. As you have learned, ethnic tension leading to revolution or civil war was the usual result in nations with ethnically diverse populations, such as Austria-Hungary or Yugoslavia. Racial and ethnic prejudice against immigrants is definitely on the rise in Europe, and there are frequent outbreaks of race-based violence.

Foreign Relations

Alliances during and after the two world wars firmly established a close and friendly connection between the United States and Western Europe. This changed soon after Saudi terrorists attacked the United States in September 2001. U.S. foreign policy immediately became aggressive—so much so that the initially sympathetic European states began to view it with alarm. Although European troops participated in the Iraq war, some enthusiastically (for example, Britain), others reluctantly, the general bent of the European Union would have been for a more restrained response. A 2008 change of leadership in the White House has gone some way toward mending the transatlantic friendships; however, it is impossible to predict what the near future will bring.

In addition, Europe and the United States no longer have a monopoly on nuclear weapons. China, India, Israel, North Korea, and Pakistan all possess strategic nuclear weapons—a fact that European heads of state must constantly keep in mind. Mutual hostility between India and Pakistan is particularly evident as of this writing. Since nuclear war might very possibly wreak destruction across the globe, all nations must use care in negotiations.

European Union Membership

The European Union includes twenty-seven members, all of which have agreed to abide by its requirements. These include the observance of basic human rights, the maintenance of a free-market economy, and the establishment of a popularly elected representative government (see Chapter 20).

Among states that have applied for membership but have not yet been accepted, the case of Turkey is the most controversial. Many European heads of state have grave concerns over admitting a nation that would be one of its largest members. The size of Turkey's population would guarantee it the largest number of seats in the European Parliament, significantly changing the current balance of power. Some member nations argue that Turkey should not be eligible on the grounds that almost all its landmass is in Asia, with only a small corner in Europe. Others argue that with its Muslim population, Turkey is culturally non-European and does not belong in the EU. Still others point to Turkey's practice of censorship and its other controls over the lives of its people. Discussion over admitting Turkey to the EU has been going on since 1987 with little likelihood that it will soon be settled.

Apart from the Baltic republics, none of the former states of the USSR has been admitted to the EU. These nations have still not recovered economically or socially from the long era of Communist domination. Although the former Soviet republics have their own union, the Commonwealth of Independent States (see Chapter 20), their exclusion from the EU may become a significant issue in the future.

Within Europe, the people appear to have a mixed view of the EU. While many enjoy the advantages it brings, others express concerns. Principally, there is a fear that the member states will lose their unique individual cultural identities and that Europe will become a second United States—a federal republic whose states all share one central government and whose people consider themselves all one nationality. Only time will determine the influence the EU will have over its members and over the future of Europe as a whole.

Answer Key

CHAPTER 1
QUIZ
1. A   2. D   3. A   4. B   5. C   6. A   7. A   8. B   9. D   10. B

CHAPTER 2
QUIZ
1. B   2. A   3. C   4. A   5. D   6. C   7. C   8. B   9. D   10. C

CHAPTER 3
QUIZ
1. B   2. A   3. D   4. B   5. C   6. D   7. A   8. B   9. B   10. A

CHAPTER 4
QUIZ
1. C   2. D   3. C   4. B   5. D   6. D   7. B   8. A   9. B   10. B

CHAPTER 5
QUIZ
1. B   2. A   3. B   4. A   5. D   6. C   7. A   8. C   9. D   10. C

CHAPTER 6

QUIZ

1. A   2. C   3. B   4. B   5. A   6. A   7. D   8. C   9. A   10. D

CHAPTER 7

QUIZ

1. D   2. B   3. D   4. A   5. C   6. D   7. C   8. A   9. C   10. A

PART I EXAM

1. D   2. B   3. C   4. C   5. B   6. C   7. D   8. C   9. C   10. A   11. A
12. A   13. B   14. D   15. B   16. A   17. C   18. B   19. C   20. A   21. A
22. A   23. B   24. B   25. D   26. A   27. C   28. B   29. C   30. C   31. D
32. B   33. C   34. D   35. B   36. B   37. B   38. D   39. A   40. C   41. A
42. D   43. A   44. C   45. B   46. C   47. B   48. B   49. B   50. B

CHAPTER 8

QUIZ

1. C   2. D   3. C   4. A   5. D   6. B   7. C   8. B   9. B   10. A

CHAPTER 9

QUIZ

1. D   2. C   3. C   4. B   5. D   6. C   7. A   8. B   9. A   10. C

CHAPTER 10

QUIZ

1. B   2. C   3. D   4. B   5. B   6. A   7. D   8. A   9. B   10. A

CHAPTER 11

QUIZ

1. C   2. B   3. C   4. B   5. D   6. C   7. C   8. A   9. B   10. A

CHAPTER 12

QUIZ

1. C   2. A   3. D   4. B   5. C   6. B   7. A   8. D   9. A   10. C

CHAPTER 13

QUIZ

1. C   2. A   3. B   4. A   5. B   6. C   7. D   8. C   9. D   10. D

CHAPTER 14

QUIZ

1. C   2. B   3. B   4. A   5. D   6. B   7. C   8. A   9. B   10. A

PART II EXAM

1. C   2. C   3. B   4. B   5. A   6. B   7. D   8. B   9. C   10. D   11. A
12. D   13. A   14. A   15. D   16. B   17. C   18. C   19. D   20. B   21. C
22. C   23. B   24. D   25. D   26. D   27. A   28. A   29. B   30. D   31. A
32. C   33. C   34. B   35. B   36. A   37. B   38. D   39. B   40. D   41. B
42. C   43. B   44. A   45. A   46. D   47. B   48. A   49. B   50. A

CHAPTER 15

QUIZ

1. C   2. A   3. B   4. C   5. B   6. A   7. D   8. C   9. C   10. D

CHAPTER 16

QUIZ

1. A   2. D   3. B   4. B   5. C   6. C   7. B   8. A   9. A   10. C

CHAPTER 17

QUIZ

1. D   2. A   3. D   4. C   5. D   6. D   7. C   8. C   9. D   10. A

CHAPTER 18

QUIZ

1. B   2. D   3. D   4. D   5. A   6. C   7. C   8. A   9. D   10. B

CHAPTER 19

QUIZ

1. A   2. A   3. C   4. B   5. C   6. D   7. C   8. D   9. D   10. B

CHAPTER 20

QUIZ

1. C   2. A   3. B   4. A   5. B   6. C   7. D   8. B   9. C   10. B

PART III EXAM

1. A   2. B   3. B   4. D   5. B   6. C   7. C   8. D   9. D   10. D   11. B
12. A   13. C   14. B   15. D   16. B   17. C   18. B   19. B   20. B   21. D
22. C   23. D   24. B   25. C   26. B   27. D   28. D   29. C   30. A   31. A
32. C   33. B   34. C   35. C   36. A   37. B   38. C   39. A   40. D   41. A
42. D   43. A   44. B   45. D   46. B   47. B   48. B   49. D   50. A

FINAL EXAM

1. B   2. D   3. D   4. B   5. B   6. C   7. A   8. B   9. D   10. B   11. A
12. D   13. C   14. A   15. B   16. A   17. B   18. B   19. C   20. A   21. B
22. B   23. D   24. A   25. B   26. B   27. A   28. A   29. A   30. C   31. D
32. C   33. D   34. B   35. C   36. B   37. A   38. D   39. B   40. C   41. C
42. D   43. C   44. A   45. C   46. A   47. A   48. B   49. C   50. C   51. B
52. C   53. D   54. C   55. D   56. B   57. A   58. B   59. A   60. C   61. B
62. B   63. B   64. C   65. B   66. C   67. A   68. C   69. C   70. A   71. C
72. C   73. A   74. A   75. B   76. D   77. A   78. C   79. D   80. A   81. B
82. B   83. D   84. A   85. B   86. A   87. C   88. C   89. A   90. A   91. A
92. C   93. D   94. B   95. A   96. D   97. C   98. B   99. D   100. C

Bibliography and Sources for Further Reading

General Works on European History

Davies, Norman. *Europe: A History*. London: Pimlico Books, 1997.
———. *Oxford Atlas of World History: Concise Edition*. London: Oxford University Press, 2002.
Roberts, J. M., and Odd Arne Westad. *The New Penguin History of the World*, 5th ed. New York: Penguin Books, 2007.
Howard, Michael. *War in European History*. Updated ed. Oxford: Oxford University Press, 2001.

Histories of Individual European Nations

Beller, Steven. *A Concise History of Austria*. Cambridge: Cambridge University Press, 2006.
Clogg, Richard. *A Concise History of Greece*. 2nd ed. Cambridge: Cambridge University Press, 2002.
Duggan, Christopher. *A Concise History of Italy*. Cambridge: Cambridge University Press, 1994.
Freeze, Gregory L., ed. *Russia: A History*. 2nd ed. Oxford: Oxford University Press, 2002.

Hibbert, Christopher. *The Story of England*. London: Phaidon Press, 1992.

Jones, Colin. *The Cambridge Illustrated History of France*. Cambridge: Cambridge University Press, 1999.

Kent, Neil. *A Concise History of Sweden*. Cambridge: Cambridge University Press, 2008.

Lawrence, John. *A History of Russia*. 7th ed. New York: Meridien/Penguin Books, 1993.

Lukowski, Jerzy, and Huber Zawadzki. *A Concise History of Poland*. 2nd ed. Cambridge: Cambridge University Press, 2006.

Phillips, William, and Carla Phillips. *A Concise History of Spain*. Cambridge: Cambridge University Press, 2010.

Schulze, Hagen. *Germany: A New History*. Cambridge, MA: Harvard University Press, 1998.

Chapter 1: The Renaissance, 1350–1517

Brotton, Jerry. *The Renaissance: A Very Short Introduction*. Oxford: Oxford University Press, 2006.

Hale, J. R., ed. *A Concise Encyclopedia of the Italian Renaissance*. New York: Oxford University Press, 1981.

Hibbert, Christopher. *The Rise and Fall of the House of Medici*. New York: Penguin Books, 1974.

Viroli, Maurizio. *Niccolò's Smile: A Biography of Machiavelli*. New York: Hill and Wang, 2000.

Zuffi, Stefano, ed. *Michelangelo: The Sistine Chapel*. New York: Rizzoli International Publications, 1999.

Chapter 2: The Reformation, 1455–1600

MacCulloch, Diarmaid. *The Reformation: A History*. New York: Penguin Books, 2004.

Marino, John. *Early Modern Italy, 1550–1796*. Oxford: Oxford University Press, 2002.

Scarisbrick, J. J. *Henry VIII*. Berkeley: University of California Press, 1968.

Woodhead, Linda. *Christianity: A Very Short Introduction*. Oxford: Oxford University Press, 2004.

Chapter 3: Early Czarist Russia, 1380–1613

De Madariaga, Isabel. *Ivan the Terrible: A Short History.* 2nd ed. New Haven, CT: Yale University Press, 2006.

Halperin, Charles J. *Russia and the Golden Horde: The Mongol Impact on Medieval Russian History.* Indianapolis: Indiana University Press, 1987.

Chapter 4: Europe to 1618

Hanson, Neil. *The Confident Hope of a Miracle: The True History of the Spanish Armada.* New York: Vintage Books, 2003.

Knecht, Robert. *The French Religious Wars, 1562–1598.* Oxford: Osprey Publishing, 2002.

Reston, James, Jr. *Dogs of God: Columbus, the Inquisition, and the Defeat of the Moors.* New York: Anchor Books, 2006.

Chapter 5: The Thirty Years' War, 1618–1648

Bonney, Richard. *The Thirty Years' War, 1618–1648.* Oxford: Osprey Publishing, 2002.

MacCulloch, Diarmaid. *The Reformation: A History.* New York: Penguin Books, 2004.

Wedgwood, C. V. *The Thirty Years' War.* New York: New York Review Books, 2005. First published 1938.

Wheatcroft, Andrew. *The Habsburgs: Embodying Empire.* New York: Penguin Books, 1996.

Wilson, Peter H. *The Thirty Years' War: Europe's Tragedy.* Cambridge, MA: Belknap Press/Harvard University Press, 2009.

Chapter 6: The Age of Monarchy

Bushkovitch, Paul. *Peter the Great.* New York: Rowman and Littlefield Publishers, 2002.

De Madariaga, Isabel. *Catherine the Great: A Short History.* 2nd ed. New Haven, CT: Yale University Press, 2002.

Goubert, Pierre. *Louis XIV and Twenty Million Frenchmen.* New York: Vintage Books, 1972.

Chapter 7: The Age of Expansion, Exploration, and Colonization, 1492–1787

Bawlf, Samuel. *The Secret Voyage of Sir Francis Drake, 1577–1580*. New York: Penguin Books, 2003.

Colley, Linda. *Captives: Britain, Empire, and the World, 1600–1850*. New York: Anchor Books, 2004.

Ronald, Susan. *The Pirate Queen: Queen Elizabeth I, Her Pirate Adventurers, and the Dawn of Empire*. New York: Harper Perennial, 2008.

Weber, David J. *The Spanish Frontier in North America*. New Haven, CT: Yale University Press, 1992.

Chapter 8: The Scientific Revolution and the Enlightenment, 1543–1789

Drake, Stillman. *Galileo: A Very Short Introduction*. Oxford: Oxford University Press, 1996.

Fara, Patricia. *Pandora's Breeches: Women, Science & Power in the Enlightenment*. London: Random House, 2004.

Gay, Peter. *The Enlightenment: An Interpretation*. Vol. I, *The Rise of Modern Paganism*. New York: W.W. Norton and Company, 1966.

———. *The Enlightenment: An Interpretation*. Vol. II, *The Science of Freedom*. New York: Alfred A. Knopf, 1969.

———. *Voltaire's Politics: The Poet as Realist*. 2nd ed. New Haven, CT: Yale University Press, 1988.

Harkness, Deborah E. *The Jewel House: Elizabethan London and the Scientific Revolution*. New Haven, CT: Yale University Press, 2008.

Maury, Jean Pierre. *Newton: The Father of Modern Astronomy*. New York: Harry N. Abrams, 1992.

Starobinski, Jean. *Jean-Jacques Rousseau: Transparency and Obstruction*. Chicago: University of Chicago Press, 1988.

Chapter 9: The French Revolution and the Napoleonic Wars, 1789–1815

Fisher, Todd. *The Napoleonic Wars: The Empires Fight Back, 1808–1812*. Oxford: Osprey Publishing, 2001.

———. *The Napoleonic Wars: The Rise of the Emperor, 1805–1807*. Oxford: Osprey Publishing, 2001.

Fremont-Barnes, Gregory. *The French Revolutionary Wars*. Oxford: Osprey Publishing, 2001.

———. *The Peninsular War, 1807–1814*. Oxford: Osprey Publishing, 2002.

Furet, François. *The French Revolution, 1770–1814*. Oxford: Blackwell Publishers Limited, 1992.

Johnson, Paul. *Napoleon*. New York: Penguin Books, 2002.

Walter, Jakob. *The Diary of a Napoleonic Foot-Soldier*. New York: Doubleday, 1991.

Chapter 10: The Industrial Revolution, 1750–1914

Dalziel, Nigel. *The Penguin Historical Atlas of the British Empire*. New York: Penguin Books, 2006.

Murray, Janet. *Strong-Minded Women and Other Lost Voices from 19th-Century England*. New York: Pantheon Books, 1982.

Weightman, Gavin. *The Industrial Revolutionaries: The Making of the Modern World*. New York: Grove Press, 2010.

Chapter 11: European Revolutions, 1815–1849

Gay, Peter. *The Dilemma of Democratic Socialism*. New York: Collier Books, 1962.

Horne, Alistair. *The Terrible Year: The Paris Commune, 1871*. London: Phoenix/Orion Books Ltd., 2004.

Marx, Karl, and Friedrich Engels. *The Communist Manifesto*. Many editions.

Chapter 12: Empires of Eastern Europe: Austria-Hungary and Russia to 1914

Lincoln, W. Bruce. *Nicholas I: Emperor and Autocrat of All the Russias.* DeKalb: Northern Illinois University Press, 1989.

Radzinsky, Edvard. *Alexander II: The Last Great Tsar.* New York: Free Press, 2006.

Schorske, Carl E. *Fin-de-Siècle Vienna: Politics and Culture.* New York: Vintage Books, 1980.

Chapter 13: German and Italian Unification, 1815–1871

Di Scala, Spencer M. *Italy from Revolution to Republic, 1700 to the Present.* Boulder, CO: Westview Press, 1995.

Kertzer, David I. *Prisoner of the Vatican: The Popes, the Kings, and Garibaldi's Rebels in the Struggle to Rule Modern Italy.* Boston: Houghton Mifflin, 2004.

Riall, Lucy. *The Italian Risorgimento: State, Society and National Unification.* New York: Routledge, 1994.

Wawro, Geoffrey. *The Franco-Prussian War: The German Conquest of France in 1870–1871.* Cambridge: Cambridge University Press, 2005.

Chapter 14: World Trade and Empires, 1839–1914

Dalziel, Nigel. *The Penguin Historical Atlas of the British Empire.* New York: Penguin Books, 2006.

Rowe, William T. *China's Last Empire: The Great Qing.* Cambridge: Belknap Press/Harvard University Press, 2009.

Chapter 15: The Great War (World War I) and Its Aftermath, 1914–1919

Audoin-Rouzeau, Stéphane, and Annette Becker. *14–18: Understanding the Great War.* New York: Hill and Wang, 2003.

Fussell, Paul. *The Great War and Modern Memory.* Oxford: Oxford University Press, 1975.

Howard, Michael. *The First World War: A Very Short Introduction.* Oxford: Oxford University Press, 2002.

Keegan, John. *The First World War.* New York: Vintage Books, 2000.

MacMillan, Margaret. *Paris 1919: Six Months That Changed the World.* New York: Random House, 2003.

Manchester, William. *The Last Lion: Winston Spencer Churchill; Visions of Glory, 1874–1932.* New York: Dell, 1988.

Chapter 16: Revolution in Russia: 1917 to the Eve of World War II

Figes, Orlando. *A People's Tragedy: The Russian Revolution, 1891–1924.* New York: Penguin Books, 1998.

Reed, John. *Ten Days That Shook the World.* New York: Penguin Books, 1977. First published 1919.

Service, Robert. *Stalin: A Biography.* Cambridge, MA: Belknap Press/Harvard University Press, 2006.

Smith, S. A. *The Russian Revolution: A Very Short Introduction.* Oxford: Oxford University Press, 2002.

Chapter 17: The Rise of Totalitarianism, 1919–1939

Beevor, Anthony. *The Battle for Spain: The Spanish Civil War, 1936–1939.* Rev. ed. New York: Penguin Books, 2006.

Fest, Joachim C. *Hitler.* New York: Vintage Books, 1975.

Manchester, William. *The Last Lion: Winston Spencer Churchill; Alone, 1932–1940.* New York: Dell, 1988.

Overy, Richard. *The Penguin Historical Atlas of the Third Reich.* New York: Penguin Books, 1996.

Paxton, Robert O. *The Anatomy of Fascism.* New York: Vintage Books, 2004.

Chapter 18: World War II, 1939–1945

Beevor, Anthony. *The Fall of Berlin, 1945.* New York: Penguin Books, 2002.

Churchill, Winston. *Blood, Toil, Tears, and Sweat: The Speeches of Winston Churchill.* Edited by David Cannadine. New York: Houghton Mifflin, 1989.

Collins, Larry, and Dominique LaPierre. *Is Paris Burning?* New York: Warner Books, 1999. First published 1965.

Fest, Joachim C. *Hitler.* New York: Vintage Books, 1975.

Overy, Richard. *The Penguin Historical Atlas of the Third Reich.* New York: Penguin Books, 1996.

Watt, Donald Cameron. *How War Came: The Immediate Origins of the Second World War, 1938–1939.* New York: Pantheon Books, 1989.

Chapter 19: The Cold War, 1945–1968

Churchill, Winston. *Blood, Toil, Tears, and Sweat: The Speeches of Winston Churchill.* Edited by David Cannadine. New York: Houghton Mifflin, 1989.

Furet, François. *The Passing of an Illusion: The Idea of Communism in the Twentieth Century.* Chicago: University of Chicago Press, 1999.

Gelb, Norman. *The Berlin Wall.* New York: Dorset Press, 1986, 1990.

Hitchcock, William I. *The Struggle for Europe: The Turbulent History of a Divided Continent, 1945 to the Present.* New York: Anchor Books, 2003.

Kemp, Anthony. *Escape from Berlin.* London: Boxtree Limited, 1987.

McMahon, Robert. *The Cold War: A Very Short Introduction.* Oxford: Oxford University Press, 2003.

Williamson, D. G. *Germany from Defeat to Partition, 1945–1963.* Harlow: Pearson Education Limited, 2001.

Sebestyen, Victor. *Twelve Days: The Story of the 1956 Hungarian Revolution.* New York: Vintage, 2007.

Taylor, Frederick. *The Berlin Wall: A World Divided, 1961–1989.* New York: Harper Perennial, 2006.

Chapter 20: The Fall of Communism, 1945–1989

Darnton, Robert. *Berlin Journal, 1989–1990.* New York: W.W. Norton and Company Inc, 2001.

Furet, François. *The Passing of an Illusion: The Idea of Communism in the Twentieth Century.* Chicago: University of Chicago Press, 1999.

Hitchcock, William I. *The Struggle for Europe: The Turbulent History of a Divided Continent, 1945 to the Present.* New York: Anchor Books, 2003.

McMahon, Robert. *The Cold War: A Very Short Introduction*. Oxford: Oxford University Press, 2003.

Taylor, Frederick. *The Berlin Wall: A World Divided, 1961–1989*. New York: Harper Perennial, 2006.

The Internet

The Internet can be a useful, even superb, tool for research—**when used with caution!** It is rich in texts of original primary source documents, many of which are difficult to find in print.

However, the secondary source material online varies greatly in quality. Anyone can post anything he or she wishes on the Internet; it does not have the fact-checking, quality-control process that goes into the publication of nonfiction books. Therefore, the student is cautioned to use good judgment when consulting online secondary sources in the field of European history; and no matter how impressive an Internet site appears, it is always best to confirm the information in a print source.

The World Almanac

A current world almanac is an excellent desktop resource for the history student. It is a one-volume, highly reliable source of facts and information. In the almanac, you can find brief histories of all the nations of the world, up to the present day. You can also find such items as complete lists of monarchs of all nations going back to the early civilizations, as well as lists and brief explanations of major scientific and technological discoveries throughout history. The current world almanac is an unbeatable source for the student who needs to look up a fact quickly.

Relevant Works of Literature

Presented here is a highly selective list of works of literature—dramas, novels, and poetry—dealing with many of the central issues and events of modern European history. Many of these works were written in the times they describe.

Of course, the student should not rely on fiction for exact accuracy of facts and dates. However, reading historical fiction and drama can enormously enrich a student's understanding of a period. Great historical fiction can bring an era to life and provide a vivid picture of a time and place.

Reformation

Robert Bolt, *A Man for All Seasons*

English Renaissance

William Shakespeare, *Complete Plays*

Scientific Revolution

Bertolt Brecht, *Galileo*

Enlightenment

Voltaire, *Candide*

Napoleonic Wars

Leo Tolstoy, *War and Peace*

Industrial Revolution

Charles Dickens, *Hard Times*
Emile Zola, *Germinal*

Italy in the Nineteenth Century

Giuseppe de Lampedusa, *The Leopard*

France in the Nineteenth Century

Victor Hugo, *Les Misérables*

Franco-Prussian War

Emile Zola, *The Debacle*

British Occupation of India

E. M. Forster, *A Passage to India*

World War I

Erich Maria Remarque, *All Quiet on the Western Front*
Wilfred Owen, *Collected Poems*

Russian Revolution

Boris Pasternak, *Dr. Zhivago*

Weimar Republic

Christopher Isherwood, *Berlin Stories*

World War II

Erich Maria Remarque, *Arch of Triumph*
Thomas Keneally, *Schindler's List*

Soviet Union Under Stalin

Alexander Solzhenitsyn, *One Day in the Life of Ivan Denisovich*

The Cold War

John le Carré, *The Spy Who Came In from the Cold*
Josef Skvorecky, *The Miracle Game*

Index